25

BICYCLE TOURS
in the Texas Hill Country
& West Texas

25 BICYCLE TOURS
in the Texas Hill Country
& West Texas

adventure rides for road and mountain bikes

Norman D. Ford

Backcountry Publications
Woodstock · Vermont

An invitation to the reader

Although it is unlikely that the roads you cycle on these tours will change much with time, some road signs, landmarks, and road conditions may. If you find that such changes have occurred, please let us know, so that corrections can be made in future printings. Please be sure to let us know the edition and printing you are using, as we continually update our guides. Other comments and suggestions are also welcome. Address all correspondence to:

Editor, 25 Bicycle Tours™ Series
Backcountry Publications
PO Box 175
Woodstock, VT 05091-0175

Library of Congress Cataloging-in-Publication Data

Ford, Norman D., 1921–
      25 bicycle tours in the Texas Hill Country and West Texas: adventure rides for road and mountain bikes / Norman D. Ford; photographs by Norman and Shirley Ford.
         p.   cm.
      ISBN 0-88150-324-X
      1. Bicycle touring—Texas—Guidebooks. 2. Texas—Guidebooks. I. Title. II. Title: Twenty-five bicycle tours in the Texas Hill Country and West Texas.
      GV1045.5.T4F67 1995
      796.6'4'09764—dc20   94-43435
                                                   CIP

10 9 8 7 6 5 4 3 2 1

Printed in the United States of America
Text and Cover Design by Sally Sherman
Cover photo by Lori Adamski Peek/Tony Stone Images
Interior photographs by Norman and Shirley Ford
Text composition by Kate Mueller
Maps by Dick Widhu, © 1995 The Countryman Press, Inc.

Published by Backcountry Publications,
a division of The Countryman Press, Inc.,
PO Box 175
Woodstock, Vermont 05091-0175

Acknowledgments

For their invaluable guidance and advice on the most worthwhile and rewarding bicycle routes and trails in a huge area of Texas, the author would like to express his appreciation to members of the Kerrville and San Antonio Wheelmen Bicycle Clubs and especially to Colonel and Mrs. Otto Benner, Kristina Coates, Mike Long, Bob Thorne, Lawrie Nomer, Charles Hunsucker, and Dick Mauldin, all of Texas; and to Jerry Brown of Durango, Colorado. Without their intimate knowledge of the back roads and byways of the Hill Country and West Texas, this book could not have been written. Special thanks goes to my wife, Shirley, for her patience and skill in photographing many of the bicycle scenes in which I was the model.

Contents

The Bicyclist's Last Frontier · 9

THE HILL COUNTRY   23

1 · Hill Country State Natural Area (mountain bike) · · · · · · · 27
2 · State Mountain–Poli's Chapel (mountain bike) · · · · · · · · 33
3 · Seco Valley Loop (mountain bike) · · · · · · · · · · · · · · · 39
4 · Mason County Loop (mountain bike) · · · · · · · · · · · · · 43
    Cross-Country Capsule Routings · · · · · · · · · · · · · · · · · 47
5 · Cherry Springs Loop (road bike) · · · · · · · · · · · · · · · · 51
6 · Lady Bird Johnson Park–Comfort Loop (road bike) · · · · · 57
7 · Willow City Loop (road bike) · · · · · · · · · · · · · · · · · · 65
8 · Fredericksburg-Harper Loops, Longer Version (road bike) · 71
    Shorter Version #1 · 76
    Shorter Version #2 · 76
    Shorter Version #3 · 78
    Wendell-Jung Loop (road bike) · · · · · · · · · · · · · · · · · · 78
9 · West Hill Country Loop: A 5-Day Tour (road bike) · · · · · 79
10 · Leakey–Camp Wood Mountain Loop (road bike) · · · · · · 91
11 · Hill Country to West Texas: A 6-Day Tour (road bike) · · · · 95

WEST TEXAS   113

12 · Sawmill Mountain Loop (mountain bike) · · · · · · · · · · · 117
13 · Old Maverick Road–Santa Elena (mountain bike) · · · · · · 125
14 · Old Ore Road (mountain bike) · · · · · · · · · · · · · · · · · 131
15 · Pinto Canyon (mountain bike) · · · · · · · · · · · · · · · · · 137
16 · Terlingua Ranch–Lake Ament Loop (mountain bike) · · · · 143
17 · Lajitas to San Carlos, Mexico (mountain bike) · · · · · · · · 149

18 · Mariscal Mine via River Road (mountain bike) · · · · · · · · 153
19 · Mariscal Mine via Black Gap Road (mountain bike) · · · · · 159
20 · County Road–Hen Egg Mountain Loop (mountain bike) · 165
21 · Stillwell's Ranch to La Linda, Mexico (road bike) · · · · · · · 171
22 · Fort Davis to Balmorhea State Park (road bike) · · · · · · · 175
23 · Davis Mountains Loop (road bike) · · · · · · · · · · · · · · · · 179
24 · West Texas Loop: A 5-Day Tour (road bike) · · · · · · · · · · 183
25 · Candelaria by the "Other" River Road (road bike) · · · · · 201

How to Plan a 21-Day, 1184-Mile Bicycle Adventure · · · · · · 205
City and Resource Directory · 209

The Bicyclist's Last Frontier

"The last frontier of adventure cycling," is how a British couple described the Texas Hill Country and West Texas after spending their entire month's vacation touring every corner of the area by bicycle. And, indeed, the wonderful bicycling available in this sparsely populated corner of Texas must be the best-kept secret in American cycling.

Compared to the thousands of bicyclists who trek annually to Vermont, Crested Butte, Durango, or Moab, only a few hundred have discovered the often equally great bicycling in the Texas Hill Country and West Texas. Yet those who do come here and ride find an extravaganza of hill, river, and mountain scenery plus an amazing variety of wildlife, thousands of miles of lightly traveled roads, plenty of inexpensive motels not too far apart, and a long fall-winter-spring season with the best cycling available at a time when most of the US is buried under snow.

My purpose in this book is to pinpoint the best road- and mountain-bicycle rides—whether a half-day or an all-day ride or a multiday tour—in this huge and uncongested area. By way of explanation, the Hill Country is a region of scenic wooded hills, valleys, and canyons almost 200 miles across, located immediately west of Austin and San Antonio in west central Texas. And West Texas is a huge chunk of mountains, deserts, and deep river canyons lying west of, and adjacent to, the Hill Country. Put together, I call this vast region the "un-country": underpopulated, unchanged, unspoiled, and undeveloped, all qualities that help to make it one of the best all-around bicycling areas in the US.

As a resident of the Hill Country for 8 years, I've ridden just about every paved and unpaved road and trail in the Hill Country and in adjacent West Texas. And whether you ride a road or mountain bike, you'll find an exciting choice of outstanding rides over routes that were carefully chosen for minimal traffic.

You may find this hard to believe, but some of the West Texas mountain-bike rides in this book take you so far off the beaten path that you may not meet another person or vehicle all day. Both road- and mountain-bike rides take you to forgotten ghost towns and some of the most remote and isolated communities in the US. Rides of this caliber cannot be found within a short drive of big cities like Austin or San Antonio (although some of our Hill Country rides are within 2 hours of these cities); cycling in West Texas is something most people must do on vacation.

So one goal of this book is to get you thinking about spending an entire vacation adventure-cycling in the Hill Country and West Texas. While researching this book, for instance, I spent several vacations in West Texas, staying a week at a time at a motel in Presidio or Alpine, Study Butte or Fort Davis, or tent camping in Big Bend National Park, each day making a road- or mountain-bike ride out and back in a different direction. At other times I took overnight tours lasting from 5 to 21 days. On the 21-day ride I toured much of the Hill Country, the Davis Mountains, and the Rio Grande and Big Bend Country of West Texas. Each night I stayed at a comfortable motel, and the longest day's ride was under 70 miles.

All these tours are described in this book with routing instructions for carrying them out and a list of motels and campgrounds where you can stay.

This book is divided into three sections:
- the Hill Country (including rides in this region)
- West Texas (including rides in this region)
- City and Resource Directory (giving basic information about the sight-seeing and bicycling resources in each city in the Hill Country and West Texas plus phone numbers and locations of one or more motels and campgrounds of interest to cyclists).

Each ride description is confined to routing information and comments about the country you pass through. When you come to a city, you are referred to the City and Resource Directory at the back of the book for further information.

Before starting to ride, however, I recommend reading the rest of this chapter. Covering mostly topics that are unique to Texas bicycling, it introduces you to information that could be vital to the success of your rides.

Changes

This book reports on facts and conditions as they existed just prior to publication. Expect some changes to occur during the life of this edition. Narrow roads may be widened, highway signs removed by souvenir

This marker, found along the route of Tour 9,
commemorates the McLauren massacre of 1881.

hunters, a small café may become a McDonald's, a black iron gate may have been replaced by a green wooden gate or a cattle guard, and an economy motel may have become a Days Inn. Motels, restaurants, and stores may change names, ownership, phone numbers, locations, or go out of business. We'll catch these changes in our next edition. Meanwhile, call ahead to verify anything important.

Dogs

Dogs are not a big problem in Texas. Most are chained up or kept behind fences to prevent them from chasing livestock, deer, and game. However, dogs often run loose in Mexico, so take some dog repellent if you ride across the border. If a dog harries you in Mexico, stop, get off the bike, and throw a few rocks at the dog.

Early Starts

Usually the earlier in the day you begin biking, the better. Traffic is lighter, you cycle in the cooler part of the day, and arriving earlier at your destination gives you a better choice of motel rooms or campsites.

Fitness

I assume you are familiar with riding skills and that, despite hills, head-winds, heat, and long distances, you have the energy and experience to complete the rides in this book. Thus, they are intended for energetic bicy-clists with some experience. They are not for beginners or someone whose energy may flag. If you have doubts about going the distance, I recommend riding shorter segments of some of the easier rides. Suggestions for short-er rides are given under some of the ride descriptions.

Getting to Texas by Public Transportation

After considerable inquiry, I've concluded that if you're flying to San Antonio, bring your bike with you on the plane only if you rent a car at the airport sufficiently large to carry your boxed bike in. Otherwise you'd probably be better off to ship it ahead by UPS to a motel in Kerrville or other small Hill Country town where you plan to begin cycling. In any case, having a car along is a huge help in reaching the starting points of many of the rides in this book.

Before shipping a boxed bike by UPS to a motel, phone and get the motel keeper's approval. You should also ship the bike well ahead of UPS's delivery estimate to ensure its arrival by the time *you* arrive. If you ship your bike to a motel and have the keeper store your bike box during a tour, you will be expected to spend your first and last nights there. Most motels will also store your car while you're on a bicycle tour provided you stay at the motel on your first and last nights.

If you're heading for West Texas by train or bus, both AMTRAK and continental bus lines serve Alpine, hub city for the Big Bend and Davis Mountains country.

Hills

Don't expect flat terrain. This is the Hill Country, and much of West Texas is quite mountainous. However, most steep hills are relatively short, and most longer hills have an easier grade you can ride up. If you're not confi-dent about hills, your gears may be too high. Whether road or mountain bike, I use a low gear of 19 inches—which translates into a 24-tooth chain ring driving a 32-tooth cog—on *all* my bikes.

If you're over 40, or have any doubts about your hill-climbing ability, I recommend installing a 24-tooth chain ring and a 32-tooth cog. You'll be amazed at the ease with which you can pedal uphill.

This overlook high above the Rio Grande provides a grand view of the river, with Mexico on the left and Texas on the right.

Horses

Thousands of Texans own horses and enjoy riding in state natural areas (undeveloped state parks), where they share the trails with hikers and mountain bikers. As a mountain biker in Texas, it's important to know how to meet or overtake someone riding a horse on a trail. State park regulations call for mountain bikers to yield to both hikers and equestrians, and the regulations prohibit bikes from being ridden in a manner dangerous to other trail users.

Some horses may spook or be hard to control at the sight of a bike. Trying to get off the trail and "hide" from the horse is not recommended. The horse can still sense your presence and may shy.

Instead, stop well in advance of meeting a horse and move aside to allow it to pass. A friendly greeting will identify the biker to the horse as a human and a friend rather than as something silent and frightening. On a steep slope, step off the trail on the downhill side, stay in plain sight, announce your presence, and allow the horse to pass.

To overtake someone on a horse, call ahead and announce your intention to pass. "Good-day, I'm on a bicycle. May I pass?" sounds better than "Bicycle coming through!" or "Bicycle on your left!". If the horse's ears are swiveled back listening, the horse is aware of your presence. If the horse's ears are flattened all the way down, the horse may kick. So stay well clear of the horse—keep at least 6 feet away if you can—and pass on the left.

Information, Maps, Cyclocomputers

For more information about any city in this book, the phone number and address of its convention and visitors bureau, or chamber of commerce, is given in the City and Resource Directory at the back of this book. Ask for a street map; list of accommodations, bed & breakfasts, and tent camping sites; a local county road map; and a map of the city's historic district if it has one.

Although the maps in this book are all you normally need to follow our ride routes, if you plan to ride elsewhere you will find the half-inch-to-the-mile series of Texas county road maps invaluable. The labyrinth of farm-to-market and ranch roads that web the Hill Country and other areas are not shown on the state highway map. Having a county map may also enable you to see other options and possibilities beyond those covered by the maps in this book.

Half-inch-to-the-mile maps of all Texas counties are available at a nominal price from the Texas Department of Transportation, PO Box 5020, Austin, TX 78762-5020. Write for their index map and price list. For a free state map, and a copy of the "Texas State Travel Guide," call or write the Texas Department of Transportation, Division of Travel & Information, PO Box 5064, Austin, TX 78763-5064 (512-389-4400).

US Geological Survey topographical maps, which show rivers, mountains and contour lines as well as roads, are usually sold by local sports and outdoor stores. Or you can order them by mail from Distribution Branch, US Geological Survey, Box 25286, Federal Center, Denver, CO 80225 (303-236-7477). Request a Texas map index and catalog.

An excellent free map of Gillespie County, which has more paved back roads than anywhere else in the Hill Country, is available from the convention and visitors bureau in Fredericksburg (see the City and Resource Directory). This map is really invaluable (and far superior to the regular county highway map) because the name of every back road appears on the map, and every public road in Gillespie County has a corresponding green metal name sign at every intersection (private roads have red signs).

To follow the routings on our rides you must have a reasonably accurate cyclocomputer on your bike. Road signs may not exist in some back-country areas, and you must rely on the mileage recorded by your computer to keep track of your position.

Loop Rides versus Out-and-Back Rides

While every bicyclist prefers a loop ride, the sheer size of Texas and the distances involved often make it necessary to do an out-and-back ride over the same road rather than a loop or circular ride. But, in fact, a loop ride isn't always ideal. I can think of a half-dozen popular loop rides in the Hill Country that route you over a scenic back road for part of the loop, then complete the loop by routing you over a featureless, high-traffic road.

The well-known Willow City Loop (Tour 7) is a case in point. For 13 miles you ride a superbly scenic back road; then, in the belief that every ride must be a circular loop, the standard itinerary routes you the rest of the way on TX 16, a major highway with narrow shoulders.

Frankly, I *never* ride this version of the Willow City Loop. Instead, I ride the 13-mile back road on the way out, then turn around and ride back on the same 13-mile back road. This way I get 26 miles of exciting scenery and challenging hills instead of having to ride partway on busy TX 16.

Thus I submit that an out-and-back ride on an exciting road may be far superior to a loop ride consisting partly of a scenic low-traffic road and partly of a monotonous high-traffic road—which is the case with all too many loop itineraries. Even though you may have just ridden over a road, going back and seeing it all again from a different direction often makes the return ride seem like an entirely new trip. So in many cases an out-and-back ride gives you a double exposure to some really outstanding scenery that you'd see only once if riding a loop.

Parking

Some of our rides require parking your car in a remote area where the ride begins. We've never had a car touched while parked, but if you have an expensive, prestigious car, you might not want to leave it unattended out in the country. One alternative may be to park your car in a community along the ride route, and start and end your ride there. In any case, it's prudent to use a wheel lock and leave nothing of value in the car. With the exception of the Mexican border, the areas covered by this book are generally low-crime areas. When parking near the Mexican border, try to park within plain view of traffic passing on a highway or national park road.

Public Roads, Private Land

Even though you may be riding on a public road, paid for and maintained by county taxpayers, the land on both sides is almost always privately owned. It's a good rule when riding any back road to stay *on* the road and *off* the land on either side. Because ranchers have lost livestock to cattle thieves, and poachers trespass on their land to hunt deer, turkey, or *javelina,* you may see No Trespassing or Keep Out signs along roads that are obviously county roads open to the public. One Kimble County road has a gate (unlocked) with a Keep Out sign on it right next to a county sign clearly identifying the road as county maintained and, therefore, open to public travel. Due to lack of road signs in the backcountry, it's always possible to stray onto a private road. But most of the time these Keep Off type signs are there to discourage cattle thieves and poachers, not bicyclists.

Rain

Graded dirt roads and narrow trails are often impassable after a heavy rain, not only to bikes but also to motor vehicles, and they may remain impassable for several days. Thus you should postpone any type of off-road riding for a day or two after a heavy or prolonged rain. In much of the Hill Country and West Texas, the thin soil consists of *caleche,* which sets like concrete in dry weather but dissolves swiftly in water to resemble wet cement with an amazing propensity to stick to your bicycle stays, wheels, and tires and completely immobilize the bike. So avoid getting far out on a dirt road if a rainstorm seems imminent. A flash flood can also put a normally dry low-water crossing under a torrent of water several feet deep, and it can stop all traffic for several hours. Few Texans carry raingear, and 95 percent of the time it isn't necessary. But if you're hit by hail or cold winter rain without having raingear, you *could* get hypothermia within half an hour.

Repairs

Most rides in this book take you a hundred miles or more from a bike shop. To be self-sufficient, you must carry basic tools and a pump and be able to change a tube or replace a broken cable or spoke. Only one bike shop exists in the entire area covered by this book, namely Mountain Sports at Kerrville. Other bike shops are located at Austin, Lubbock, and San Antonio. Makeshift mountain-bike tires and tubes may be found in

Pinto Canyon Road as it runs along the canyon bottom: Ride it on Tour 15.

Western Auto or similar stores in most small towns. Because I often ride alone, I carry three spare tubes, a spare derailleur and brake cable, 6 feet of strong cord, four spare spokes, one rim tape, and a piece of old tire to use as a patch if a tire splits. When my rear derailleur recently lost its inner pulley 20 miles from the car, I used the cord to lash the derailleur in place with the chain set on one of the larger cogs. Then by shifting the front derailleur across the three chain rings, I was able to ride back using three different gears.

Reservations

Bikers staying at motels need a confirmed reservation before cycling to a locale with only one or two small motels. Such places include Balmorhea, Iraan, Leakey, Presidio, Rocksprings, Sheffield, Study Butte, or anywhere in the Big Bend or Davis Mountains regions. You can't afford to arrive only to discover every room is taken. Larger motel centers like Alpine, Fort Stockton, Fredericksburg, Junction, Kerrville, Ozona, or Sonora usually have vacancies on weekday nights. But on weekends or holidays you may need a reservation even at these. During rodeos, chili cook-offs, festivals, and similar special events, every motel for 50 miles around is often fully reserved weeks in advance. The first 2 weeks of deer-hunting season (November in the Hill Country; Thanksgiving into December in West Texas) also see an increased demand for motel space. Campsites and lodges at Big Bend National Park and several state parks are also fully booked during spring break vacations in March and early April.

Outside of resort areas such as the Davis Mountains and Big Bend, motel rates in the Hill Country and West Texas are among the lowest in America. If you stay for a week at a motel while cycling in the area, you can often qualify for an economical weekly rate.

Tent camping is possible at most places. Many smaller communities permit tent camping in the city park. Some RV travel parks also have tent sites as do all KOA Kampgrounds and state parks and natural areas.

Undoubtedly, Texas's state parks and natural areas provide the best tent camping. To avoid the (as of recently) $6 daily entrance fee, I recommend purchasing a Conservation Passport ($35 a year as this was written). A similar State Parklands Passport is free to anyone over 65. Campsites can be reserved at all parks by calling the Central Reservations Center at 512-389-8900 between 8–5 on weekdays. You must call at least 2 days ahead of arrival and pay with a Visa card or MasterCard. The overnight camping fee was recently $11 including electricity and $8 without. Campsites have tables with overhead shelters, while toilets and hot showers are close by. For information about state parks or a folder on any specific park, call 1-800-792-1112 (in Austin call 389-8950) or write to Park Information, 4200 Smith School Road, Austin, TX 78744.

Road Surfaces

Texas's highways are among the best in the nation, and most major roads have paved shoulders 4 to 7 feet in width. By contrast, the majority of two-lane farm-to-market and ranch roads lack paved shoulders. As much as possible I've avoided using any two-lane road that carries appreciable traffic for the rides in this book. Since this isn't always feasible, I strongly recommend using a rearview mirror and wearing an approved bicycling helmet. Should a potentially dangerous situation occur, such as a truck overtaking you from behind while another vehicle is passing in the opposite lane, you can usually ride off the road onto the dirt shoulder. That's because in Texas road edges are flush with the shoulder, and—should the need ever arise—this maneuver can usually be done safely even when riding a road bike with skinny tires.

On secondary roads and country lanes, low-water crossings (causeways) are frequently used instead of a bridge to carry a paved road across a creek. Most low-water crossings are normally dry and are flooded only for a few hours following heavy rain. But water runs across some crossings for months at a time and sometimes permanently. Usually the water is only an inch or two deep, but the water's constant presence allows algae to grow on the crossing. Algae is extremely slick, and virtually any bike—including one with fat tires—may slip sideways and slide out from under you.

To traverse a slick low-water crossing, stay in one of the tracks cut by car tires where algae is less. Disengage any clipless pedals and cross at walking speed. Ride straight and avoid braking or pedaling. Walking across may not be the answer because your feet can slide as readily as can a bike. Many low-water crossings are also narrow, and traffic is one-way. It's best to give cars rights-of-way at both low-water crossings and cattle guards.

Cattle guards consist of a grid of widely spaced metal pipes or rails placed across a road at fence lines to prevent livestock from crossing. Most cattle guards consist of 3-inch steel pipe spaced 2 inches apart, and almost all bike wheels and tires can cross them safely. To do so, however, you *must* cross at right angles. The pipes are usually laid across the road at a 90-degree angle—but not always. Some may be at an oblique angle of 80 degrees, or even 75. These could be hazardous, especially when wet. If you meet one, maneuver your bike so that you *do* cross at right angles.

Most cattle guards have a smooth leading edge, but some may not, and the resulting bump could cause a pinch-flat in a very skinny tire. The best way to cross a cattle guard is to slow down until you can clearly see that all the rails are in place and there is no leading edge bump. Then stop pedaling, level the pedals, and stand up with knees bent to cushion any shock.

Occasionally in sheep and goat country a rancher may stretch an automobile inner tube across and above a cattle guard. The tube will be about 6 inches above the cattle guard, which may be fine for trucks but not for bikes. If you see an inner tube across a cattle guard, stop and walk your bike over.

Loose, pea-sized gravel may be scattered on some paved secondary roads as a cheap way to repave. The weight of passing cars and trucks eventually smooths down the gravel. Since traffic is often extremely light on these roads, this process can take weeks or months. Usually you can ride

The tower of a ruined adobe mission stands beside the general store in the border village of Ruidosa.

in the tracks created by cars. But if you must pull onto the road edge, you could find yourself riding in deep gravel.

Some unpaved roads in Big Bend National Park have been surfaced with larger river-bottom gravel to prevent washboarding. Even cars and trucks sink into this stuff. To provide maximum flotation for a mountain bicycle, you'll want to fit 2.35- or 2.5-inch tires both front and rear.

Tire sizes? A 1.5-inch tire will take a hybrid or mountain bike over most graded county roads. But for riding on single track or across creek beds, or in state parks or Big Bend National Park, knobby 2.35- to 2.5-inch tires are best. For road riding, a 700 x 28- or a 27 x 1.25-inch tire will negotiate most cattle guards without a pinch-flat.

Texas Highway Classifications

Paved highways in Texas with two or more lanes are classified as follows and these abbreviations are used in the ride descriptions in this book:

- Farm-to-market roads. These bear four digits (FM 2138, for instance) and are usually narrow and shoulderless. In rural areas most are lightly traveled.

- Ranch roads. These bear three digits (RR 765) and usually lack shoulders. They serve as secondary roads in rural areas. Many, though not all, are lightly traveled.
- State roads. These bear two digits (TX 16). The majority are two lane with a wide shoulder.
- US highways. These bear a two- or three-digit number (US 377). In Texas most have a wide shoulder, and they are usually main roads. However, not all are heavily traveled.
- Interstates (I-10). In rural areas of Texas you may ride on the interstate shoulder provided no alternative route exists and you keep far right.

Touring Companies and Touring Equipment

To join a group bicycle tour of the Hill Country or West Texas, contact one of these commercial tour operators and ask for a list of their upcoming tours (mention does not imply our endorsement): Country Roads Bicycle Tours, Route 2, Box 186-B, Fayetteville, TX 78940 (1-800-366-6681); or Coyote Bicycle Tours, Box 1832, Austin, TX 78767 (512-474-2714).

For touring equipment such as bicycle bags and clothing, and lightweight tents and sleeping bags, contact REI—Recreational Equipment, Inc., 1112 North Lamar Blvd, Austin, TX 78703 (512-474-2393).

A Final Word

I'd like to conclude by stating that this book is published solely to inform you of the existence of certain bicycle routes. What you do with this information is entirely up to you. Neither the author nor the publisher can be held responsible for any mishaps that may occur while riding the routes in this book. It's up to you to recognize your limitations, to always stay within them, to wear an approved helmet, and at all times to practice the principles of safe and effective bicycling.

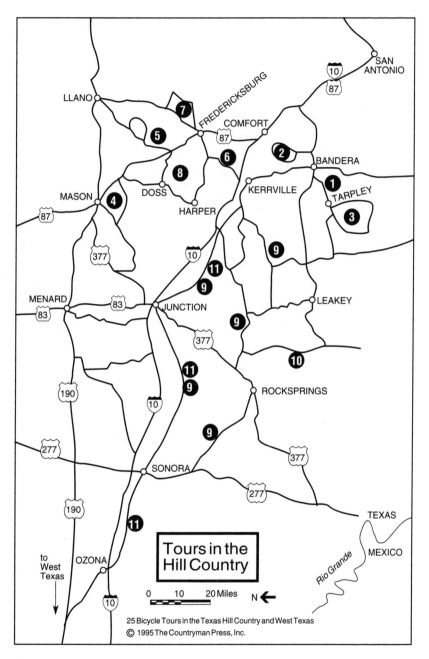

SAN ANTONIO

LLANO

FREDERICKSBURG

COMFORT

BANDERA

7

5

2

6

1 TARPLEY

8

KERRVILLE

3

MASON

4

DOSS

HARPER

87

377

9

10

11

MENARD

83

9

JUNCTION

LEAKEY

83

377

9

10

190

11

10

9

ROCKSPRINGS

277

9

377

190

SONORA

277

TEXAS

11

Tours in the
Hill Country

MEXICO

to
West
Texas

OZONA

0   10   20 Miles   N ←

Rio Grande

10

25 Bicycle Tours in the Texas Hill Country and West Texas
© 1995 The Countryman Press, Inc.

22

THE HILL COUNTRY—
ONE OF AMERICA'S
LAST GREAT PLACES

Calling the Hill Country the largest of America's Last Great Places, The Nature Conservancy describes it as "an enormous crescent of land that stretches across Central Texas—18,000 square miles, the size of New Hampshire and Vermont combined."

Lying west of Austin and San Antonio, and bordered by the cities of Llano, Mason, and Junction, this part of West Central Texas has some of the best year-round bicycling in America. Hundreds of miles of almost traffic-free back roads offer unlimited riding on both paved and graded county roads, while several state parks and privately owned ranches provide challenging and technical single-track mountain biking.

The Hill Country is part of the Edwards Plateau, an undersea bedrock formed by prehistoric seas. In the north, granite and marble domes expose some of the world's oldest rocks, while the Hill Country's southern boundary consists of the Balcones Escarpment, a layer cake of limestone deposits honeycombed with caves and sinkholes. By seeping through this eerie underworld, billions of gallons of water have collected 100 feet underground to form the Edwards Aquifer. Much of the water bubbles to the surface to form the hundreds of springs and clear flowing rivers that lace the Hill Country and that have carved deep limestone canyons through the monumental hills.

Native Americans, who had lived in the Hill Country for 7000 years, fiercely resisted both the Spanish friars who built missions here in the 1700s and the Anglos who began settling the hills in the 1840s. Historic markers all across the southern hills describe massacres of Anglo women and children tending livestock in the fields. While all this was going on, a group of 120 German immigrants led by former nobleman John O.

Riding on a single track around the Twin Peaks in the
Hill Country State Natural Area

Meusebach founded Fredericksburg and settled much of the northern hills. By signing a peace treaty with the Native Americans, the Germans avoided any massacres, and today the northern Hill Country is filled with churches, farmhouses, barns, and fences built of native limestone rock by these sturdy pioneers. Other visible relics of frontier history are the numerous roadside cemeteries containing the graves of hundreds of victims of diptheria and influenza epidemics that swept through the area a century ago.

Meanwhile, smaller cities like Comfort, Fredericksburg, Llano, and Mason still have town squares and well-preserved historic districts dotted with homes, churches, stores, and other buildings dating from the 1880s or even earlier. Chambers of commerce in these cities distribute free tour maps, enabling you to tour the historic districts on foot or by bicycle.

Instead of heavy industry and agribusiness, ranching, tourism, and retirement checks power the Hill Country's economy. Longhorn cattle, buffalo, and exotic game graze in roadside pastures, and the Hill Country has become home to the world's largest herds of endangered cleft-footed animals. Shaggy bearded aoudad sheep, black buck antelope with spiral horns, spotted axis deer, llamas, and gentle fallow deer often feed along fence lines close to the road. The Hill Country is also home to the nation's largest herd of white-tailed deer. Perky rock and black squirrels and even coyotes are as common as scissor-tailed flycatchers and scarlet male cardinals. Turkey vultures and hawks soar on updrafts overhead.

But it is the trees and flowers that perpetually flood the hills with color. From mid-March until late May the sides of many roads are ablaze with a succession of bluebonnets, pink evening primrose, red Indian paintbrush, and the reds and golds of Indian blanket, firewheels, and Mexican sombreros. Mountain laurel blooms at higher elevations in April and fills the mountainsides with its heady scent. In summer, sunflowers and the ripening purple prickly-pear tunas maintain a pageant of color, while in fall the hills are splashed with the crimson of sumac and red oak and the golds of sycamore and cottonwood. Even in winter the scarlet berries of yaupon stand out against the vivid green of cedar. Peak season for bluebonnets is April 1–21 and until May 21 for other wildflowers.

With an average total snowfall of perhaps 1 inch every other year, Hill Country weather allows bicycling throughout the year. Admittedly, summer afternoons can be hot, and it pays to cycle early in the day. Occasionally, too, in winter and spring a blustery norther may be followed by several days of rain. From May through July, and periodically at other times, heavy thunderstorms may occur with torrential rain and sometimes golfball-sized hail. The media is usually able to warn of upcoming violent storms, and most state-park tables are equipped with overhead shelters that protect against hail. Nevertheless, spring and fall are eminently suited for bicycling, and most of us who live here ride throughout the year.

It is these and similar factors that have made the Hill Country one of the most uncrowded, unspoiled, and best locales for bicycle day rides and touring in America today. Sample a few of the rides that follow and see if you don't agree.

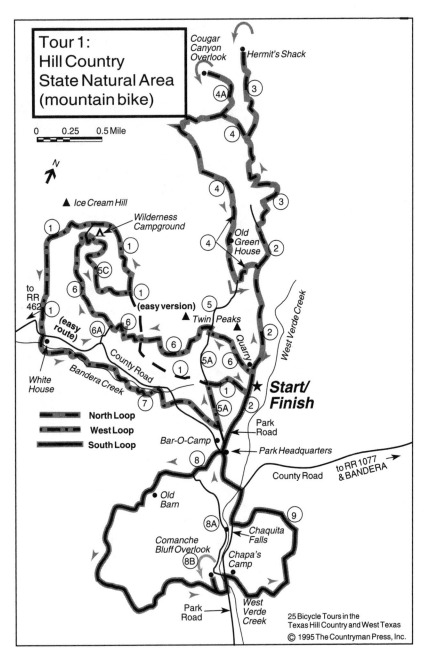

**Tour 1:
Hill Country
State Natural Area
(mountain bike)**

0   0.25   0.5 Mile

N

▲ *Ice Cream Hill*

*Cougar
Canyon
Overlook*

Hermit's Shack

④A

③

④

④

③

④

*Old
Green
House*

②

*Wilderness
Campground*

① △

①

⑤C

①

⑥

① **(easy version)**

⑤

to
RR
462

①

**(easy
route)**

⑥A

⑥

▲ *Twin Peaks*

West Verde Creek

②

⑥

*White
House*

Bandera Creek

County Road

①

⑤A

⑥

Quarry

②

⑦

①

★ ***Start/
Finish***

⑤A

②

North Loop
West Loop
South Loop

Bar-O-Camp

*Park
Road*

⑧

← *Park Headquarters*

to RR 1077
& BANDERA

County Road

*Old
Barn*

⑧A

⑨

*Chaquita
Falls*

*Comanche
Bluff Overlook*

⑧B

*Chapa's
Camp*

*Park
Road*

*West
Verde
Creek*

25 Bicycle Tours in the
Texas Hill Country and West Texas

© 1995 The Countryman Press, Inc.

1
Hill Country State Natural Area
(mountain bike)

Distance: *22.0 miles*
Terrain: *This all-day, three-stage ride offers technical challenges for intermediate or advanced riders yet can also be ridden by partly experienced beginners. Go 7, 15.3, or the full 22 miles.*
Nearest city: *Bandera*
Map: *Hill Country State Natural Area trail map*

A 5400-acre preserve of rocky hills, shallow creeks, and ancient oak groves, Hill Country State Natural Area is one state park that is seldom crowded. That's because only primitive campsites are available and almost everyone who comes here is an equestrian, a hiker, or a mountain biker. With 32 miles of trail, most of which is open to mountain biking, the natural area has a variety of challenging single-track trails with plenty of steep climbs and descents, stair-step ledges, large and small rocks, and creeks to ride through. Beginners with rudimentary skills can also enjoy these trails by simply walking around the gnarly and technical places.

Formerly the Merrick Bar-O Ranch, the present natural area was donated in 1979 with the provision that all 5400 acres be kept far removed and untouched by modernity, with everything left intact and put to a useful purpose. Since the park was opened in 1984, equestrians, hikers, and mountain bicyclists have closely cooperated to maintain these principles. To ensure that these conditions are preserved, I urge you to read the advice for bicyclists on the back of the natural area trail map, especially regarding cooperation with other trail users. You should also read the advice under "Horses" in the introduction to this book. Because trails can be damaged when wet, and because some areas may be flooded, I suggest not riding for a day or so after a heavy rain.

A free trail map is available at the natural area or can be obtained by mail beforehand. The natural area is closed on Tuesdays and Wednesdays. During winter it may be closed at times for hunting. The natural area office is open 8–5 daily on days the park is open. For more information, call the natural area at 210-796-4413, or write Hill Country State Natural Area, Route 1, Box 601, Bandera, TX 78003. Primitive camping is available by permit on Thursday, Friday, Saturday, and Sunday nights.

The natural area is about an hour's drive from Kerrville or a half hour from Bandera. To get there, head south out of Bandera on RR 173 for 0.5 mile, turn right onto FM 1077 and drive 8 miles southwest on a paved road, then drive 2 more miles on a graded dirt road and follow signs into the park. The parking area is 0.6 mile north of the natural area office on a graded road.

Each trail is numbered and identified by signs that are also keyed into the park map. For a full day of riding, I suggest making three separate loop rides from the parking area. At the car after each ride you can have a drink and snack before starting on the next loop. These are the three loops:

1. The North Loop: Hermit's Trace–Cougar Canyon–Twin Peaks

Distance: *7 miles*

0.0   *From the parking area, ride north on Trail #2, actually a graded road.*

1.3   *Turn right onto Trail #3, an interesting single track that climbs and winds uphill and across two steep dips. At Mile 1.8 turn right onto a double track, still designated as Trail #3.*

2.5   *Junction with Trail #4. Stay right on Trail #3, and pedal another 0.5 mile to the Hermit's Shack, an old line cabin in a forest clearing. The two-room cabin is usually open. Return south on Trail #3 for 0.7 mile.*

3.2   *Junction with Trail #4. Turn right. Alternately single then double track, Trail #4 passes a shelter on the right.*

3.5   *Junction with Trail #4A. Turn right onto #4A and ride up this rocky single track to the top of Cougar Canyon Overlook, one of many spectacular viewpoints in the natural area. Return to Trail #4; turn right and continue on #4. Climbing steadily, Trail #4 crosses a low*

By walking the difficult parts of the trail, even beginners can enjoy mountain biking in Hill Country State Natural Area.

pass, then descends a long double-track section to a Trail 4 sign pointing right. Stay on Trail #4.

After passing an old, green house on the left, Trail #4 winds under tall trees along a valley bottom, then crosses a creek and stays on the gravel creek bed for 100 yards.

6.0   *Turn right onto Trail #2, a graded road, and ride south.*

7.0   *The parking area and end of this ride.*

2. The West Loop: Twin Peaks–Wilderness Campground–Bandera Creek

Distance: *5.3 or 6.8 miles*

Basically, this loop consists of a 5.3-mile ride on a generally smooth double-track trail with no formidable hills or obstacles. To ride it, take Trail #1 from the south side of the parking lot and follow it west, then south, for 3 miles until you meet a graded, two-lane county road. An abandoned white farmhouse on the south side of the county road identifies this intersection.

Turn left here and ride 1.75 miles east on the county road to park headquarters; then turn left and ride 0.6 mile north on Trail #2 back to the parking lot.

A more interesting and challenging version can be made on single-track trails as described below.

0.0   *From the parking lot, ride north on Trail #2, a graded road, for 100 yards to a quarry on the left. Turn left into the quarry and ride about 50 yards west until you see an arrow and a single-track trail. By some oversight, this trail is not shown on current natural area maps, nor is the trail numbered at this end. However, this is Trail #6. Start riding west and uphill on #6. This trail climbs high up on the side of the Twin Peaks until it meets Trail #5A.*

0.75   *Turn right onto Trail #5A, go 50 yards north, then turn left onto single-track Trail #6.*

Wide panoramas of forested hills unfold as you ride around the shoulder of the Twin Peaks, then drop steeply down to meet Trail #1.

1.5   *Cross Trail #1 and continue riding Trail #6.*

The next 0.5 mile includes some of the most technical riding in the natural area with steep climbs and descents over twisted rocks and rough ledges. Most beginners elect to walk these.

1.9   *At this junction, Trail #6A forks left. Stay right on #6.*

For the next 0.8 mile, Trail #6 is a smooth double track with no significant challenges.

2.7   *Fork right here onto single-track Trail #5C.*

In just under a mile, #5C takes you on a roller-coaster ride up, over, and down the steep sides of three different hills.

3.6   *Here Trail #5C meets Trail #1. Turn left onto double-track Trail #1 and ride west. At Mile 4.25, you pass a wilderness campground on your left. Then at Mile 4.5, with Ice Cream Hill looming high on your right, Trail #1 winds around a small pond. As you ride down Trail #1, off to the right you see a ranch home beside a small lake.*

5.5   *At this junction Trail #1 ends and intersects with a two-lane, graded county road. Trail #7 also crosses the county road here. A white*

abandoned farmhouse on the south side of the county road identifies this intersection. On the west side of the farmhouse you will find
single-track Trail #7. Ride Trail #7 south for 100 yards to Bandera
Creek and continue.

Negotiating numerous tight bends, Trail #7 crosses and recrosses
Bandera Creek at least a dozen times.

7.0 *Here Trail #7 crosses the county road and continues on the other
side. Stay on single-track Trail #7.*

For 0.5 mile Trail #7 twists through groves of gnarled oaks and
emerges at the Bar-O Camp close to park headquarters.

7.5 *At the Bar-O Camp turn left onto Trail #5A.*

A fairly smooth double track, Trail #5A climbs steadily uphill to
meet trail #1.

8.0 *Turn right here onto double track Trail #1.*

8.3 *Trail #1 reaches the parking area, end of this ride.*

3. The South Loop: Comanche Bluff–Pasture Loop–Chaquita Falls

Distance: *6.6 miles*

Its slow, rocky terrain has earned this trail the nickname of "Interstate Ten."
Yet not all of the South Loop is rough and rocky. At least a mile consists of
a graded road.

0.0 *From the parking lot, ride south on Trail #2, a graded road, to park
headquarters, and continue straight across the county road onto Trail
#8.*

0.9 *Trail #8A branches left here. Stay right on double-track Trail #8.
Riding on sections of rock below tall trees, #8 passes through a
fence with an old metal barn on the left. Here the double track
becomes single track, and you plunge down a rock-strewn slope.*

Threading through deep woodland groves, Trail #8 provides a
bumpy ride on a rocky trail. At Mile 2.3 you commence a steep
descent over a series of contorted rocks and challenging ledges.
Most novices prefer to walk this stretch.

At the bottom you turn right beside a round metal water tank and begin riding on a smoother double track. At Mile 3.6 Trail #8B branches left to climb a short hill to Comanche Bluff Overlook. Ride up if you like, then return to Trail #8.

3.7 *Here Trail #8 meets a graded park road and ends. Turn left onto the graded road.*

One tenth of a mile along this road you pedal through a wide ford about 9 inches deep across West Verde Creek. The river bottom is rocky, so stay in low gear and keep pedaling. Immediately across the creek and on the right are the buildings of Chapa's Group Camp, used by equestrian groups.

3.8 *Beside Chapa's Camp, Trail #9 forks right. Turn right onto this single-track trail.*

Known for tight turns, and with barely enough room to ride between tree branches, Trail #9 makes a fairly level 1.75-mile loop through a pasture and back to the graded road.

5.25 *Trail #9 rejoins the graded park road here.*

Before turning right onto the graded road, turn left for 150 yards to Chaquita Falls campground. The low waterfall can be seen on the west side of the road. Then ride north for 0.3 mile and turn left across a low-water crossing (which is frequently slick). From here, signs direct you along a graded park road to park headquarters.

6.0 *Turn right at park headquarters onto Trail #2, and ride north on this graded park road.*

6.6 *The parking area and end of this tour.*

2
State Mountain–Poli's Chapel
(mountain bike)

Distance: *35.8 miles*
Terrain: *A moderately strenuous ride on hilly, unpaved back roads*
Nearest cities: *Bandera, Kerrville*
County maps: *Bandera, Kerr*

This backcountry ride takes you far from traffic and through a beautiful area of wooded hills to historic Poli's Chapel. Tucked away in a forest clearing, the chapel was built in 1882 by Methodist minister Policarpo "Poli" Rodriguez, a former Texas ranger, army scout, and Indian fighter who finally settled on nearby Privilege Creek.

En route, you ride up and around State Mountain, the most challenging of several steep and demanding hills along the way. Though nontechnical, this ride crosses numerous cattle guards and several low-water crossings that are under water, and often slick, for much of the year. Several picnic tables at Poli's Chapel invite you to stop and enjoy some munchies.

Much of this ride is on graded county roads, which are smooth enough to be ridden on 1.5-inch tires or on a hybrid bike. The ride begins at the junction of RR 173 and Elm Pass Road, approximately 14 miles south of Kerrville and 6 miles north of Bandera. If you prefer, you can park 4 miles east of Bandera at the junction of TX 16 and Privilege Creek Bridge, and begin the ride there (Mile 21 in the road log). Ample parking exists on the highway shoulder at both locations. A glance at the map will suggest several ways to shorten this ride if you prefer not to go the full distance.

0.0 *Starting from RR 173, ride northeast on paved, two-lane, shoulderless Elm Pass Road across flat fields.*

After passing Elmwood Estates subdivision on the right at Mile 2,

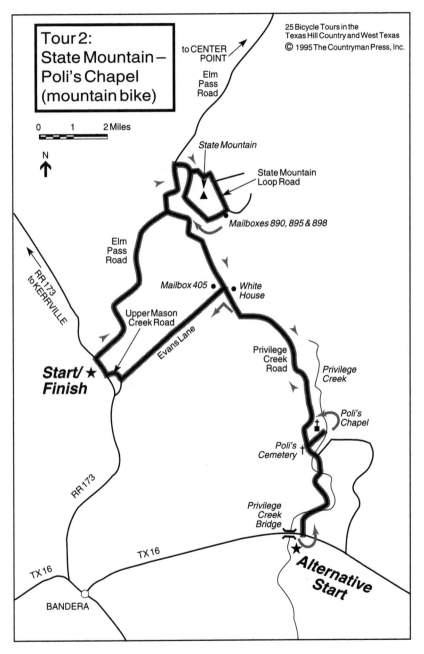

Tour 2:
State Mountain –
Poli's Chapel
(mountain bike)

0   1   2 Miles

N

25 Bicycle Tours in the
Texas Hill Country and West Texas
© 1995 The Countryman Press, Inc.

to CENTER POINT

Elm Pass Road

State Mountain

State Mountain Loop Road

Mailboxes 890, 895 & 898

Elm Pass Road

RR 173 to KERRVILLE

Mailbox 405 • • White House

Upper Mason Creek Road

Evans Lane

Privilege Creek Road

Privilege Creek

Poli's Chapel

Poli's Cemetery

**Start/ ★
Finish**

RR 173

Privilege Creek Bridge

★

*Alternative
Start*

TX 16

TX 16

BANDERA

Elm Pass Road enters rolling hills and continues unpaved for 1.5 miles. As paving resumes again at Mile 4, the round mass of State Mountain looms close on your right, and you can clearly see the road you will later be riding down this mountain.

4.3   *An unpaved and unsigned road branches right here and heads south. Bear left and stay on paved Elm Pass Road.*

Elm Pass Road then climbs a 0.5-mile hill and drops down through tall, verdant oaks.

5.3   *Turn right onto a two-lane, unpaved road that branches off here.*

Though unsigned, this is the State Mountain Loop Road. It immediately dips across a paved low-water crossing and begins a gradual climb.

5.8   *Turn left at this Y-fork and continue on unpaved State Mountain Loop.*

On through tall oaks, and surrounded by wooded hills and ravines, your road begins a steep 0.5-mile climb up the side of State Mountain.

6.75   *Turn right at this triangular road junction identified by two signs that each point left and read Ingenhuett.*

Stay on State Mountain Loop and disregard the driveway at Mile 7 that leads to a private home. Far-flung panoramas of hills and valleys are revealed at every turn as the road plunges steeply downhill.

7.3   *Turn right at this T-junction identified by three mailboxes numbered 890, 895, and 898.*

More great Hill Country views reach away as you spin in low gear up another 0.5-mile hill, then drop steeply down again.

8.5   *Turn left at this fork that you previously passed (at Mile 5.8). Retrace the route you followed earlier back to Elm Pass Road, turn left, and descend Elm Pass Road for 1 mile.*

10.0   *Turn left onto an unpaved one-lane road that branches south here. This is the same road you passed earlier at Mile 4.3.*

For the next 2.25 miles, disregard any turns to the left and stay on this very scenic but unmarked road that winds up and down through wooded hills.

12.25 *Turn left at a triangle-shaped junction here, identifiable by a black mailbox at one corner numbered 405. To further confirm your position, you should pass a white house close to the road on the left and a cattle guard about 200 yards after leaving the junction.*

No road signs exist, but you are now on Privilege Creek Road, and at Mile 13 you commence a 0.25-mile climb up a very steep hill. At the top of the hill on the right is a white building with a paved driveway.

15.0 *Stay right at a series of intersections here where several roads branch left and a sign points left to Privilege Creek Ranch. (Northbound riders stay left.)*

From here on, Privilege Creek Road hugs a series of ridgetops before descending to the Poli's Chapel turnoff. If you reach a low-water crossing, you have gone too far.

18.2 *At a cattle guard, turn left onto a narrow dirt road, and ride 0.25 mile to Poli's Chapel.*

Poli's native stone chapel stands in a clearing beside several tree-shaded picnic tables. A medallion describes how Poli was converted to the Methodist faith in 1858 and built the chapel with his own hands some 24 years later. The chapel is sometimes open; you may enter, but, please, do not play the piano or tug the bell rope.

18.5 *Ride back to Privilege Creek Road, and continue straight across it for 50 yards to Poli's Cemetery.*

Park and walk in through the gate. Poli's grave is the first on the left, and the inscription tells an inspiring story. Also here are clusters of other local family graves. Back on Privilege Creek Road, head south, descend a hill and ride over a low-water crossing, the first of three across Privilege Creek. Immediately south of the crossing is a road fork.

18.75 *Turn right at this road fork. (Northbound riders will find signs here pointing left to Poli's Chapel.)*

Past low limestone cliffs, etched on the right by Privilege Creek, the road runs south for another 2.25 miles.

21.0 *Here, Privilege Creek Road meets TX 16 and ends. You turn around here and ride back the way you came to the same triangular junc-*

tion you passed earlier at Mile 12.25. Bicyclists starting Tour 2 from TX 16 simply follow the itinerary from here to Mile 35.8, then continue to ride from Mile 0.0 back to this point.

32.0 *Turn left at this triangular junction (the same one you passed earlier on the ride at Mile 12.25) identified by a black mailbox numbered 405.*

Though unsigned, the road you are now riding is Evans Lane. Stay on this unpaved, two-lane road for just over 3 miles.

35.0 *Turn right onto unsigned Upper Mason Creek Road, go 100 yards, and turn right onto RR 173 and head north.*

It's 0.75 mile on this paved but shoulderless highway back to your car.

35.8 *Junction with Elm Pass Road and the end of this ride.*

Bicyclists who started from TX 16 should turn back to Mile 0.0 of this ride and follow the itinerary around State Mountain and back to their starting point.

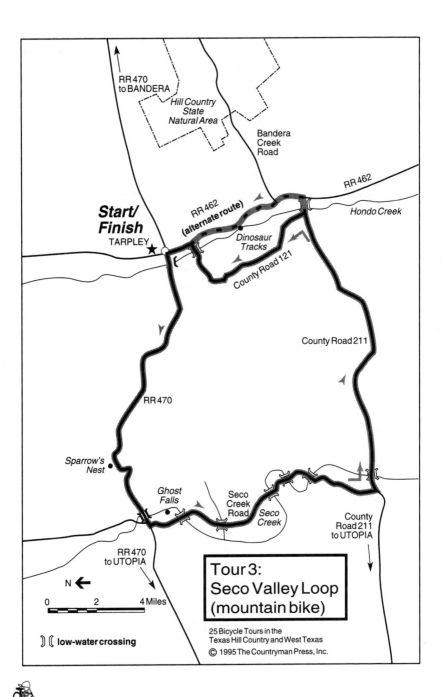

RR 470
to BANDERA

Hill Country
State
Natural Area

Bandera
Creek
Road

RR 462

Hondo Creek

RR 462
(alternate route)

Start/
Finish
TARPLEY

Dinosaur
Tracks

County Road 121

County Road 211

RR 470

Sparrow's
Nest

Ghost
Falls

Seco
Creek
Road

Seco
Creek

County
Road 211
to UTOPIA

RR 470
to UTOPIA

N ←

0   2   4 Miles

Tour 3:
Seco Valley Loop
(mountain bike)

25 Bicycle Tours in the
Texas Hill Country and West Texas
© 1995 The Countryman Press, Inc.

) (**low-water crossing**

38

3

Seco Valley Loop (mountain bike)

Distance: *37.3 miles*
Terrain: *Moderate cycling—first 11 miles of hilly highway, then 26 miles of more level, graded dirt road with six or seven creek crossings*
Nearest city: *Bandera*
County maps: *Bandera, Medina, Uvalde*

Ranging through a remote southwestern section of the Hill Country, this ride takes you through a scenic medley of clear creeks; tall, conical hills; and sinkholes ringed by circles of moss-draped oaks. The ride begins at Tarpley, a hamlet (with a café) at the junction of RR 462 and RR 470, 12 miles west of Bandera.

You then ride 11 miles west on RR 470 on a paved highway that snakes up, down, and across range after range of rugged hills. For the next 9 miles, you head south on a narrow dirt road and you ride across Seco Creek at least five times. Still on a narrow dirt road, you ride east through forested hills for 10.6 miles to Hondo Creek. You complete the loop by riding 7 miles north, either on a dirt road or on RR 462, which passes some dinosaur tracks more than 80 million years old.

You'll enjoy this ride best if you follow the itinerary in a counterclockwise direction and ride RR 470 first. Later in the day, and especially on weekends or holidays, this shoulderless two-lane road carries an appreciable amount of traffic, including RVs, and it has many blind curves. Once on the dirt roads, some creek crossings may be slick, so cross slowly and stay in car tracks. In winter or spring the water can be 9 inches deep. Finally, carry plenty of food and water because none is available en route.

You can park almost anywhere on the shoulder at Tarpley.

0.0 *From Tarpley, ride west on RR 470.*

Don't let the terrific scenery distract you from keeping an eye open for overtaking traffic. Winding, twisting, and plunging over rocky hills and past deep ravines, RR 470 climbs to the top of a pass known as Sparrow's Nest. It then descends and crosses Seco Creek.

11.0 *Watch for an unmarked dirt road that branches left here across a cattle guard. A small telephone company building on the southeast side of the junction helps identify this road as does a stop sign on the dirt road. Turn left here onto Seco Creek Road.*

As you ride south through tall cedars you glimpse Seco Creek flowing between low bluffs on your left. Visible on the left at Mile 12.3 is Ghost Falls, where water flows silently over a limestone ledge. At Mile 13.8 a hill leads down to Seco Creek, and you ride across on a mixture of gravel and bedrock. From here on the creek flows between limestone bluffs on your right, while cattle (and sometimes zebras) graze on deep pastures surrounded by forested hills.

At Mile 15.5 you ride across a tributary of Seco Creek on a wide slab of bedrock framed by low bluffs. At Mile 17 you ride across the creek again on a submerged low-water crossing, and at Mile 17.5 you ride through the creek once more on a wide expanse of gravel. At Mile 18.9 you again pedal over shallow Seco Creek on a wide but often slick slab of limestone bedrock. A final paved low-water crossing may be dry in summer.

20.3 *A T-junction. Turn left here onto unmarked County Road 211, and ride across Seco Creek one last time on yet another paved low-water crossing that is usually dry in summer. (The right fork leads 10 miles west to the village of Utopia and its Lost Maples Cafe.)*

One-quarter mile from the low-water crossing you pass a group of three houses on the left. Without climbing any significant hills, County Road 211 cuts through a verdant region of sprawling oaks and cedars sandwiched between high, rocky hills. At Mile 28.5 a gate on the left leads to Texas Mountain Ranch, and Road 211 becomes two lanes.

30.3 *Intersection with County Road 121. Roads 121 and 211 are identified by numbers on a post here. Tarpley lies 7 miles north. You can return there by riding flat, narrow, unpaved County Road 121 through*

During the Seco Valley Loop Ride, bikers cross
Seco Creek at least six times.

*groves of big trees, followed by a ride across shallow Hondo Creek on
a slab of bedrock. A final ride of 0.9 mile on RR 462 takes you back
into Tarpley.*

SIDE TRIP: Continue east on County Road 211, which crosses
Hondo Creek on a paved low-water crossing, then intersects with RR
462. Turn left onto RR 462—a shoulderless two-lane highway with
fairly light traffic—and ride north. At Mile 32 you pass unpaved
Bandera Creek Road on your right (which leads 6 miles east to Hill
Country State Natural Area). On the left at Mile 34.7 a sign at a parking turnout marks the location of the dinosaur tracks.

The three-toe tracks are clearly visible in the bedrock of Hondo
Creek in about 6 inches of water. Paleontologists consider them to
be at least 80 million years old. Tarpley is 2.6 miles north of here
on RR 462.

37.3 Tarpley, end of this ride.

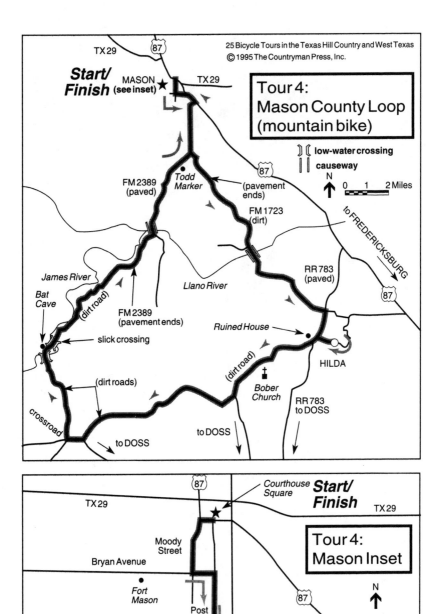

25 Bicycle Tours in the Texas Hill Country and West Texas
© 1995 The Countryman Press, Inc.

Start/Finish (see inset)

MASON

TX 29

TX 29

87

Tour 4: Mason County Loop (mountain bike)

)(**low-water crossing**
‖ **causeway**

N

0   1   2 Miles

FM 2389 (paved)

Todd Marker

87 (pavement ends)

FM 1723 (dirt)

to FREDERICKSBURG

87

James River

RR 783 (paved)

Bat Cave

(dirt road)

Llano River

FM 2389 (pavement ends)

slick crossing

Ruined House

HILDA

(dirt roads)

(dirt road)

Bober Church

RR 783 to DOSS

crossroad

to DOSS

to DOSS

Courthouse Square **Start/Finish**

87

TX 29

TX 29

Moody Street

Bryan Avenue

Fort Mason

Post Hill Street

Rainey Street

87

Tour 4: Mason Inset

N

4
Mason County Loop (mountain bike)

Distance: *47.5 miles*
Terrain: *A fairly level ride with 34 miles of graded dirt road and 13.5 miles of paved road*
Nearest city: *Mason*
County map: *Mason*

Don't look for dramatic mountain scenery. But this all-day loop tour takes you on graded county roads through a land of gentle hills and rivers that saw bloody conflicts between settlers and Native Americans in the 1870s and, a few years later, a desperate range war between ranchers and bands of cattle rustlers. Most of rural Mason County still looks much as it did back in those days, and many back roads carry almost zero traffic.

The ride begins on Courthouse Square in Mason, a pleasant small town with a well-preserved 19th-century square and an extensive historic district that you ride through on this tour. This is a true backcountry ride on narrow dirt roads with no cafés or convenience stores en route, so carry plenty of food and at least two 24-ounce bottles of water. While it's possible to make this ride on 1.5-inch tires, I recommend 1.95-inch tires. The ride includes one of the slickest river crossings in Texas, so be prepared to walk when you reach it, and don't be surprised if you get your feet wet. This crossing is one of several reasons why you should *not* make this ride for several days after a heavy rain.

If this ride sounds rather long, consider a shorter out-and-back ride over a single section. Starting from Mason, for example, ride south on FM 1723 and FM 2389, and continue riding south along the James River. Ride to the bat cave (see Mile 31.5); then turn around, and ride back to Mason for a total round trip of 31.0 miles.

0.0 *From the southwest corner of Mason's Courthouse Square, ride 2 blocks south on Moody Street to Bryan Avenue. Turn left onto Bryan, and ride 1 block east to Post Hill Street. Turn right onto Post Hill and ride south. Many of Mason's most historic homes line Post Hill Street. Ride 4 blocks south on Post Hill to Rainey Street and turn left. Ride east on Rainey Street for 0.5 mile to US 87. Turn right onto US 87, and ride south on its wide shoulder for 0.25 mile.*

1.0 *Paved FM 1723 branches right. Turn right here.*

Gradually, the outlying houses of Mason thin out, the light traffic becomes lighter, and soon you're pedaling between low rolling hills through the heart of rural Mason County.

3.0 *At this Y-intersection with FM 2389, stay left on paved FM 1723.*

Paving continues for another 2 miles; then you're riding on the hard-packed red soil of a graded county road. Watch for patches of drift sand. At Mile 12 you dip down to the wide, rocky Llano River and ride across on a smooth concrete causeway.

13.4 *Intersection with RR 783. Turn right and ride south on this paved, two-lane, shoulderless highway with extremely light traffic flow.*

15.0 *A signed dirt road branches left here to the tiny community of Hilda. Turn left and ride 0.25 mile to the Hilda church. When you return to RR 783, turn left, and ride 0.1 mile south.*

A brief visit to the well-kept cemetery beside the church reveals that this area was largely settled by German pioneers. A medallion on the stone church identifies it as Hilda Bethel Church, built in 1862 and the second-oldest church in Mason County.

15.1 *An unmarked dirt road forks right here. Turn right and head southwest on this graded county road.*

At Mile 15.5 the still-imposing ruins of a once-elegant stone house stand beside the road on the right. The house, which apparently burned, appears to be almost a carbon copy of a similar house with a facade of tall pillars that faces the Hilda church.

On the left at Mile 16.5 you pass another historic limestone building, Bober Church, followed in the next 2 miles by three handsome farm residences. Narrow now, with patches of washboard, the road winds across flat countryside. Ignore two dirt roads that

A typical low-water crossing in the Hill Country. A flood gauge shows the depth of water that may pour across the road following a rainstorm.

branch left at Mile 20.4 and Mile 21.3.

26.3 *Y-intersection with a dirt road that branches left (and leads 16.5 miles east to Doss). Stay right.*

Turkey and deer abound in this wild, remote area.

27.0 *Four dirt roads meet at this isolated crossroad. Turn right and ride north toward Mason.*

Pedal another 2 flat miles; then begin a series of dips across dry creek beds. Next, you ride down several gravel-strewn hills, and at Mile 31.5 you meet the James River. During dry weather the James is little more than a creek. I've always found it safe to carefully ride across the river here on its flat, rocky bed.

Watch for patches of pulverized dust as you pedal up a hill to a sign that points left and reads: Eckert James River Bat Cave Preserve. Open summer Thursday–Sunday 6–9 PM. Phone 347-5970.

Unfortunately, bat-viewing hours don't coincide with the best time of day for bicycling. In case you decide to visit the cave later by car, it's home to some 6 million Mexican free-tailed bats that migrate here from Central Mexico each March. In early June each female bears a pup, and by late October mother and pup migrate back to Mexico. Although the cave is 0.25 mile from the road, you can often see bats flying here during daylight.

32.4 *Second crossing of the James River.*

This is the slick one! Stay left as you approach the river and ride out on a flat rock spit. Dismount before reaching the water. Push your bike through the shallow water while you walk across on a narrow rock ledge that is dry much of the year. Don't be surprised if your bike slides sideways out of your hands. If the river is high, and the rock ledge is covered, you may still be able to walk across safely since it takes some days for algae to build up and become slick. Otherwise, consider walking across a few feet downstream. Whatever you do, take care—and don't say we didn't warn you.

Once back on dry land, continue riding north through low, red hills. At Mile 35 you ride across a series of dips, each with an unpaved (and often dry) low-water crossing.

35.1 *The paved road that forks left here goes to a ranch. Ignore it and stay right on the dirt road.*

Off to the left you may see corrals and another ranch and more evidence of cattle raising activity.

37.6 *The road is paved from here on and is designated as FM 2389, a shoulderless, two-lane farm road.*

Continue to ride through low, rolling, cedar-dotted hills with views of the James River over to the left. Ignore a dead-end dirt road that branches right and stay on FM 2389.

39.5 *Here you ride on a concrete causeway across the wide, rocky Llano River.*

For a while FM 2389 roller coasters up and down across a series of dips. Then it flattens out, and a marker on the right commemorates another Native American massacre, this one of three members of the Todd family in 1864. The foundations of the Todd homestead are visible 100 yards east of the road at the foot of a hill known as Todd Mountain.

44.0 *Here FM 2389 meets FM 1723. Stay left and continue north on FM 1723.*

46.5 *Intersection with US 87. Turn left onto US 87 and ride northwest on the wide shoulder into Mason.*

The shoulder exists almost all the way to the Courthouse Square. On the left at Mile 47.0, a grocery store sells cold drinks.

47.5 *Courthouse Square in Mason, end of this ride.*

Cross-Country Capsule Routings

Kerrville to Mason, 60 miles—partly dirt

County maps: Gillespie, Kerr, Mason

Tracing parts of Tours 4 and 8, this fairly level backcountry route avoids traffic but requires a mountain or hybrid bike, or a touring bike capable of traversing dirt roads. It starts at Ingram, 4 miles west of Kerrville via TX 27. From Ingram ride northwest on the shoulder of TX 27 for 7 miles. Turn right and ride 4 miles north on RR 479 to I-10 (water, drinks) and continue north for 4 more miles on RR 479 to where Resolution Road branches right. Turn right and ride Resolution Road east and north for 5 miles to an intersection with US 290. Turn right and ride 4 miles east on the shoulder of US 290 to Harper (café, convenience store, market) and continue 4 miles east on the shoulder of US 290 to where Old Harper Road branches left (café on right). Turn left onto Old Harper Road and ride 6.4 miles east to junction with Maner Road. (Look up Tour 8, Longer Version, Mile 25.35 to Mile 39.75.) Turn right on Maner Road and ride 9.3 miles north to junction with RR 783. Turn right and ride 1.7 miles north to Doss (water, drinks) and continue north on RR 783 for 6 miles to Hilda. From Hilda, follow the itinerary of Tour 4 in reverse from Mile 15.0 to Mile 0.0, which takes you right into the center of Mason. (If you have a road bike and don't mind a bit of traffic, continue north from Hilda on RR 783 to the junction of US 87, turn left onto US 87 and ride northwest on this highway into Mason. US 87 has a wide shoulder for part of the way. This way you can ride on paved roads the entire distance.)

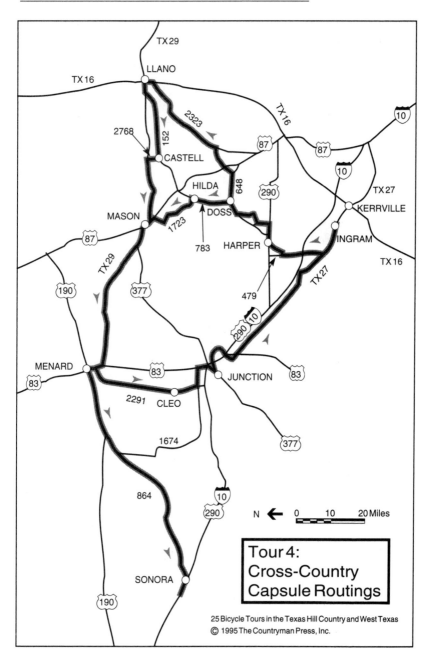

Tour 4:
Cross-Country
Capsule Routings

25 Bicycle Tours in the Texas Hill Country and West Texas
© 1995 The Countryman Press, Inc.

Kerrville to Llano, 75 miles—all paved

County maps: Gillespie, Llano

From Kerrville/Ingram follow the same itinerary just described as far as Doss. At Doss, turn right onto RR 648 and ride 4.8 miles east to the junction with Doss Cherry Springs Road. Turn left here and stay on Doss Cherry Springs Road for 8.7 miles until it intersects with FM 2323. (This route is described in Tour 5 from Mile 0.0 to Mile 8.7.) Turn left onto FM 2323 and ride 21 miles northeast toward Llano. One mile before reaching Llano, turn left onto Wright Street and ride into the center of Llano on quiet residential streets.

Llano to Mason and Menard, 75 miles—all paved

County maps: Llano, Mason, Menard

Leave Llano west on RR 152 and ride 18 miles to Castell (water, drinks). At Castell turn right onto FM 2768 and ride 3 miles north to TX 29. Turn left onto TX 29 and ride west on the shoulder for 16 miles to Mason and for 16 additional miles to the Menard County line. Here the shoulder widens to 7 feet. Continue west on TX 29 to its junction with US 87. Turn right onto US 87 and ride the wide shoulder north for 4 miles into Menard.

Menard to Junction, 39 miles—all paved

County maps: Kimble, Menard

Leave Menard south on FM 2291 and ride this paved, low-traffic road for 32 miles through Cleo to the junction with FM 1674. Turn left onto FM 1674 and ride 5 miles east to the junction with US 83. Turn right onto US 83 and ride 1 mile south on this four-lane road into downtown Junction.

Junction to Kerrville, 48 miles—all paved

Follow the itinerary of Tour 11, Day 1, in reverse.

Menard to Sonora, 58 miles—all paved

County maps: Menard, Sutton

Leave Menard by riding west on US 190 for 17 miles. Turn southwest onto RR 864 for 37 miles, and enter Sonora on Loop 467. Twenty-three miles west of Menard, this generally low-traffic route passes Fort McKavett State Historical Site (water available), a well-preserved frontier fort in service from 1852 to 1883.

From this network of cross-country routes you can easily design a tour of several days. You could then add this tour to the 5-day Hill Country trek in Tour 9; or you could add it to the 6-day Hill Country to West Texas ride in Tour 11. For street maps and accommodations, look up Junction, Kerrville, Llano, Mason, and Menard in the City and Resource Directory at the back of this book.

5
Cherry Springs Loop (road bike)

Distance: *34.2 miles*
Terrain: *Hilly and moderately strenuous back roads with short, steep hills and a steady 2-mile climb*
Nearest city: *Fredericksburg*
County map: *Gillespie*

For a delightful, low-traffic ride through an unspoiled part of the Hill Country, you can't beat the Cherry Springs Loop. Riding narrow back roads through open range—where sheep and goats wander freely on the road—you pass several stone farmhouses a century or more old, some still inhabited by descendents of the original German settlers. You also pass a typically European church built here by German families in 1912. But this is still a sparsely populated region, and save for some Sunday morning churchgoers, it's unusual to meet more than half a dozen vehicles during the entire ride.

Most of the roads you'll be riding are paved country lanes with many cattle guards and low-water crossings. Watch for some cattle guards that are laid obliquely—that is, not exactly at right angles to the road. Deer may also dash out in front of you at any time. But that about covers all the possible hazards. Every road is marked by a metal sign, and a good road map can be had free from the Fredericksburg Convention and Visitors Bureau. Carry adequate food and water because none is available.

The ride starts at the junction of RR 648 and Doss Cherry Springs Road, located 4.6 miles east of Doss and 16 miles northwest of Fredericksburg in Gillespie County. Park on the shoulder of Doss Cherry Springs Road close to the fence.

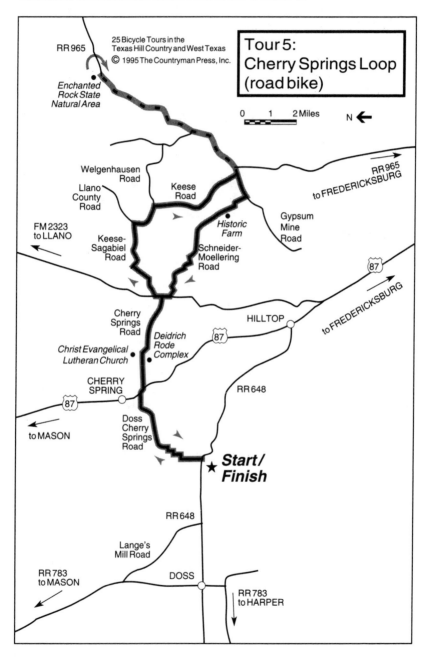

RR 965

25 Bicycle Tours in the
Texas Hill Country and West Texas
© 1995 The Countryman Press, Inc.

Tour 5:
Cherry Springs Loop
(road bike)

Enchanted Rock State Natural Area

0   1   2 Miles

N ←

Welgenhausen Road

Keese Road

Llano County Road

RR 965
to FREDERICKSBURG

FM 2323
to LLANO

Keese-Sagabiel Road

Historic Farm

Gypsum Mine Road

Schneider-Moellering Road

87

to FREDERICKSBURG

Cherry Springs Road

HILLTOP

Deidrich Rode Complex

87

Christ Evangelical Lutheran Church

RR 648

CHERRY SPRING

87

to MASON

Doss Cherry Springs Road

★ *Start/ Finish*

RR 648

Lange's Mill Road

RR 783
to MASON

DOSS

RR 783
to HARPER

0.0   *Ride north on Doss Cherry Springs Road.*

One lane wide, and with almost zero traffic, Doss Cherry Springs Road immediately tunnels under a canopy of live oak trees and crosses a series of narrow low-water crossings. Threading between wooded hills, you ride over two low passes.

4.5   *Intersection with US 87. Go straight across US 87 and continue riding on Doss Cherry Springs Road.*

Riding across level fields, you pass Marschall Cemetery on the left and, on the right at Mile 5.8, come to a three-story farmhouse built of native limestone with several other rock outbuildings nearby. A marker identifies these as the Deidrich Rode Complex, completed in 1880 by Deidrich Rode, a native of Germany. The upper floor of the house was used for storing wool and cotton raised on the land.

Visible just beyond, on the left at Mile 6, is the metal steeple of the gothic revival style Christ Evangelical Lutheran Church, built of native limestone by local church members in 1912. A marker gives the history of the church and of the German Lutherans who settled here in the late 1840s. Until the 1950s, all services were in German. Arriving one Sunday morning before the service began, we were invited into the church to view the magnificent stained-glass windows.

8.7   *Junction with FM 2323. Turn left and go 75 yards north on FM 2323, then turn right onto Keese-Sagabiel Road.*

Several times while riding on Keese-Sagabiel Road I've had to shoo large herds of woolly Angora goats off the road before I could pass. Along here, sprawling groves of live oaks mingle with green hills, and you cross several bubbling creeks on narrow low-water crossings. At Mile 12.6, a sign points right to Saddle Mountain Ranch, still owned by the Sagabiel family.

13.0   *T-intersection with Keese Road. Turn right here and head south on Keese Road.*

Starting at Mile 13.5, you begin a steady 2-mile ascent through a verdant woodland region. Several varieties of cacti grow beneath the trees.

14.0   *Welgenhausen Road branches left. Stay right on Keese Road.*

You continue pedaling uphill through the same magnificent woodland scenery uphill for another 1.5 miles. The next 2.5 miles take you across a level woodland plateau. Suddenly, at Mile 17.5, the road drops steeply down, revealing a fertile green valley below with a farmhouse in the center. In just 0.25 mile you make a steep descent into the valley.

Quite unexpectedly, you find yourself riding on a bedrock surface across a wide but shallow creek. A very steep hill begins immediately on the other side of the creek, so shift into low gear while still crossing the creek.

18.0 **Turn right at this T-intersection, and continue southwest on Gypsum Mine Road.**

SIDE TRIP: Just 75 yards east of this intersection, Keese Road intersects with RR 965. On weekdays, but never on weekends or holidays, you might consider riding 5 miles northeast on shoulderless, two-lane RR 965 to Enchanted Rock State Natural Area and back. Enchanted Rock is a huge, pink granite dome over 400 feet high with hiking trails, and an extensive, tent-only campground nearby. Soft drinks are available at and near the park.

Continuing southwest on Gypsum Mine Road, the next mile is a roller-coaster ride through groves of oaks and forests of cedar.

19.3 **At this T-junction, turn right onto Schneider-Moellering Road.**

One-quarter mile along Schneider-Moellering Road you pedal right through the yard of an abandoned historic farm. A large stone farmhouse is on the left, and next to it a stone barn bears the date 1899. On across scenic creeks, Schneider-Moellering Road climbs to a forested plateau. At Mile 24.5 you descend steeply into a wide valley and come to the junction of FM 2323.

25.5 **Turn right onto FM 2323, and ride 75 yards north to Doss Cherry Springs Road. Turn left.**

You are now back on Doss Cherry Springs Road at the same place as you were at Mile 8.7 earlier in the ride. From here, you retrace your earlier ride but in reverse. At Mile 28.2 you reach the Lutheran Church, and at Mile 29.7 you cross US 87 a second time. The final 4.5 miles takes you back to your car through a picturesque region of rounded, rocky hills.

34.2 **Junction with RR 648 and end of this ride.**

This marker outside the Lutheran church on the Cherry Springs Loop Tour describes its construction in 1912 by local German residents.

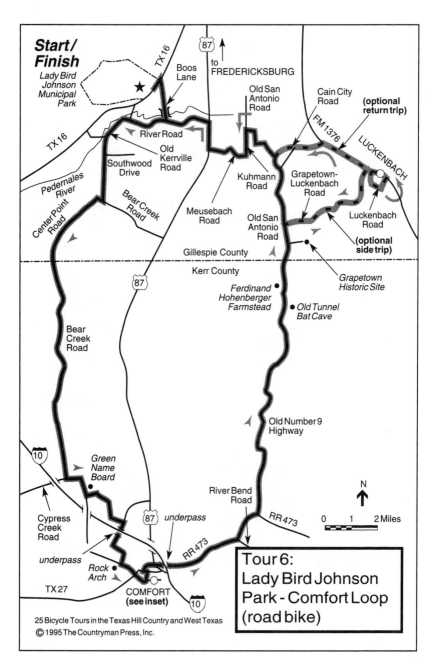

Start / Finish

Lady Bird Johnson Municipal Park

TX 16

Boos Lane

87

to FREDERICKSBURG

Old San Antonio Road

Cain City Road

(optional return trip)

FM 1376

LUCKENBACH

River Road

TX 16

Old Kerrville Road

Southwood Drive

Pedernales River

Center Point Road

Bear Creek Road

Meusebach Road

Kuhmann Road

Grapetown-Luckenbach Road

Luckenbach Road

Old San Antonio Road

(optional side trip)

Gillespie County

Kerr County

87

Ferdinand Hohenberger Farmstead

Old Tunnel Bat Cave

Grapetown Historic Site

Bear Creek Road

Old Number 9 Highway

10

Green Name Board

River Bend Road

N

Cypress Creek Road

87

underpass

RR 473

RR 473

0   1   2 Miles

underpass

Rock Arch

TX 27

COMFORT
(see inset)

10

**Tour 6:
Lady Bird Johnson
Park - Comfort Loop
(road bike)**

25 Bicycle Tours in the Texas Hill Country and West Texas
© 1995 The Countryman Press, Inc.

6
Lady Bird Johnson Park–Comfort Loop (road bike)

Distance: *56.7 miles*
Terrain: *Fairly strenuous and hilly with an optional 12-mile side trip*
Nearest city: *Fredericksburg*
County maps: *Gillespie, Kendall, Kerr*

Mix together miles of picturesque creeks, groves of live oaks and ancient cypresses, dozens of stone farmhouses built by German pioneers, a ride through the historic district of Comfort, a visit to a famous bat cave, and an optional side trip to whimsical Luckenbach, Texas, and you have an idea of the variety available on this all-day Hill Country ride.

The ride starts at Lady Bird Johnson Municipal Park near Fredericksburg and at lunchtime puts you in Comfort, a community of 1500 people, where you can eat in a café, a convenience store, or at the city park. The return itinerary offers an optional side trip of 12 miles (round-trip) to Luckenbach, Texas. Because of the crowds and traffic there on Friday, Saturday, and Sunday afternoons, I suggest avoiding Luckenbach at these times. However, by starting early and pedaling Tour 6 clockwise, you could probably visit Luckenbach on any weekend morning, and get back out before the traffic builds up. Drinks and snacks are available at Luckenbach, though not on Sunday morning.

Whichever way you go, this is apt to be a long ride, and an early start is recommended. (For a shorter trip, consider riding the Center Point Road–Bear Creek Road side of the loop, starting either at Lady Bird Johnson Park or at Comfort. Ride as far as you like; then turn around and return.)

The ride starts from Lady Bird Johnson Municipal Park, located 3 miles south of Fredericksburg on TX 16. Park as close to the entrance as possible.

(You can also bicycle here from Fredericksburg on TX 16; if so, don't ride all the way to the park; instead, 0.5 mile north of the park, turn left onto Boos Lane, and you'll be at Mile 0.5 on the road log below.)

0.0 *From Lady Bird Johnson Park turn left onto four-lane TX 16, and ride northeast on the wide shoulder for 0.5 mile.*

0.5 *Turn right onto Boos Lane and ride south. If the sign has been removed by souvenir hunters, this is the first paved road on your right, and it angles sharply south.*

Boos Lane runs straight and flat for 2 miles, then dips down and across the Pedernales River on a paved low-water crossing.

2.5 *At this triangular junction, turn right onto River Road.*

This narrow country lane runs through farms and past a pair of twin black silos.

4.2 *Turn left at this T-junction onto Old Kerrville Road.*

Old Kerrville Road follows the tree-clad south bank of the Pedernales River.

5.5 *Turn left at this T-junction, and head south on Center Point Road.*

A quiet, paved back road, Center Point Road climbs up a fairly easy mile-long hill. En route, ignore Southwood Drive, which branches left at Mile 6.0.

8.0 *At this hilltop T-junction, Bear Creek Road branches left. Stay right on Center Point Road.*

Traversing several low-water crossings, Center Point Road winds up and down through wooded hills and follows creeks past farms with windmills spinning in the breeze. Cattle guards are numerous, but traffic is usually very light. At Mile 10.5, Center Point Road meanders for a mile under tall oaks beside a picturesque creek with vignettes of historic farmhouses through the trees. After entering Kendall County, Center Point Road becomes Bear Creek Road.

At Mile 13.5 watch for llamas in a fenced pasture on the right. They often have young. At Mile 14.5 a long, steep downgrade is followed by a roller-coaster ride through wooded hills.

18.5 *Turn left at this intersection onto shoulderless, two-lane Cypress Creek Road and ride 1 mile.*

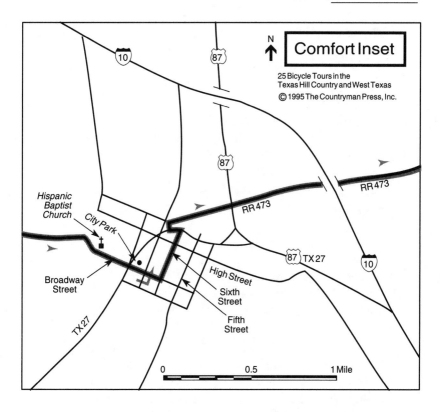

Comfort Inset

25 Bicycle Tours in the
Texas Hill Country and West Texas

© 1995 The Countryman Press, Inc.

19.5 *At this intersection turn left onto an unnamed road. This junction can be identified by a large, green board listing the names of some 30 residents who live on the road. For further identification, 50 yards past the intersection on Cypress Creek Road is a Speed Zone Ahead sign. The unnamed road makes several right-angle turns.*

21.5 *At this intersection, fork right onto another unnamed road, and go through an underpass beneath I-10.*

None of the roads here carry identifying signs. This is a delightful, narrow paved road with very light traffic that winds along a creek and corkscrews over two low-water crossings.

24.5 *At this T-intersection, identified by a small rock arch, turn left onto another unnamed road.*

After 1 mile this unnamed road enters the town of Comfort and becomes Broadway Street. Continue along Broadway. On the left you pass the Hispanic Baptist Church, then the two-story, brick August Faltin House, built in 1894 and one of Comfort's most prestigious mansions.

25.5 *A stop sign and intersection with four-lane TX 27. Go straight across TX 27 and continue down Broadway for 2 blocks to Sixth Street. On the left you pass City Park, ideal for a picnic. Turn left at Sixth Street and go 2 blocks to High Street.*

High Street is the center of Comfort's extensive historic district. One block north on TX 27 is a convenience store, while nearby you'll find a small supermarket (which may be closed Sundays) and two cafés.

Settled in the 1880s by German freethinkers, Comfort's 15 blocks of historic homes and buildings form the best-preserved historic district in the Hill Country. Between Fifth and Eighth Streets, High Street is lined by homes, stores, and buildings dating back to the 1800s. More information is available from the Chamber of Commerce, PO Box 777, Comfort, TX 78013 (210-995-3131).

25.7 *To continue your ride, head north to TX 27—also called Front Street—turn left, and go 100 yards to the junction of RR 473. Turn sharp right onto RR 473, a shoulderless two-lane road. RR 473 crosses US 87 and at Mile 27.8 passes under I-10 and heads across open fields. At Mile 29.5 you pass a large, stone, pioneer-era farmhouse on the left.*

30.2 *River Bend Road branches right. Stay left on RR 473.*

31.0 *Here RR 473 makes an abrupt 90-degree turn to the right. Bear left and go straight ahead on a shoulderless two-lane road marked Old Number 9 Highway.*

The road soon narrows to become a country lane, and traffic diminishes to almost zero. Old Highway 9 winds up and down and along creek beds beside limestone bluffs. Long stone fences border the road, and every half mile or so you glimpse a two-story stone farmhouse built over a century ago by German pioneers. Traversing numerous low-water crossings, Old Highway 9 serpentines between low, wooded hills.

Atop a hill at Mile 39, turn right into a parking area next to a sign

Llamas with their young are a common sight along the route of Tour 6.

reading: Old Tunnel Wildlife Management Area Viewing Platform. A marker at the platform explains that below is a railroad tunnel built in 1913 to link Fredericksburg with San Antonio. After the railroad ceased operating in 1942, millions of bats took over the tunnel. They live there between June and October, emerging each evening at dusk and returning at dawn. Even if you don't see any bats, the panoramic Hill Country view from the platform is worth a stop, while the flat rocks nearby make a good place to rest and munch a snack. As you continue north you can see the old railroad bed on the left.

Behind a long stone fence on the left at Mile 40.5 is the privately owned Ferdinand Hohenberger Farmstead. Consisting of a stone farmhouse and outbuildings, the complex dates from the 1870s and was formerly used as a post office and store. Huge oaks shade this splendidly preserved property, and a marker describes the history of the Hohenberger family.

More historic farms glide past as you pedal north through verdant hills. At Mile 41.6 you enter Gillespie County and Old Highway 9 becomes Old San Antonio Road.

61

42.1 *A side road on the right leads 50 yards to Grapetown Historic Townsite, complete with its original stone schoolhouse and teacher's house plus a large ranch house and other buildings. A plaque states that the schoolhouse was completed in 1884 and all seven grades were taught by one teacher. Continue north on Old San Antonio Road.*

42.9 *At this intersection, Grapetown-Luckenbach Road branches right. (The sign may be missing since virtually all signs with the Luckenbach name are taken for souvenirs.) If you wish, you can turn right here and take a 12-mile round-trip excursion to Luckenbach and return. Otherwise, continue straight ahead on Old San Antonio Road.*

SIDE TRIP TO LUCKENBACH: Turn right at the intersection, and ride 5 flat miles northeast on narrow Grapetown-Luckenbach Road; then turn right onto FM 1376, a shoulderless two-lane road with considerable traffic. Go 0.5 mile on FM 1376, turn right onto quieter Luckenbach Road, and follow it for 0.5 mile to Luckenbach.

Shaded by huge oaks, the small community of Luckenbach, with its unpainted plank buildings, looks much as it did in the 1880s. Except, that is, on weekend afternoons when crowds of country-western fans descend on Luckenbach to enjoy a beer or two and lots of rock, blues, and country music. Known as the town where everybody is somebody, Luckenbach owes its fame to the lyrics of Willie Nelson and Waylon Jennings in their song "Luckenbach, Texas." Snacks and drinks are available, but everything is closed on Sunday mornings and on Wednesdays. Worth seeing is the saloon, the old general store, and the monument to storyteller Hondo Crouch.

You can save a mile or two by returning to the main route via FM 1376 and the Luckenbach–Cain City Road. Because of traffic, however, I recommend returning via the same low-traffic route that you came by and resuming the itinerary below.

42.9 *Intersection of Old San Antonio Road and Grapetown-Luckenbach Road. Turn right onto Old San Antonio Road and ride north.*

44.1 *Junction with Cain City Road on right; a second branch of this same road forks right at Mile 44.4 Neither is marked. Stay left on Old San Antonio Road.*

Old San Antonio Road descends a hill for 1 mile, then makes a sharp

90-degree turn left followed by an equally sharp turn to the right.

47.4 *Exactly at the sharp turn to the right, a paved one-lane road branches left, crosses a cattle guard, passes several houses, and crosses two more cattle guards. Turn left onto this road, which is Kuhmann Road. A mile farther on Kuhmann Road becomes Meusebach Road. Stay on this road as it crosses flat farmland to US 87.*

50.2 *Turn right onto US 87, a busy four-lane highway with no shoulder, and ride 1.4 miles north. Use care, and a rearview mirror, in riding this major highway. Just before crossing the bridge over the Pedernales River, a green sign points left to River Road.*

51.6 *Turn left onto River Road and ride west.*

This narrow country lane follows the south bank of the Pedernales River, passing through several farmyards en route.

54.0 *At this triangular junction, fork right onto Boos Lane, cross the Pedernales River on a low-water crossing, ride 2 miles north to TX 16, turn left, and ride the shoulder of TX 16 for 0.5 mile back to Lady Bird Johnson Park.*

56.7 *Entrance to Lady Bird Johnson Park, end of this ride.*

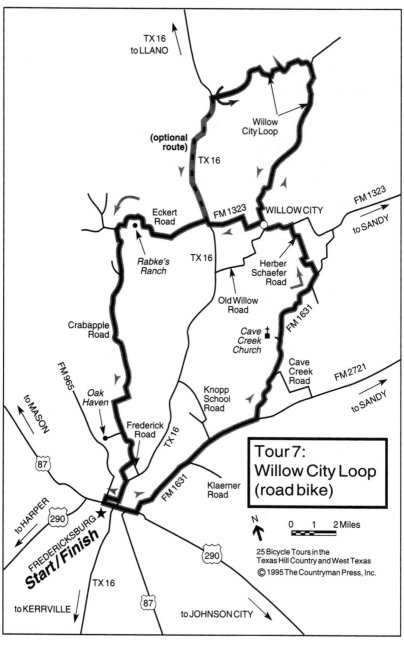

TX 16
to LLANO

Willow
City Loop

**(optional
route)**
TX 16

Eckert
Road

FM 1323

WILLOW CITY

FM 1323

to SANDY

*Rabke's
Ranch*

TX 16

Herber
Schaefer
Road

Old Willow
Road

FM 1631

*Cave
Creek
Church*

Crabapple
Road

Cave
Creek
Road

FM 2721

to SANDY

FM 965

to MASON

*Oak
Haven*

Frederick
Road

Knopp
School
Road

TX 16

87

to HARPER

290

FM 1631

Klaerner
Road

FREDERICKSBURG
Start/Finish ★

TX 16

to KERRVILLE

87

290

to JOHNSON CITY

Tour 7:
Willow City Loop
(road bike)

N

0   1   2 Miles

25 Bicycle Tours in the
Texas Hill Country and West Texas
© 1995 The Countryman Press, Inc.

64

7
Willow City Loop (road bike)

Distance: *65 miles*
Terrain: *Moderately strenuous with steep and demanding hills; a shorter*
26-mile version is easier but still has some steep, challenging climbs
Nearest city: *Fredericksburg*
County map: *Gillespie*

In a distance of 13 miles, the Willow City Loop packs an extraordinary diversity of Hill Country scenes. Not only are the roadsides ablaze with masses of wildflowers in spring, but throughout the year you pass a scenic jumble of clear streams rippling over rocky shelves and ledges, verdant groves of live oak, and rocky, cedar-sheathed hills. Deer bound gracefully over tall fences, and it's not unusual to see a tom turkey followed by a harem of admiring females. En route you pedal through a countryside that hasn't changed much since German pioneers settled here a century and a half ago.

Sound good? It's so good, in fact, that on weekends during the bluebonnet season—usually around Easter—hundreds of motorists, including large RVs and busloads of sightseers descend on the Loop. They create such congestion that the Kerrville Easter Hill Country Bike Rally no longer schedules rides through here. However, on weekdays traffic is much less intense. And after the bluebonnet season, the flow of tourist cars slows to a trickle despite the masses of red and gold wildflowers continuing to bloom along this loop into late May and sometimes early June. Wildflowers or not, this loop is always a spectacular and rewarding ride, and I've enjoyed it most in midwinter.

The scenic section extends for 13 miles, from Willow City north to TX 16 (see map). Thus, the really scenic stretch isn't actually a loop. To complete the loop, you must ride back on TX 16 and share it with everything from 18-wheelers to oversize RVs and speeding cars. Though you ride less than 6 miles on TX 16, those are all uphill miles through a featureless landscape and on a narrow shoulder.

If you're willing to ride an extra 10 miles, consider retracing your route back to Willow City and riding the dramatically scenic section for a second time. There's one really steep, long hill to climb back up, but I personally always go this way. And invariably I find that viewing the Willow City Loop from the opposite direction is like making an entirely new ride.

Water and drinks are available at the Willow City post office weekdays from 8:30–4:30 and on Saturdays till 1 PM. The Corner Post Cafe, also in Willow City, serves barbecue, beer, and soft drinks from 11 AM–8 PM Wednesday through Sunday. Soft drinks and sandwiches are also usually available at Rabke's Ranch, located on the homeward route about 13 miles north of Fredericksburg. However, Rabke's may not always be open.

For a shorter, 26-mile version of the Willow City Loop, drive to Willow City, park there, and ride the 13-mile length of the Loop as far as TX 16. Then turn around and return the same way. This, too, gives you a double exposure to the most scenic section of Tour 7. Another shorter version of this route would be to skip the Willow City Loop but ride the rest.

The full-distance tour begins in Fredericksburg. If staying in Kerrville, you can drive to Fredericksburg in 45 minutes. The mileage below includes riding the Willow City Loop both out and back. If you return via the shortcut on TX 16, the distance is only 55 miles.

0.0   *Park in downtown Fredericksburg outside the public library. Ride east on East San Antonio Street for 3 blocks to South Washington Street, turn left and ride 1 block to Main Street. Turn right onto Main Street and ride 4 blocks east to a sign pointing left to FM 1631. Turn left at this sign onto North Olive Street (FM 1631) and head northeast out of town. Disregard any of the side roads with German names that branch off FM 1631 and stay on two-lane, shoulderless FM 1631 until you reach Mile 7.4.*

Expect to meet a few cars and pickup trucks as you ride out of Fredericksburg and head past farms and fields.

7.4   *Y-junction of FM 1631 and FM 2721. Fork left and stay on FM 1631.*

Again disregarding all obvious side roads, stay on two-lane, shoulderless FM 1631 as it continues through low hills and past more farms. Traffic is fairly light here but may increase on Sunday mornings when folks drive to St. Paul Lutheran Cave Creek Church, on the left at Mile 10.4. A medallion on the church explains that this frame church, with its tin brick siding, was built between 1884–1890 and is the oldest rural Lutheran church in Gillespie County.

14.4 *Turn left onto Herber Schaefer Road.*

For 3 very scenic miles, this narrow country lane winds and twists across tree-shaded creeks and through farmyards.

17.2 *Turn left at this T-junction and ride northwest on two-lane, shoulderless FM 1323 into Willow City.*

Consisting of a dozen houses, a post office, and the Corner Post Cafe, Willow City was named in the 1870s for the abundant willows found here.

18.5 *At Willow City, turn right off FM 1323 and ride north up the narrow Willow City Loop.*

The loop starts out flat, but soon you're swooping up and down hills and negotiating cattle guards and narrow low-water crossings. Almost everyone stops at the top of a hill at Mile 22.4 to admire the stunning views of a valley below, carpeted with bluebonnets in spring. Then you're off on a long, steep descent down a rock-strewn hillside.

Several ranchers have erected metal fences to keep out poachers and sightseeing crowds, and signs along the way ask you to please stay on the road. For miles the loop runs a wild, roller-coaster course through verdant forests and between high, wooded hills. "A tumultuous jumble of scenery," one British bicyclist called it.

An occasional house glides past, and at Mile 29 you pass twice under a power line. From here on, you see pink boulders on the hillsides, and at Mile 30 a free-standing rock pinnacle is visible on the left.

31.3 *T-junction with TX 16. If you wish to loop south on this highway, turn left onto TX 16, and ride 5.7 miles south to Eckert Road. Turn right onto Eckert Road, and resume the log of Tour 7 at Mile 47 below. Via the recommended itinerary, turn around and ride back over this 13-mile stretch of dramatically scenic road to Willow City.*

The big climb back up the rock-strewn hillside begins at Mile 38.5. Whether you stand up and honk or spin your cranks in lowest gear, almost everyone is able to ride back up. (If you can't, your climbing gears are too high for your fitness level.) Besides letting you ride the Willow City Loop twice, this routing also permits a second stop at the Corner Post Cafe in Willow City (unless it's a Monday or Tuesday).

44.0 *At Willow City, turn right onto FM 1323, and ride a flat 3 miles west until you come to TX 16.*

47.0 *Turn right onto TX 16, ride 70 yards north, then turn left onto narrow but paved Eckert Road.*

As everywhere in Gillespie County, virtually every back road is paved and identified by a green metal name sign. Whether or not it's wildflower season, for the next 18 miles traffic should be very light. One reason is that wildflowers are fewer on Eckert and Crabapple Roads.

Passing Great Escape Farm on your left, Eckert Road crosses a wide expanse of wooded hills. On the left at Mile 50.7, and beside a picturesque creek, is the entrance to Rabke's Ranch. The ranch is usually open, and they sell ready-to-eat sandwiches of smoked turkey and ham, sausage, beef breast, bacon, or jerky, and cold drinks. On across more low-water crossings, Eckert Road intersects with Crabapple Road.

51.7 *At this T-junction, turn left onto narrow Crabapple Road and ride south.*

More great views unfold as you crest a series of hilltops, then speed downhill toward Fredericksburg. At Mile 60.7, a road leads right into Oak Haven subdivision. Occasional cars now begin to pass as you climb a mile-long hill. Then, with the church steeples of Fredericksburg in sight, you soar down another hill to a Y-junction.

62.4 *At this fork, turn left onto Frederick Road if you need a cool drink fast. If not, stay right on Crabapple Road. Both roads meet TX 16 0.8 mile beyond. But the Frederick Street route takes you past a convenience store.*

63.2 *Turn right onto North Llano Road (TX 16).*

Wide North Llano Road has ample room for bicycles.

64.7 *Immediately after crossing a bridge, turn right onto East Austin Street, and ride past the octagonal church (it's on your left) to North Crockett Street. Turn left onto North Crockett, cross Main Street, and turn left onto Nimitz Parkway.*

Pedal a few yards east, and you should be outside the public library and close to your car.

65.0 *Downtown Fredericksburg and end of this ride.*

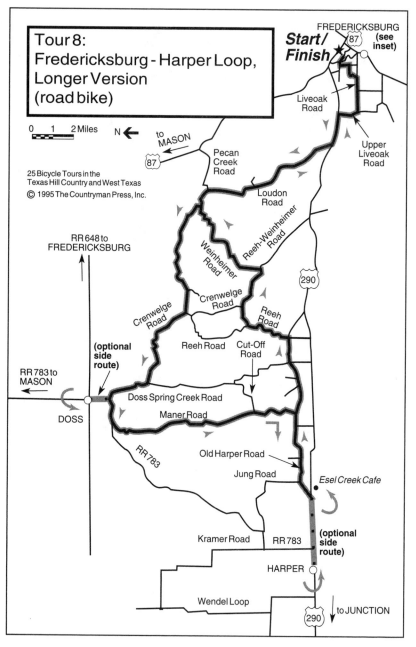

Tour 8:
Fredericksburg - Harper Loop,
Longer Version
(road bike)

0 1 2 Miles   N ←

25 Bicycle Tours in the
Texas Hill Country and West Texas
© 1995 The Countryman Press, Inc.

FREDERICKSBURG (see inset)
87
Start / Finish

Liveoak Road

Upper Liveoak Road

to MASON
87

Pecan Creek Road

Loudon Road

Reeh-Weinheimer Road

RR 648 to FREDERICKSBURG

Weinheimer Road

290

Crenwelge Road

Crenwelge Road

Reeh Road

(optional side route)

Reeh Road   Cut-Off Road

RR 783 to MASON ←

DOSS

Doss Spring Creek Road

Maner Road

RR 783

Old Harper Road

Jung Road

Esel Creek Cafe

(optional side route)

Kramer Road   RR 783

HARPER

Wendel Loop

290   to JUNCTION

8
Fredericksburg-Harper Loops, Longer Version (road bike)

Distance: *71.7 miles*
Terrain: *A fairly strenuous, hilly, all-day ride*
Nearest city: *Fredericksburg*
County map: *Gillespie*

Today you can ride a high-tech bike over a network of winding Hill Country lanes through a land that was settled by German pioneers in the 1840s and that remains timeless and unspoiled. Most roads bear German names, and many ranches are still owned by descendents of the original German settlers. Located in a triangle between Fredericksburg, Harper, and Doss, this smoothly paved back-roads network offers a choice of at least five different loop rides far from frenetic freeways and with almost zero traffic.

These roads are often unfenced. Expect to find large herds of sheep, goats, and cattle wandering around, deer bounding out in front of your bike, and turkeys and jackrabbits scuttling for cover—plus hawks and vultures wheeling overhead. Expect, too, plenty of cattle guards, low-water crossings, and hills of all sizes.

Altogether, I describe how to ride five different loops: Longer Version, 71.7 miles; Shorter Version #1, 29.8 miles; Shorter Version #2, 34.0 miles; and Shorter Version #3, 44.2 miles. Additionally, I describe the Wendel-Jung Loop of 26.35 miles. All take you awheel through hills sheathed with cedar and live oak into a quiet, pastoral world far from the trials of urban living.

To get started on the Longer Version, park in the center of Fredericksburg on or near Nimitz Parkway and close to the public library.

0.0 *From Fredericksburg public library go 1 block south to West San Antonio Street and ride 4 blocks west. Turn left onto South Bowie Street. After two blocks, South Bowie Street curves to the right and dips across a low-water crossing. One-quarter mile beyond this crossing turn left onto Postoak Road and head south to a stop sign. Here, turn right onto Liveoak Road and ride west, disregarding any side roads.*

4.0 *At this T-junction, turn right onto Upper Liveoak Road and ride 1 flat mile north.*

5.0 *At this T-junction, turn left onto four-lane US 290 (no shoulder) and carefully ride 1 mile west. After crossing Liveoak Creek Bridge, climb a hill and look on the right for a turnoff to Loudon Road.*

6.0 *Turn right onto Loudon Road.*

After crossing a concrete bridge, Loudon Road enters an unspoiled pastoral region of meandering, cypress-bordered creeks, rambling stone fences, and sprawling oaks. Through the trees you glimpse historic German farmhouses built of native limestone. All in all, Loudon Road provides 6 superbly scenic miles of hilly riding on a narrow country lane through the Teutonic heart of Gillespie County.

12.8 *Turn left onto Pecan Creek Road.*

This is free range, so don't be surprised to find large herds of goats and sheep on the road.

13.7 *Junction with Weinheimer Road. Stay right on Pecan Creek Road.*

For 5.75 hilly miles, Pecan Creek Road climbs, dips, and twists its way through amazingly unchanged and unspoiled backcountry. Ignore a junction on the right marked Nixon Creek Road, and stay left on Pecan Creek Road. Some of the farmhouses you pass are obviously uninhabited.

19.45 *At this junction turn right onto Crenwelge Road.*

Barely one lane wide yet smoothly paved and virtually traffic-free, Crenwelge Road is typical of Gillespie County's back roads. For almost 4 miles it climbs up and down some challenging hills through a countryside that seems almost uninhabited.

23.35 *At this junction turn right onto Doss Spring Creek Road.*

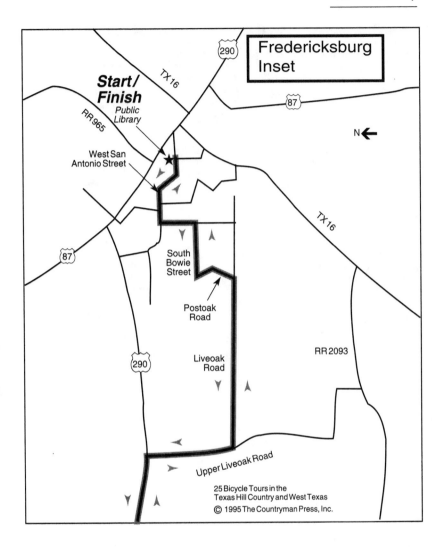

At Mile 25 you emerge into a wide valley, and a mile to the north you see across the meadows the steeple of Doss church.

25.35 Junction with RR 783.

OPTIONAL SIDE TRIP TO DOSS: If you like, you can pedal an extra mile north on shoulderless two-lane RR 783 to the hamlet of

Fredericksburg's octagonal "coffee mill" church is a replica
of the original Vereins Kirche built in 1847.

Doss. Two small stores here, one on RR 648, sell soft drinks and
candy (but are closed on Sundays). Read the medallion on Doss's
handsome Gothic revival church, and if the church happens to be
open, ask if you can view the stained-glass windows from inside.
Elementary students at Doss's one-room schoolhouse recently
scored highest in the state for academic achievement. Return south
on RR 783 to the junction of Doss Spring Creek Road, and resume
the following itinerary.

25.35 *Ride west on RR 783 for 1 mile.*

26.35 *Turn left onto Maner Road, the first paved road on the left.*

Passing small farms and meandering along creeks, Maner Road provides another 9.3 miles of virtually traffic-free cycling. Watch for an
unpaved low-water crossing at Mile 31.65. Shift into low gear, and
pedal across the shallow creek at 3 MPH. From the farther bank
Maner Road abruptly climbs a steep, 1-mile hill. At Mile 33.65, disregard Cut-Off Road, which branches left.

35.65 *At this T-junction, turn right onto Old Harper Road. Disregard Jung Road which branches right at Mile 38.65.*

39.75 *Junction with four-lane US 290.*

If it's Thursday, Friday, Saturday, or Sunday, cross US 290, and turn left for 50 yards to the entrance to Esel Creek Cafe (210-864-4464), open 8 AM–9 PM, Thursday through Sunday.

OPTIONAL SIDE TRIP TO HARPER: On other days—or if you prefer to go anyway—you may elect to ride an additional 4 miles west on the 4-foot shoulder of US 290 to the community of Harper. Founded in 1880 by George Franklin Harper, this is a ranching community and high school center with two cafés (closed Sunday afternoons), a convenience store, and a market (closed Sundays). Return on US 290 to Esel Creek Cafe and the junction with Old Harper Road.

39.75 *From Esel Creek Cafe, cross US 290, turn left for 50 yards, then turn right onto Old Harper Road. Ride east for the next 7.5 miles, and ignore all turns to both left and right. Lightly traveled Old Harper Road traverses rolling farmland, staying 1 mile or so north of US 290.*

46.15 *At this T-junction with Doss Spring Creek Road, stay right on Old Harper Road if you're riding the Longer Version or Shorter Version #2 or #3. (If you're following Shorter Version #1, turn left here onto Doss Spring Creek Road.)*

47.25 *At this T-junction, turn left onto Reeh Road, and ride north for 2.1 miles.*

49.35 *At this T-junction, turn right onto Reeh-Weinheimer Road.*

50.5 *Here Crenwelge Road forks left. To follow the Longer Version and Shorter Version #3, stay right on Reeh-Weinheimer Road for another 2.25 miles. (To follow Shorter Version #2, turn left onto Crenwelge Road.)*

52.75 *At this T-junction, turn left onto Weinheimer Road.*

On past both new and ancient farmhouses, some with crumbling stone fences and pioneer barns, others with whirring windmills, Weinheimer Road winds through a picturesque 5.25-mile cross section of the German Hill Country.

58.0 Here you rejoin Pecan Creek Road at the same spot that you passed earlier at Mile 13.7. If you're following the Longer Version, return to Fredericksburg by turning right and retracing this part of the itinerary in reverse from Mile 13.7 back to Mile 0.0. You should have no trouble doing this since you rode this same route just a few hours previously. (To follow Shorter Version #3, turn left onto Pecan Creek Road.)

71.7 Downtown Fredericksburg and end of this ride.

Fredericksburg-Harper Loop: Three Shorter Versions (road bike)

Distance: Shorter Version #1: 29.8 miles. Shorter Version #2: 34.0 miles. Shorter Version #3: 44.2 miles

Terrain: Hilly on all three versions

To take these shorter loop rides, park at or near Esel Creek Cafe, located on the south side of US 290, 4 miles east of Harper or about 16 miles west of Fredericksburg (and also easily accessible from Kerrville). The Esel Creek Cafe is open only Thursday through Sunday, 8 AM–9 PM. A café in Harper serves an earlier breakfast 7 days a week. If for some reason you cannot park at the Esel Creek Cafe, park on the shoulder of Old Harper Road, which lies immediately north of the café across US 290.

Start by following the route of Tour 8, Longer Version, at Mile 39.75 (Esel Creek Cafe) and continue riding east on Old Harper Road. You then have the three following options:

Shorter Version #1
At Mile 46.15, turn left onto Doss Spring Creek Road, and ride north on this road for 7.1 miles to the intersection with Crenwelge Road. This is the same intersection as that at Mile 23.35 in the Longer Version. Turn left and follow the itinerary of the Longer Version from Mile 23.35 around to Maner Road and back to the Esel Creek Cafe. Total distance 29.8 miles.

Shorter Version #2
Follow the itinerary of the Longer Version to Mile 50.5, which is the junction of Reeh-Weinheimer and Crenwelge Roads. Turn left here onto Crenwelge Road, and ride north for 3 miles to the intersection of Pecan

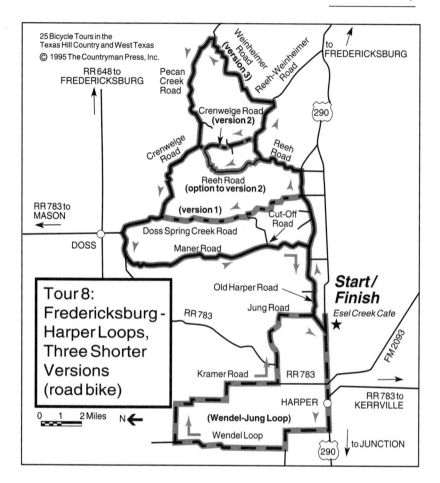

25 Bicycle Tours in the Texas Hill Country and West Texas
© 1995 The Countryman Press, Inc.

RR 648 to FREDERICKSBURG

Pecan Creek Road

Weinheimer Road **(version 3)**

Reeh-Weinheimer Road

to FREDERICKSBURG

290

Crenwelge Road **(version 2)**

Crenwelge Road

Reeh Road

Reeh Road **(option to version 2)**

(version 1)

Cut-Off Road

RR 783 to MASON

Doss Spring Creek Road

DOSS

Maner Road

Tour 8: Fredericksburg - Harper Loops, Three Shorter Versions (road bike)

Old Harper Road

Jung Road

RR 783

Start/ Finish
Esel Creek Cafe
★

FM 2093

Kramer Road

RR 783

HARPER

RR 783 to KERRVILLE

0   1   2 Miles   N ←

(Wendel-Jung Loop)

Wendel Loop

290

to JUNCTION

Creek Road. This is the same intersection as the one at Mile 19.45 on the Longer Version itinerary. Turn left and follow the Longer Version from Mile 19.45 around to Maner Road and back to the Esel Creek Cafe. Total distance: 34.0 miles.

Note: If you've noticed on your map that Reeh Road parallels Crenwelge Road, go ahead and ride Reeh instead of Crenwelge. It adds an extra mile of very scenic, hilly cycling.

Shorter Version #3

Follow the itinerary of the Longer Version to Mile 58, the junction of Weinheimer Road and Pecan Creek Road. This is the same intersection as that at Mile 13.7 in the Longer Version itinerary. Turn left onto Pecan Creek Road and follow the routing of the Longer Version from Mile 13.7 around to Maner Road and back to the Esel Creek Cafe. Total distance: 44.2 miles.

Wendel-Jung Loop (road bike)

Distance: *26.35 miles*

Terrain: *Fairly level but with about 10 miles of very hilly terrain*

Here's yet another loop ride available from the Esel Creek Cafe.

0.0   From the Esel Creek Cafe, turn left onto US 290 and ride west on the 4-foot shoulder of US 290 for 6 miles, passing through the village of Harper (cafés, convenience store) and continuing to a green highway sign pointing right and reading Wendel Loop.

6.0   Turn right onto the Wendel Loop, and ride this low-traffic country lane past several sheep and goat ranches for 14.2 miles of roller-coaster dips and climbs to the intersection of RR 783.

20.6   Turn left onto shoulderless, two-lane RR 783, and ride this low-traffic road for 0.75 mile to where Jung Road forks right.

21.35 Turn right onto Jung Road, a single-lane backcountry road with numerous cattle guards, and cycle past several ranch houses and across a mile of open range to a T-junction with Old Harper Road.

25.35 Turn right onto Old Harper Road, and cycle 1 mile back to a Y-junction with US 290 and the Esel Creek Cafe.

26.35 Esel Creek Cafe, end of this ride.

78

9

West Hill Country Loop: A 5-Day Tour (road bike)

Distance: *275 miles*
Terrain: *A multiday loop tour with strenuous rides on Days 1 and 2, slightly less strenuous but hilly rides on Days 4 and 5, and a level, somewhat easier ride on Day 3. Daily stages range from 48 to 59 miles.*
Nearest cities: *Kerrville, Leakey, Rocksprings, Junction*
County maps: *Edwards, Kerr, Kimble, Real, Sutton*

In 275 miles, this 5-day, 4-night tour takes you through the highest hills and the most rugged river canyons in the Hill Country. You ride generally low-traffic roads, and you spend each night at a modest but comfortable small-town motel. (Because campgrounds are rather inconveniently located, I suggest staying at motels on this tour.)

The first day takes you west from Kerrville along the cool, clear Guadalupe River to Lost Maples State Natural Area, then over a true mountain highway to the picturesque community of Leakey for overnight (59 miles). The second day you ride another challenging mountain road the length of scenic West Frio Canyon to Rocksprings for overnight (53 miles). The third day, admittedly less scenic, takes you to Sonora for overnight (56.5 miles). The fourth day you ride low-traffic Hill Country back roads east to Junction for overnight (58 miles). And the fifth day you ride a hilly route back to your starting point at Ingram or Kerrville (48–52 miles).

I've made this tour almost annually for the past 8 years and for the cost of 4 nights at small-town motels, it's one of the least expensive 5-day vacations available.

When to go? I've done this tour in July, but the best months are mid-October through mid-May. In early fall or late spring carry plenty of water.

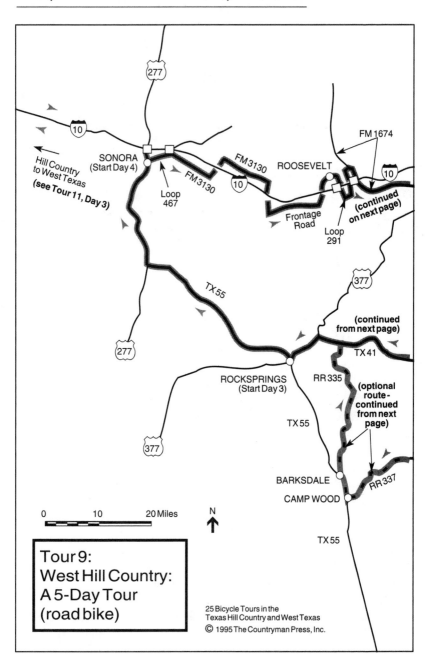

Tour 9:
West Hill Country:
A 5-Day Tour
(road bike)

25 Bicycle Tours in the
Texas Hill Country and West Texas
© 1995 The Countryman Press, Inc.

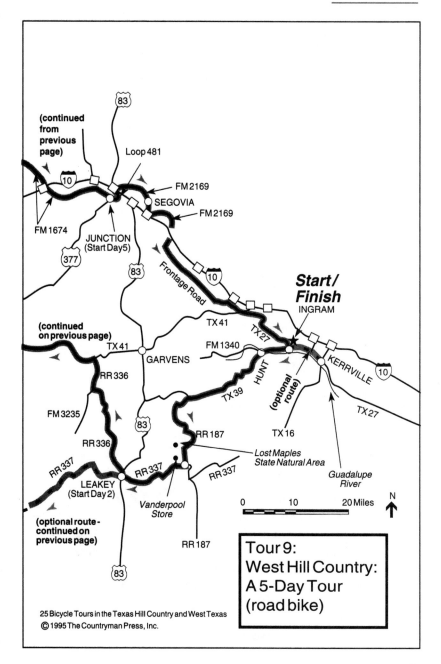

(continued from previous page)

Loop 481

FM 2169

SEGOVIA

FM 2169

FM 1674

JUNCTION
(Start Day 5)

(continued on previous page)

Frontage Road

Start / Finish

INGRAM

TX 41

TX 27

GARVENS

FM 1340

HUNT

(optional route)

KERRVILLE

RR 336

TX 39

FM 3235

RR 187

TX 16

RR 336

Lost Maples
State Natural Area

Guadalupe
River

RR 337

LEAKEY
(Start Day 2)

RR 337

RR 337

(optional route -
continued on
previous page)

Vanderpool
Store

RR 187

0   10   20 Miles   N

Tour 9:
West Hill Country:
A 5-Day Tour
(road bike)

25 Bicycle Tours in the Texas Hill Country and West Texas
© 1995 The Countryman Press, Inc.

Confirmed advance reservations are essential at Leakey and Rocksprings and everywhere on weekends or holidays or during the fall deer-hunting season. Because of increased traffic to state parks in the Leakey area on weekends and holidays, I suggest starting this tour on a non–holiday weekday.

The itinerary given here covers only the first 3 days of the 5-Day West Hill Country Loop. The final 2 days are described under Day 2 and Day 1 of Tour 11, the Hill Country to West Texas tour. Here is how to put together the full 5-day itinerary:

First day: Kerrville/Ingram to Leakey, Tour 9, Day 1;

Second day: Leakey to Rocksprings, Tour 9, Day 2;

Third day: Rocksprings to Sonora, Tour 9, Day 3;

Fourth day: Sonora to Junction, Tour 11, Day 2 in reverse;

Fifth day: Junction to Ingram/Kerrville, Tour 11, Day 1 in reverse.

Tour 9 begins at the junction of TX 27 and TX 39 at the center of Ingram, and all mileages are from this point. To reach Ingram from Kerrville, ride west on the wide shoulder of TX 27. Assuming you start from a motel on the west side of Kerrville, or from the KOA Kampground, the distance varies from 3–5 miles.

DAY 1: Kerrville/Ingram to Leakey
Distance: *59 miles*
Terrain: *A fairly strenuous ride with two major climbs; food and drink available at Mile 6 and Mile 44*
County maps: *Kerr, Real*

0.0 **The ride begins at the Y-fork of TX 27 and TX 39 in downtown Ingram. Fork left onto TX 39.**

As you start to ride, immediately on your right are a series of murals painted on the walls of T.J. Moore's lumberyard depicting the early history of West Kerr County. Also on the right, approximately 100 yards farther on, is River Road Cafe (which serves breakfast) and Hunter House Motor Inn (210-367-2377). TX 39 is a two-lane highway with an 18-inch shoulder and a moderately steady flow of cars and pickup trucks. By starting early, however, most of the traffic will consist of people driving to work in Kerrville, which means it will be in the opposite lane.

At Mile 1, the Guadalupe River appears on your left, and TX 39 hugs this river for the next 20 miles, crossing and recrossing it time after time on narrow low-water crossings. Along the way, you ride through a narrow, river-carved valley wide enough in places for fields and pastures; yet much of the way the Guadalupe is squeezed between high limestone bluffs and steep rocky hills. Elegant riverside homes, youth camps, and plush resorts glide by as you pedal west. At Mile 5.4, TX 39 reaches Schumacher's Crossing, a popular picnic area under tall cypress trees beside a deep river pool.

6.0 *The community of Hunt. FM 1340 forks right here. Stay left on TX 39.*

Just past this intersection on the right is a combined convenience store–deli, where you can enjoy a drink and snack at a polished wood table before a log fire. It's 38 miles to the next convenience store, so this is your last chance for a beverage or snack for a while.

Traffic begins to diminish as you leave Hunt and TX 39 serpentines under ancient cypress trees beside the river. At Mile 12, the 18-inch shoulder ends, and TX 39 begins to cross from one bank of the Guadalupe to the other on a series of narrow low-water crossings. Some crossings are one lane wide and one-way, so watch for cars. By now, however, most of the traffic should have disappeared.

Threading a picturesque course past steep limestone cliffs and verdant hills, TX 39 stays close to the rocky riverbed. In spring, golden and bald eagles often nest in the cliffs that border the river. Finally the river peters out and you ride for several miles across undulating open land.

26.0 *At this T-junction, fork left onto RR 187.*

Passing an occasional ranch entrance gate, two-lane shoulderless RR 187 crosses rolling hills for the next 11.5 miles. Traffic is normally very light, but may be heavier on weekends since this is a feeder road to a state park. At Mile 37.5 you pass two shaded picnic tables on the left.

RR 187 then winds along a ridgetop with steep ravines below on both sides. At Mile 39 the road plunges down a steep, mile-long grade between sheer limestone walls 100 feet high. Layer upon layer of sedimentary rocks are revealed in this deep highway cut.

At the foot of the hill, a road branches right into Lost Maples State Natural Area (210-966-3414), a 2208-acre preserve of rugged limestone canyons, clear springs, and high wooded hills with stands of bigtooth maple trees. Water is available at the Visitor Center, 100 yards from RR 187. The park also has 30 campsites, all available to tenters. During the fall foliage season, the park is crowded every day, but at other times it draws crowds only on weekends and holidays. If you ride in, all low-water crossings are likely to be slick.

Continuing south, RR 187 follows the clear Sabinal River between high wooded hills and past two bed & breakfasts, and two commercial campgrounds to an intersection and a convenience store. Expect some traffic along this 4-mile stretch of RR 187, especially on weekends.

44.0 At this T-junction, turn right onto RR 337.

Also at this junction is the Vanderpool Store, a convenience store with packaged snack food, soft drinks, coffee, restrooms, and, on weekends, barbecued beef sandwiches. Fill up on calories here because a real workout lies ahead.

Immediately upon leaving the store, RR 337 begins to climb between rocky, verdant hills. At Mile 45 you start one of the longest and steepest ascents in the Hill Country. High on your right are layers of stratified rock revealed by a deep highway cut, while the left side of the road drops into a steep wooded valley. At Mile 46 you can rest at a shaded picnic table beside the road. RR 337 then follows a ridgetop with stunning panoramas of hills and valleys on both sides. At Mile 47.3 you begin a steep, twisting descent down a mountainside that, in sheer scenic splendor, rivals North Carolina's Blue Ridge Parkway.

In the next 4 miles you repeat it all again, climbing yet another spectacular mountain, winding along another ridgetop with an extravaganza of views, and making another wild descent down a steep mountain road. From the bottom, a straight 5-mile run through a green valley brings you out on a hilltop. Ahead, Leakey's tall, white water tower is visible among distant treetops, and you smell the fragrance of cedar from the city's cedar oil plant 0.5 mile ahead. You fly down this hill and across the Frio River into Leakey.

59.0 *Intersection with US 83 in downtown Leakey. Turn left and ride south on the wide shoulder of US 83 for 0.25 mile to the markets, café, and the Welcome Inn Motel. Today's ride ends here.*

Look up Leakey in the City and Resource Directory.

DAY 2: Leakey to Rocksprings
Distance: *53 miles*
Terrain: *A fairly strenuous ride with three major climbs; food and water are unobtainable en route*
County maps: *Edwards, Real*

0.0 *From downtown Leakey ride north on the wide shoulder of US 83.*

Two markers tell the history of Real County Courthouse, which you pass on the right.

0.8 *Fork left at this Y-intersection onto RR 336.*

Usually traffic is very light to almost nonexistent on two-lane, shoulderless RR 336. Within a couple of miles you're riding up West Frio Canyon past groves of ancient oaks and cypress and between high wooded hills. At Mile 6.8 a marker commemorates the McLauren massacre of 1881, when Apaches killed Mrs. McLauren and a 15-year-old boy near this location.

Between Mile 9 and Mile 22, RR 336 weaves a roller-coaster course across a region of rugged hills and ridges. The first major climb begins at Mile 9, and you wind up the side of a mountain with an immensely deep valley on the right. Then for several miles the road hugs a ridgetop with deep ravines on both sides. From hilltops you see range after range of blue hills reaching away in every direction. It's hard to find a flat spot anywhere here. Road signs warn of steep grades, sharp curves. Hairpin bends and switchbacks take you up, down, and around a dozen rock-strewn hills. For 3 more miles the road climbs up and down short, steep hills beside the shade-dappled Frio River. Finally at Mile 19 you climb up and away from the river and pedal uphill for 2.2 miles.

21.2 *At this T-junction, FM 3235 branches left. Stay right on RR 336.*

Next you ride across 6 miles of level, wooded open range where deer and turkey often mingle with the herds of sheep and goats that wander freely on the road.

27.0 *At this T-junction, turn left onto TX 41, and ride west on the highway's 4-foot shoulder.*

The scenic excitement is over for today, and you ride west across a rolling landscape of rocky fields and cedar woods. On the right at Mile 30.5 is a phone booth, and just past it on the left is Jon's Garage, not always open, but which may have water and soft drinks. Though you may meet an occasional 18-wheeler, traffic is generally light on TX 41.

40.6 *At this T-junction, RR 335 forks left. Stay right on TX 41, and continue west for 4 more miles to the intersection of US 377. Turn left onto US 377 (at the intersection of TX 41 and US 377 are two shaded picnic tables). Ride south on the 4-foot shoulder. Expect somewhat more traffic for the next 8 miles.*

51.0 *FM 2630 branches right here. Ignore it and stay on US 377.*

A mile beyond you pass Rocksprings Cemetery on the left and a marker explains that it was founded in 1889. Another marker on the right commemorates the site of the original Rock Spring, used by wagon trains in the 1880s, for which the town was named.

52.5 *As you enter Rocksprings, turn right onto the first residential street, go 1 block, then turn left. This detour avoids the congested school area on US 377.*

53.0 *Downtown Rocksprings with the Mesa Motel, Springs Inn, IGA Store, and the town square all within a block. This ends today's ride.*

Look up Rocksprings in the City and Resource Directory.

DAY 2: Optional route via Camp Wood
Distance: *65.4 miles*
Terrain: *Very strenuous with many high hills*
County maps: *Edwards, Real*

If you like, you can ride from Leakey to Rocksprings by the very scenic alternative route described in Tour 10. This takes you from Leakey west on RR 337 to Camp Wood; north on TX 55 to Barksdale; and north on RR 335 to intersect with TX 41. The description of Tour 10 provides a mile-by-mile account of the sights and scenery you'll encounter as you ride from Mile 0.0 at Leakey until you intersect with TX 41 at Mile 53.2. Here you turn left and follow

Bicyclists enjoy grand views of the Pecos River Canyon while riding across this bridge on US 90 between Sanderson and Comstock.

Tour 9, Day 2 from Mile 40.6 into Rocksprings at Mile 53. (These are Tour 9 mileages.)

While this optional route adds a few extra miles of great scenery to Tour 9, and provides access to food and drink en route, you are less likely to encounter traffic on the standard Tour 9 itinerary.

The optional route just described is shown on the map of Tour 9. If you plan to ride it, you should read the description of Tour 10 in its entirety.

DAY 3: Rocksprings to Sonora
Distance: *56.5 miles*
Terrain: *A generally level, fast, and fairly easy ride, but with no food or water en route*
County maps: *Edwards, Sutton*

0.0 *From downtown Rocksprings head west on the shoulder of US 377.*

A marker on the right commemorates the site of the first school in Rocksprings.

0.6 *At this Y-junction turn right onto TX 55, and ride northwest on the 5-foot shoulder.*

For the next 33 miles, TX 55 crosses a lightly rolling landscape of rock-strewn fields dotted with cedar trees and populated by herds of goats and sheep. If you see a lone mule or burro grazing along with the herds, it's because these animals protect the sheep and goats from coyotes. Disregard any side roads. You may meet an occasional large truck or RV, but the wide shoulder gives good protection.

33.0 *At this T-intersection, turn right onto US 277, and ride 22 miles northwest on the highway's 7-foot shoulder.*

There are picnic tables at the intersection. Expect some traffic on US 277, including an occasional heavy truck or RV. If the wind is southerly, as it often is, you can make good speed across this level-to-slightly rolling terrain. At Mile 49.3 you pass a shaded picnic table on the left, and at Mile 51.4 a marker on the left identifies the site of Wentworth, which flourished between 1880 and 1891. Remnants of the ghost town are visible behind the marker.

At Mile 52 the outlying buildings of Sonora come into view, and traffic increases. At Mile 55 is a small grocery store with soft drinks.

56.0 *Two blocks south of Crockett Avenue (a busy intersection), turn left onto Tom Greene Avenue and ride west. At the first cross street, Chestnut Street, you'll find a large supermarket on the right. Continue west on Tom Greene Avenue as far as you can go, then turn right and ride 1 block. This low-traffic detour brings you onto Crockett Avenue, the main thoroughfare, within a block of the Twin Oaks and Zola's Motels and close to a convenience store and deli.*

56.5 *Downtown Sonora, end of today's ride.*

Look up Sonora in the City and Resource Directory.

5-Day West Hill Country Loop

Turn to Tour 11, and ride Day 2 and Day 1 in reverse back to Junction and Kerrville/Ingram. You spend your 4th night at Junction and reach Kerrville/Ingram on the afternoon of the 5th day.

Hill Country to West Texas

Turn to Tour 11 and begin on Day 3. This takes you on to Ozona, Iraan, and Fort Stockton, then to either Alpine or to Balmorhea State Park and Fort Davis.

A Good Out-and-Back Day Ride

Look up Day 2, Mile 21.2 in the preceding road log of Tour 9. Drive to this location, which is the intersection of RR 336 and FM 3235, and park on the shoulder at this infrequently visited spot. Then ride the itinerary in reverse south to Leakey. Have lunch or brunch in the Rio Frio Cafe, on the left on US 83 at the south end of Leakey, and ride back on RR 336 to your car. Total mileage is approximately 43 miles, during which you ride both ways through the West Frio Canyon, one of the most spectacular mountain rides in the Hill Country.

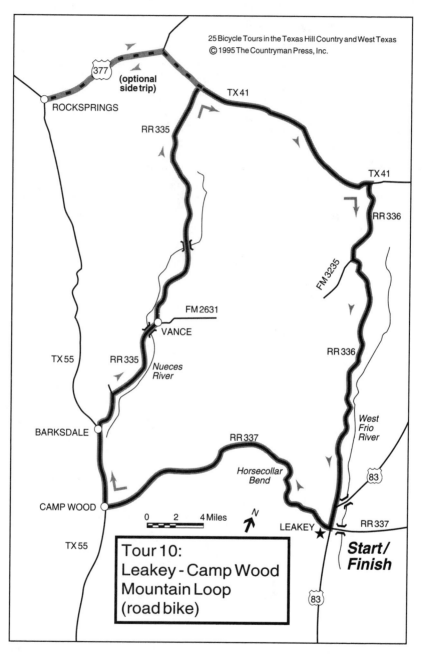

25 Bicycle Tours in the Texas Hill Country and West Texas
© 1995 The Countryman Press, Inc.

377

ROCKSPRINGS

(optional side trip)

TX 41

RR 335

TX 41

RR 336

FM 3235

FM 2631

VANCE

RR 336

TX 55

RR 335

Nueces River

RR 337

West Frio River

83

BARKSDALE

Horsecollar Bend

CAMP WOOD

0   2   4 Miles

N

LEAKEY

RR 337

TX 55

Start/ Finish

**Tour 10:
Leakey - Camp Wood
Mountain Loop
(road bike)**

83

10
Leakey–Camp Wood Mountain Loop (road bike)

Distance: *93.8 miles*
Terrain: *Very strenuous with many high hills; somewhat easier if spread over 2 days*
Nearest cities: *Leakey, Rocksprings*
County maps: *Edwards, Real*

The closest thing to a mountain century ride, this exciting trip takes you over three of the highest and most spectacular roads in the Hill Country. Skirting limestone cliffs and gorges and winding along high ridges, this ride is famed for its breathtaking vistas of isolated valleys and steep ravines. In spring, mountain laurel cloaks the hillsides with masses of purple blooms. Much of this remote highland area seems almost uninhabited, but exotic game is common, and on our survey ride we saw camels, zebras, emus, and llamas near the road.

The first 53.2 miles of this loop starts from Leakey and heads west on RR 337 to Camp Wood, then heads north through Barksdale and up RR 335 to TX 41. At the junction of TX 41 and RR 335, Tour 10 meets Tour 9, Day 2 at Mile 40.6, and you follow the itinerary of Tour 9 in reverse back to Mile 0.0 at Leakey.

You can ride this loop in either direction, but I'd recommend going clockwise. This should provide less exposure to traffic on RR 337 between Leakey and Camp Wood, a shoulderless two-lane road with many blind curves. While traffic is rarely a problem on this road, it does tend to be lighter earlier in the day.

Very strong riders can probably cover the full 93.8 miles of this loop in a single day. Other options are these:

Option 1: From Leakey ride counterclockwise around the loop, spending the night at a motel in either Barksdale or Camp Wood, a distance of 69–74 miles. Ride the remaining 20–24 miles back to Leakey the next morning.

Option 2: From Leakey ride clockwise to Camp Wood and Barksdale, and continue north on RR 335 to TX 41. Turn left onto TX 41, go 12.4 miles west into Rocksprings, and stay there overnight (see Rocksprings in the City and Resource Directory). Your first day's travel totals 65.6 miles. Next morning, follow the 53-mile itinerary of Tour 9, Day 2 in reverse from Rocksprings back to Leakey. The side trip to Rocksprings adds 24.8 miles to the loop, making a total of 118.6 miles spread over 2 days.

Riding the entire loop in 1 day involves traveling for 68 unbroken miles without access to food or water. To complete a century, ride 7 additional miles on the wide shoulder of US 83 after you return to Leakey. Regardless of where you plan to stay overnight on this route, an advance reservation is essential, especially on weekends.

0.0   *Head west from Leakey on RR 337.*

For the first 3.8 miles, this shoulderless, two-lane road threads through a verdant valley between rocky hills. RR 337 then climbs the famous Horsecollar Bend, 1.5 miles of steep mountain road full of switchbacks and abrupt bends with vistas of wooded valleys far below. Once on top, at Mile 5.3, you reach an elevation of 2350 feet, one of the highest points in the Hill Country. For the next 5 miles RR 337 makes a roller-coaster run across a series of steep dips, then at Mile 12 begins to descend. The 2-mile downhill ride is as dramatic as was the climb up Horsecollar Bend. In a wild, twisting descent, you swoop down the mountainside, then level out and continue on into Camp Wood.

20.8   *The community of Camp Wood and junction with TX 55. Turn right onto TX 55 and ride north on the 4-foot-wide shoulder.*

Camp Wood, population 550, has a convenience store, a small market, two cafés, and the Hill Country Motel (210-597-3278). Camp Wood's colorful false-fronted stores and shady park with picnic tables are all within a block of the center. A marker in the park commemorates Charles Lindbergh's landing here in 1924 while flying to California.

On the left as you leave town, a marker identifies the site of Camp Wood, an army post established in 1857 to prevent Native

American raids while another marks the site of Mission San Lorenzo La Santa Cruz, founded by Franciscan missionaries in 1762 and abandoned in 1769. Pedal another 3 flat miles on the shoulder of TX 55 to Barksdale.

24.3 The community of Barksdale and a Y-junction with RR 335. Fork right onto RR 335.

At Barksdale is a café, a filling station with soft drinks, and the Nueces River Motel (210-234-3648). Three historic markers near the motel explain that Barksdale, once called Dixie, was the site of the early-day Nix Mill and was attacked on numerous occasions by Lipan Apaches.

From Barksdale, shoulderless two-lane RR 335 runs under tall trees beside the Nueces River. Here on the right, at Las Palmas Ranch, you may see a variety of exotic African wildlife grazing near the road. At Mile 31.8 you pass through the village of Vance. On the left a marker commemorates the founding of Vance cemetery in the late 1870s.

32.5 FM 2631 forks right here. Stay left on RR 335.

For the next 4 miles RR 335 follows the east bank of the Nueces River between high hills banded by tiers of rock, and at Mile 38 it crosses the river on a wide low-water crossing. This is the largest of some 25 low-water crossings on this road, each equipped with a gauge to show the level of water during a flood. Obviously RR 335 is impassable during and after heavy rains.

RR 335 then winds through steep, wooded hills into Nueces Canyon. To describe this as a roller-coaster highway would be an understatement. For mile after mile the road swoops down into deep dips, traverses low-water crossings, then climbs steeply up again. Huge limestone cliffs and cuts tower above the road on the left, while panoramas of the cypress-bordered river reach away on the right.

At Mile 50 you pass a ranch and commence a steep 1-mile climb up the side of a mountain and onto the rimrock of the Edwards Plateau. As you pedal up, you look steeply down into deep, wooded valleys on both sides of the road. Then you pedal 2 miles across a level plateau.

53.2 A T-junction with TX 41.

To continue this loop and ride back to Leakey, turn right onto the 4-foot shoulder of TX 41 and follow Tour 9, Day 2 in reverse from Mile 40.6 back to Leakey at Mile 0.0.

To go on into Rocksprings for overnight, turn left and follow Tour 9, Day 2 from Mile 40.6 to Rocksprings at Mile 53.

11

Hill Country to West Texas:
A 6-Day Cross-country Tour (road bike)

Distance: *321.5 miles*
Terrain: *A one-way, multiday tour through generally hilly country in stages of 35 to 66.5 miles*
County maps: *Brewster, Crockett, Kerr, Kimble, Pecos, Reeves, Sutton*

This long, open-road ride links the Hill Country with West Texas. From Kerrville, the largest city in the Hill Country, it closely follows the route of I-10 to Fort Stockton in West Texas, then continues to Alpine, the largest city in the Big Bend Country. And it does so by taking you over quiet back roads or service roads; you never have to ride on I-10.

If you *are* willing to ride for a dozen miles on the shoulder of I-10, an optional branch route (Tour 11-B) takes you from Fort Stockton to Balmorhea State Park in the scenic Davis Mountains of West Texas. Whichever way you go, the final day's ride is apt to be dull and flat. But the first 2 days take you over miles of Hill Country back roads, and on the fourth day you ride through one of the largest oil fields in Texas. Almost nowhere is traffic a problem, and you can spend each night in a comfortable motel.

Though this ride is divided into six 1-day stages, given favorable conditions experienced bikers may be able to do it in 5 days. To do so, combine the rides of Day 3 (Sonora to Ozona, 35 miles) with Day 4 (Ozona to Iraan, 51 miles) into a single 1-day ride of 86 miles. If conditions change en route, and you are unable to make the full distance in 1 day, you can still stay overnight at Ozona.

If you enjoy long tours, you may already have realized that this 6-day ride to West Texas can be linked with Tour 24, our 5-Day West Texas Loop tour, to form an exciting 11-day bicycling adventure. If you have the time,

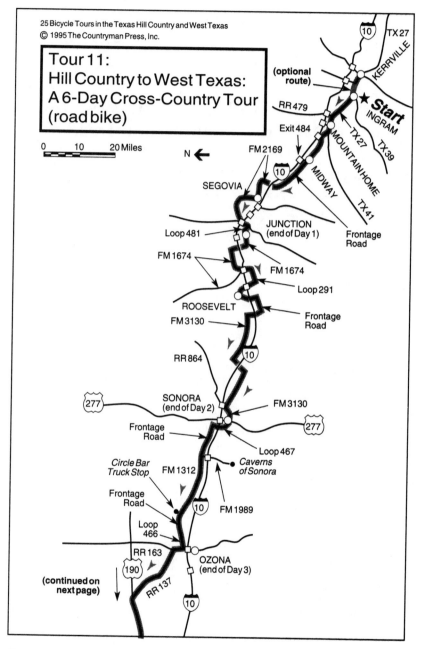

25 Bicycle Tours in the Texas Hill Country and West Texas
© 1995 The Countryman Press, Inc.

Tour 11:
Hill Country to West Texas:
A 6-Day Cross-Country Tour
(road bike)

0   10   20 Miles

N ←

TX 27

10

KERRVILLE

(optional route)

RR 479

★ Start
INGRAM

Exit 484

TX 27

TX 39

MOUNTAIN HOME

TX 41

MIDWAY

FM 2169

10

SEGOVIA

Loop 481

JUNCTION
(end of Day 1)

Frontage Road

FM 1674

FM 1674

Loop 291

ROOSEVELT

Frontage Road

FM 3130

RR 864

10

SONORA
(end of Day 2)

FM 3130

277

277

Frontage Road

Loop 467

Circle Bar Truck Stop

FM 1312

Caverns of Sonora

Frontage Road

10

FM 1989

Loop 466

RR 163

190

OZONA
(end of Day 3)

RR 137

10

(continued on next page)

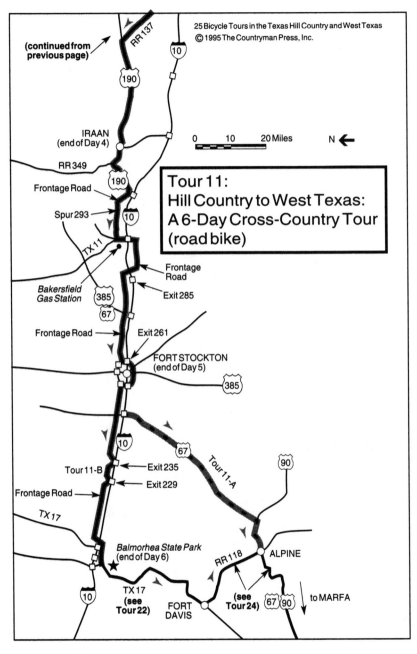

25 Bicycle Tours in the Texas Hill Country and West Texas
© 1995 The Countryman Press, Inc.

(continued from previous page)

RR 137

10

190

IRAAN
(end of Day 4)

RR 349

0   10   20 Miles   N ←

190

Frontage Road

Spur 293

10

TX 11

Tour 11:
Hill Country to West Texas:
A 6-Day Cross-Country Tour
(road bike)

Frontage Road

Bakersfield Gas Station

385

Exit 285

67

Frontage Road →

Exit 261

FORT STOCKTON
(end of Day 5)

385

10

67

Tour 11-A

90

Tour 11-B ← Exit 235

Exit 229

Frontage Road →

TX 17

Balmorhea State Park
(end of Day 6)

ALPINE

RR 118

10

TX 17
(see Tour 22)

FORT DAVIS

(see Tour 24)

67 90

to MARFA

97

and some vacation funds, you can do even more. For a review of the many touring opportunities and options available, read "How to Plan a 21-Day, 1184-Mile Bicycle Adventure." (See page 205.)

Two Good, Half-day, Out-and-Back Rides

If you lack time for an extended tour, you might consider two excellent half-day out-and-back rides along the route of Tour 11. They are:

Ride A

Drive from Kerrville or Fredericksburg to Midway, located at I-10 Exit 484, and park on the south side of the interstate near the Midway gas station and store. You are now at Day 1, Mile 17.5, of Tour 11. Ride west along the route of Tour 11 to Segovia at Mile 37.5. Have lunch at the truck-stop café, and return the same way for a very low-traffic ride of 40 miles round trip.

Ride B

Drive to Junction and park on the west side of town, close to the intersection of US 87 and FM 1674. You are now at Day 2, Mile 1.0, of Tour 11. Ride west along the route of Tour 11 to Roosevelt village at Mile 18.5. Enjoy a drink and snack on the porch of a small store here, then return the same way. This 35-mile round-trip ride along the North Llano River and between wooded hills offers a wonderfully scenic trip that is almost entirely free of hills.

Getting Started on Tour 11

Tour 11 begins at the Y-junction of TX 27 and TX 39 at the center of Ingram, and all mileages are from this point. To reach Ingram from Kerrville, ride west on the wide shoulder of TX 27. Assuming you start out from a motel or the KOA Kampground on the west side of Kerrville, the distance varies from 3–5 miles. Before leaving Ingram, see the murals on the walls of T.J. Moore's lumberyard depicting the history of West Kerr County. You ride right past these murals.

DAY 1: Kerrville/Ingram to Junction
Distance: *48 miles*

Terrain: *A not-too-strenuous but hilly ride with food and drink available en route*

County maps: Kerr, Kimble

0.0 *Fork right at the Y-junction, and ride northwest out of Ingram on the shoulder of TX 27. Varying from 3 to 7 feet in width, the shoulder borders two-lane TX 27 for 14 miles to where it meets I-10.*

Unless it's Sunday morning, you'll meet people driving to and from work at nearby ranches and camps. For the first few miles, TX 27 passes a series of rural homes, guest ranches, and RV parks.

6.5 *Intersection with RR 479, which branches right. Stay left on TX 27.*

In the next few miles, TX 27 climbs up and down through limestone hills. At Mile 8.6 two shaded picnic tables overlook Johnson Creek, and a marker here commemorates the Dowdy family massacre in the 1870s when Native Americans killed four Dowdy children who were tending sheep in the area.

11.8 *Mountain Home Post Office and a crossroads intersection with TX 41. Stay straight on TX 27.*

13.8 *Junction with I-10. Turn left here onto the shoulderless, two-lane frontage road that parallels I-10 on its south side.*

Since most drivers prefer to travel on the interstate, traffic on the frontage road varies from very light to almost nil. Though the frontage road stays within 30–50 yards of the interstate, its traffic is seldom distracting. For the next 10 miles the roadsides here are famed for their masses of vivid blue, red, and yellow spring flowers.

At Mile 17.5 on the left you reach Midway Store, a gas station and convenience store with coffee, soft drinks, hamburgers, and snacks. Then you soar over a series of hilltops with wide vistas of blue hills reaching to the horizon. At Mile 27.5 the frontage road leaves the interstate and winds up and down through deep highway cuts.

33.3 *From here on the frontage road becomes FM 2169, and it immediately makes a 90-degree turn to the right and goes through an underpass below I-10. Do not go straight ahead, which is marked: Dead End.*

34.0 *Here RR 479 branches right. Stay left on FM 2169.*

For 2 miles FM 2169 heads west between low limestone cuts, then plunges downhill for 1 mile and enters Segovia. A truck stop, two motels, two stores, a cedar-oil plant, and a few houses accurately describes the hamlet of Segovia.

37.5 *At Segovia, FM 2169 again meets I-10. Turn left at the stop sign, and cross the I-10 overpass to the truck stop and café on the south side of I-10.*

You'll find a convenience store 150 yards east of the café. Also at the café is Cedar Hills Motel (915-446-3693), popular with truck-drivers, and 0.25 mile east is the Best Western River Valley Inn Motel (E) with restaurant (915-446-3331). Across the road from the café, a marker tells how, in the 1850s, wagon trains bound from San Antonio to Fort Terrett passed nearby on the military road.

37.5 *When you're ready, return across the overpass to the north side of I-10, and continue northwest on shoulderless, two-lane FM 2169.*

For the next 10 miles FM 2169 meanders through cedar-clad hills and across cool, clear creeks out of sight of I-10. Soon the rich scent of cedar oil permeates the air and on the right you pass the chimneys of a cedar-oil plant surrounded by mountains of crushed cedar logs. As FM 2169 approaches Junction, a marker commemorates the Miller-Browning colony, a group of early pioneers who settled here in 1874 and endured as a colony until the early 1900s.

At Mile 47 you pass a convenience store on the right, and the road immediately crosses a bridge over I-10. FM 2169 then passes a Days Inn Motel and runs beside the Llano River, both on your right.

47.5 *Intersection with Loop 481. Turn right here onto Loop 481. Immediately ahead, a long steel bridge crosses the Llano River. Cross to the south side of the bridge and ride across on the walkway. At the other end of the bridge, cross back to the north side of Loop 481. From here it's 3 more blocks to the courthouse and downtown Junction.*

48.0 *Junction, end of today's ride.*

Look up Junction in the City and Resource Directory.

DAY 2: Junction to Sonora
Distance: *58 miles*

Terrain: *A long but fairly easy ride with moderate hills*
County maps: *Kimble, Sutton*

0.0   *From downtown Junction head west on US 87, and cross the Llano River on a four-lane bridge.*

1.0   *Turn left at the junction with FM 1674, and ride west on this shoulderless, two-lane road.*

For the next 17 miles FM 1674 provides frequent glimpses of the North Llano River, its limestone bedrock clearly visible through the transparent water. Huge pecan and oak trees line the river, which flows first on one side of the road, then on the other. Once away from Junction traffic is light, and the 18-mile stretch of road between Junction and Roosevelt is one of the flattest rides in the Hill Country. Markers beside the road identify the site of an 1877 Texas Rangers camp, while another marks the spot where the Marques de Rubi camped in 1767.

At Mile 11.0, FM 1674 crosses a bridge to the north side of I-10 and continues west through a scenic, wooded area.

14.2   *Here FM 1674 forks right. Stay left and continue west on the frontage road, which now becomes Loop 291.*

At Mile 15.2, Loop 291 crosses over a bridge to the south side of I-10. With the North Llano River close on the left, Loop 291 runs through tall trees for 2 miles before turning north under an I-10 underpass toward the village of Roosevelt. Just before entering Roosevelt, a marker explains that the Fort McKavett–Fort Clark Military Road ran through here in the 1870s.

Roosevelt, at Mile 18.5, is best known for the poinsettias that are raised here in greenhouses. Two small stores in the center sell soft drinks, candy, and packaged snack food. It's 40 miles to the next available drinking water. From Roosevelt you continue west on Loop 291.

19.7   *Turn left at this intersection, and cross I-10 on a bridge to the south side of the interstate, then ride west.*

The road, temporarily unnumbered, begins a roller-coaster ride, traversing deep limestone cuts and climbing several long grades. At Mile 24 the road crosses another bridge to the north side of I-10 and continues west. Now numbered as FM 3130, it continues to dip and climb through wooded hills.

28.4 *Harrell Road branches left. Stay right on FM 3130.*

You're now almost halfway to Sonora, and traffic generally ranges from very light to almost nonexistent. For the next 8.5 miles FM 3130 twists, turns, climbs, and dips through rocky hills sheathed with cedar and valleys verdant with live oak. Much of today's ride, in fact, takes you out of sight and hearing of I-10 and through a delightful cross-section of the Hill Country.

Once more, this time at Mile 36.8, FM 3130 crosses an overpass to the south side of I-10 and heads west. At Mile 44 you pass an oil storage depot, and from here on you may meet an occasional tanker truck.

45.7 *At this intersection FM 3307 branches north. Ignore it and continue west.*

FM 3130 continues flat and straight toward Sonora.

53.5 *Here RR 864 branches off to the right, and FM 3130 becomes Loop 467. Turn left onto Loop 467, and ride west on its wide shoulder.*

At Mile 56 you pass Holiday Host Motel on the right, and Loop 467 becomes a four-lane road. (Loop 467 is also known as US 290–Business Loop.)

57.5 *As Loop 467 enters Sonora, it curves right and intersects with US 277. Turn left onto US 277, go 2 blocks south, then turn right onto Tom Greene Avenue. Ride northwest until you reach West Fourth Street. Turn right onto West Fourth Street and ride a short block to four-lane Crockett Street (US 277). This low-traffic route brings you to within a block of Twin Oaks Motel, Zola's Motel, and a deli.*

58.0 *Sonora, end of today's ride.*

Look up Sonora in the City and Resource Directory.

DAY 3: Sonora to Ozona
Distance: *35 miles*
Terrain: *A fairly easy ride with relatively few hills*
County maps: *Sutton, Crockett*

0.0 *From Twin Oaks Motel in Sonora, turn left onto Loop 467, and ride*

northwest across the I-10 overpass to the north side of the interstate. Turn left here onto the shoulderless, two-lane frontage road.

Staying close to the north side of I-10, the frontage road climbs gradually uphill as it heads west. Expect some traffic for the first few miles, including a possible tanker truck. At Mile 5.5 you pass a rest area on the north side of I-10.

7.5 *At this intersection, FM 1989 branches left to the Caverns of Sonora, and the frontage road is now designated as FM 1312. Stay right on FM 1312.*

For much of the next 20 miles FM 1312 traverses wooded hills and stays well away from I-10. Traffic here is usually minimal.

14.0 *At this intersection FM 2129 branches off to the right. Stay left on FM 1312.*

17.5 *At this intersection, paved Glasscock Road branches left. Stay right on FM 1312.*

On through long, rolling wooded hills, FM 1312 returns to the north side of I-10. Here it is designated as an interstate service road, and once more it loses its number. On the right at Mile 28.3 you pass the Circle Bar Motel, café, and truck stop. As it approaches Ozona, the service road veers north and away from I-10; it immediately acquires an 18-inch shoulder and is designated as Loop 466. A few cars and pickup trucks appear as you enter Ozona, and on the right you pass the Flying W Lodge Motel, a popular place for bicyclists to stay. For the next 3 blocks Loop 466 tunnels under a canopy of huge oaks while elegant homes border both sides of the street.

35.0 *Courthouse Square in Ozona, end of today's ride.*

Look up Ozona in the City and Resource Directory.

DAY 4: Ozona to Iraan
Distance: *51 miles*
Terrain: *A generally level ride with several long uphill climbs*
County maps: *Crockett, Pecos*

If you are overnighting at motels, you should have a confirmed reservation at Iraan's Trail West Lodge Motel (915-639-2548) before starting out. It is the only motel in town. Neither food nor water is available during today's ride.

On Tours 9 and 11, murals depicting the history of West Kerr County are painted on the walls of a lumberyard at Ingram.

0.0 *From Courthouse Square in downtown Ozona, head north up four-lane RR 163.*

For 0.5 mile north of the courthouse, RR 163 runs through a canopy of ancient oaks with a row of stately homes on each side. RR 163 then becomes two lanes with a 7-foot shoulder.

3.0 *Turn left at this intersection onto RR 137, a two-lane road with 5-foot shoulders.*

As RR 137 heads northwest across a flat scrubland of low mesquite and juniper trees, you realize that you are rapidly approaching West Texas. Gone are the verdant trees and the shade-dappled rivers of the Hill Country. A harsher land lies ahead. Occasional pickup trucks and an 18-wheeler or two roll by, but traffic would still be classified as light.

17.2 *At this intersection FM 1694 branches left. Stay right on RR 137.*

20.2 *RR 137 meets US 190. Turn left onto US 190, a two-lane highway with a 5-foot shoulder.*

22.0 *At this Y-intersection, fork left onto US 190.*

A marker at the intersection commemorates Crockett County's first oil well, brought in during 1925. There are now 2000 oil wells in the county. Traffic on US 190 averages about 18 vehicles per hour in each direction, and, of course, the wide shoulder continues all the way to Iraan.

Like black wading birds dipping their beaks, oil pumps dot the wide, flat scrubland on both sides of the highway. At Mile 34 you top a rise and enjoy a mile-long downhill run. Beside the road you may see a herd of longhorn cattle grazing in an oil field. Then at Mile 40 you commence a steady 4-mile climb followed by a fast 2-mile descent with magnificent views. At the foot of the hill is a shaded picnic table with more panoramas of oil fields and ranchlands.

To your left an entirely bare hillside appears, dotted with pumping oil rigs. To the right of the hill you discern the rooftops of Iraan. At Mile 50 you cross the Pecos River, and you're officially in West Texas. It's another mile uphill into Iraan. You pass the Memory Garden Cemetery on the left and then Trail West Lodge Motel. Dusty and ringed by oil rigs and storage tanks it may be, but to anyone who has just bicycled 51 thirsty, arid miles, Iraan is a welcome oasis in the desert.

51.0 *Iraan, end of today's ride.*

Look up Iraan in the City and Resource Directory.

DAY 5: Iraan to Fort Stockton
Distance: *63 miles*
Terrain: *a moderately strenuous ride with an initial climb of 10 miles, then mostly level to moderately hilly terrain*
County map: *Pecos*

0.0 *From Iraan's Trail West Lodge, turn left onto US 190, and ride west through Iraan. Stay on US 190—a two-lane highway with 4-foot shoulders—for the next 14 miles.*

At the west end of Iraan a marker commemorates the first oil well of the Yates Oilfield, brought in during 1925, which led to establishment of the Permian Oil Basin, third largest oil field in the US. Leaving Iraan, the highway climbs through hills dotted with oil rigs and pumps. Once clear of Iraan, you should encounter very little traffic until entering Fort Stockton.

4.5 *Here RR 349 branches right. Stay left on US 190.*

US 190 continues to climb through the Yates Oilfield which, for anyone unaccustomed to oil fields, can be interesting and unusual. Traffic is normally quite light, and there are views of distant bluffs and black-topped mesas.

10.0 *Intersection with RR 305, which branches right. Stay left on US 190.*

Still gradually climbing, US 190 ascends a steep, mile-long hill followed by an equally steep and fast 1-mile descent. On the right at Mile 13 you pass the gate to Wilson Bison Ranch, but we've never seen any bison here.

14.0 *US 190 ends at I-10. Turn right onto the frontage road on the north side of I-10, and ride west on this shoulderless, two-lane road.*

On through the White-Baker Oilfield and past more oil pumps, the almost traffic-free frontage road provides vast panoramas of hills and mesas under a wide western sky.

20.0 *The frontage road veers away from I-10 and is designated as Spur 293.*

Passing more oil pumps, many close to the road, shoulderless two-lane Spur 293 heads west across a level area of low brush.

26.3 *A crossroads and junction with TX 11. Turn left onto TX 11, and go 0.25 mile south to a filling station on the right. This location is marked as Bakersfield on highway maps.*

The filling station has cold drinks, coffee, sandwiches, and rest rooms. I-10 is immediately south of the filling station.

26.8 *From the filling station, continue south on TX 11 and cross the overpass to the south side of I-10. You'll find another filling station immediately south of the I-10 bridge. Turn right here, and ride west on the shoulderless two-lane frontage road.*

You ride west on the frontage road across low hills for the next 10 miles until you see the Exit 285, McKenzie Road sign on I-10.

37.0 *Near Exit 285, you turn right on the frontage road, and cross the bridge to the north side of I-10. Turn left here, and ride west on the shoulderless two-lane frontage road.*

Across the interstate on the south side are the buildings of the Domaine Cordier vineyard. The frontage road then swoops up and down a series of hills flanked by mesas.

45.0 *Here FM 2023 branches off south across I-10. Stay right on the frontage road.*

48.4 *Intersection with US 67/US 385, which branches off to the right. Stay left on the frontage road, which continues to parallel the north side of I-10.*

From here to Fort Stockton is a flat, monotonous ride beside the interstate without trees or shelter. On the right at Mile 57.5 you pass a KOA Kampground where soft drinks are available.

60.6 *At I-10 Exit 261, also marked by an Exxon station on the frontage road, turn left and go through the I-10 underpass; then turn right onto four-lane US 385, and ride west into Fort Stockton.*

US 385 has wide shoulders and plenty of room for bicycles. It soon becomes East Dickinson Boulevard, and at Mile 61.7 you begin to pass motels.

63.0 *Downtown Fort Stockton, end of today's ride.*

Look up Fort Stockton in the City and Resource Directory.

11-A

DAY 6: Fort Stockton to Alpine
Distance: *66.5 miles*
Terrain: *A fairly easy and level ride through uninhabited country*
County maps: *Brewster, Pecos*

If made against a strong headwind, this ride could be quite strenuous. Neither food nor water are available en route, and the only rest stops are picnic tables at Miles 25.5 and 58.5.

0.0 *From central Fort Stockton head west on West Dickinson Boulevard, pass under I-10, and turn left onto the frontage road on the north side of I-10. Stay on this shoulderless two-lane frontage road for the next 8 flat, featureless miles.*

10.5 *At this intersection with US 67, bicyclists following Tour 11 to Alpine*

turn left onto US 67 and ride south. Bicyclists following Tour 11-B to Balmorhea State Park continue straight (west) on the I-10 frontage road. (For a continuation of Tour 11-B, see the end of this road log.)

US 67 is a two-lane road with shoulders 4 to 5 feet wide that continue unbroken for the next 48 miles to the junction with US 90. US 67 begins a slow, gradual climb across a scrub-covered plain toward distant hills topped by a microwave tower. After winding through low hills, the highway reaches the tower at Mile 25.5, and here, also, is a picnic area with views of several distant mountain ranges. US 67 then continues to unroll across another wide, flat plain. These desolate, featureless plains are often referred to by bicyclists as "dead zones," but I've still enjoyed the cloud effects and the somber earth tones of the landscape.

Traffic amounts to roughly 15 vehicles per hour in each direction. At Mile 32.5, the highway makes a wide S-bend, crosses a railroad track, and undulates through a series of low hills toward a distant mountain range.

58.5 *US 67 intersects here with US 90. Turn right onto US 90 (which is also US 67), and ride west on the 7-foot shoulder.*

At the intersection are several picnic tables. For the next 8 miles, US 67/US 90 runs along the base of a low mountain range with the Southern Pacific railroad tracks paralleling the highway 100 yards or so to the south. By Mile 61.5 a few houses appear, the first since Fort Stockton. The highway then descends into Alpine and becomes four lanes without shoulders. You pass a gas station and several motels and, on the right, the redbrick campus of Sul Ross State University. Here the highway divides, and you enter downtown Alpine on one-way Avenue E.

66.5 *Alpine, end of today's ride.*

Look up Alpine in the City and Resource Directory.

If you wish to continue with Tour 24, the 5-day West Texas Loop tour, stay in Alpine overnight. On the following day, pick up the itinerary of Tour 24 on Day 1 at Mile 24 (where it stops for lunch in Alpine), and follow it west for 27 miles to Marfa for overnight. Alternatively, if you prefer a slightly longer ride, consider riding 24 miles northwest to Fort Davis on RR 118, then 21 miles south to Marfa on TX 17. The route to Fort Davis is described under Day 1 of Tour 24. The 21-mile ride from Fort Davis to Marfa on TX 17 is flat and uninteresting, but this road does have 7-foot shoulders.

11-B

DAY 6: Fort Stockton to Balmorhea State Park
Distance: *59.5 miles*
Terrain: *A fairly easy, generally flat ride*
County maps: *Pecos, Reeves*

This ride takes you roughly 50 miles west of Fort Stockton along the route of I-10. All but 9 miles of that distance can be ridden on a low-traffic frontage road. But three short gaps in the frontage road must be bridged by riding on the shoulder of I-10. Provided you keep far right, bicycling on interstate shoulders is permitted in rural Texas. Carry sufficient food and water for a 50-mile ride. Do not start out for Balmorhea or Balmorhea State Park without a confirmed reservation for either a motel or a campsite.

After staying overnight at Balmorhea or the state park, you can continue on to Fort Davis by following the route of Tour 22, a scenic trip of 32 miles across Wild Rose Pass.

0.0 *For the first 10.5 miles follow the same routing as that described in Tour 11, Day 6. At the intersection with US 67 at Mile 10.5, leave the Tour 11 route, and continue straight (west) on the same I-10 frontage road you have been riding from Fort Stockton, which parallels I-10 on the north side of the interstate. Continue riding west on this shoulderless, two-lane frontage road for 8.5 more miles.*

19.0 *The frontage road ends. Begin riding on the shoulder of the westbound lane of I-10. Keep far right.*

21.2 *Take I-10 Exit 235, which returns you to the frontage road, and continue riding west.*

23.5 *Here the frontage road passes close to a rest area with toilets and picnic tables that borders I-10.*

24.7 *The frontage road ends. Begin riding on the shoulder of the westbound lane of I-10.*

27.0   Take I-10 Exit 229 (Hovey Road), which returns you to the frontage road, and keep riding west.

31.8   The frontage road ends. Begin riding on the shoulder of the westbound lane of I-10.

36.7   The frontage road recommences. Leave the interstate shoulder and continue cycling west on the frontage road. From here on the frontage road continues unbroken, taking you past miles of flat, irrigated farmland.

48.0   In the next 4.5 miles, three roads branch off to the right, namely FM 2448, TX 17, and FM 1215. Ignore them all and keep riding west on the frontage road on the north side of I-10.

52.5   Just past Exit 209, turn left and cross to the south side of I-10, then turn right onto TX 17. Stay on the wide shoulder of TX 17 through the small community of Balmorhea and for a total distance of 7 miles to the entrance of Balmorhea State Park. The park is located on the left side of the highway.

59.5   Balmorhea State Park, end of today's ride.

Look up Balmorhea and Balmorhea State Park in the City and Resource Directory.

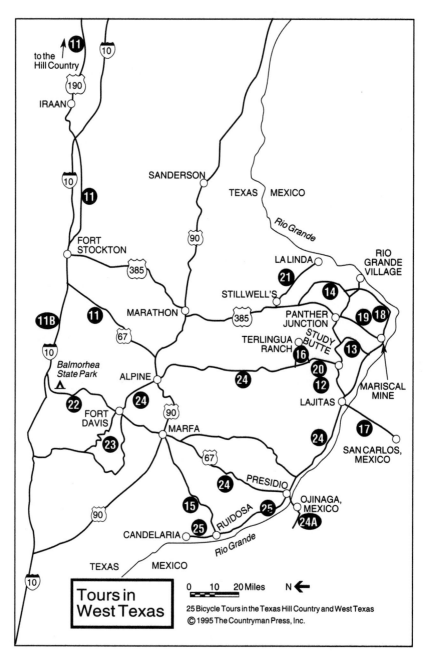

Tours in West Texas

0   10   20 Miles   N ←

25 Bicycle Tours in the Texas Hill Country and West Texas
© 1995 The Countryman Press, Inc.

WEST TEXAS—
THE EMPTY LAND

Early Spanish explorers called it the *desplobado,* the unpopulated land. That description still fits West Texas today. A railroad track and a few thin ribbons of highway linking a handful of small towns are the only signs of civilization in a land essentially unchanged from frontier days. Excluding urban El Paso, the nine Texas counties west of the Pecos are equal in area to South Carolina. Yet the population of this huge, empty region totals barely 55,000. Scores of abandoned homes in towns like Sanderson or Sierra Blanca reveal that these are ghost towns, barely hanging on. Much of West Texas is still so sparsely populated that you can pedal a mountain bike across a wild, primitive landscape of mountains and canyons without seeing another vehicle or a human habitation all day. (Yet every night you can sleep at a comfortable motel, and every day have a hearty dinner and breakfast at a friendly western café.)

While researching this book I discovered that West Texas towns like Alpine, Presidio, Study Butte, and Lajitas are among the most remote in America. Distances seem awesome, and you may be a hundred miles from a pharmacy, supermarket, or convenience store and several hundred miles from a bike shop. I also found that almost everything in West Texas is dry, tough, scrawny, and has thorns.

All this has made the people a tough breed of rugged individualists. Mexican *curanderos* still practice the healing arts in West Texas towns, while Sul Ross State University at Alpine gives credit courses in riding and roping. And the whistle of the locomotive as Southern Pacific freights roll through Alpine and Marfa still seems as lonesome as in Depression days.

Add together the declining population and the rugged scenery—West Texas has more than 90 mountain peaks over a mile high—and the region can be a mecca for the fit, experienced bicyclist. Despite the high mountains, however, West Texas is essentially a desert—the Chihuahua Desert to be exact. And while it's rarely more than 65 miles from one overnight stop to the next, headwinds and heat can sap a rider's energy. For cyclists who are unfit and unprepared, West Texas can be unforgiving.

The cyclist's West Texas falls into two parts. North of US 90 the high, cool Davis Mountains surround Mount Livermore, at 8382 feet the second highest peak in Texas. From June through September tourists flock here to escape the summer heat, and these months are less attractive for cycling. Spring and fall are ideal, however, and if you don't mind an occasional frost, biking can be enjoyable on most midwinter days. Except for Davis Mountains State Park and Fort Davis National Historic Site, all land is private, and opportunities are nil for mountain biking.

South of US 90 lies the Big Bend country, a vast, untamed region of mountain and desert reaching south to the Rio Grande and Mexico. Bordering the Rio Grande are three enormous tracts of land. To the west is state-owned Big Bend Ranch State Natural Area, 450 square miles of mountains and canyons that will eventually be open to the public and will contain some 50 miles of road and trail for mountain bicycling.

To the east lies Big Bend National Park, where the wild crags of the Chisos Mountains overlook far-flung desert panoramas dotted with abandoned quicksilver mines and relics of early ranching days. While single-track trails cannot be ridden in national parks, a series of rough and quite challenging dirt roads offer mountain bikers a unique opportuniy to explore the 1106 square miles of this huge, federally owned area. For a variety of reasons (including big climbs, long distances, RV traffic, lack of shoulders on paved park roads, the fact that campsites cannot be reserved ahead, and also because Chisos Basin Lodge—the only motel-type accommodation in the park—is booked solid most of the year) opportunities for road bicycling on the park's paved roads may be somewhat limited.

North of and between these two parklands sprawls the huge 435-square-mile expanse of Terlingua Ranch. Years ago this enormous property was subdivided into hunting tracts and sold to the public. To access these tracts, some 1100 miles of rough dirt roads were bulldozed, creating a labyrinth of double-track trails, dirt roads, and jeep trails. Provided you stay on the roads and keep off the land, all of which is privately owned, mountain bikers are welcome to explore this wonderfully scenic area. If you like, you can tent camp or stay in a motel at the ranch headquarters in the remote Christmas Mountains.

Turnoff to Terlingua Abaja on Old Maverick Road in Big Bend National Park.
Ahead is the colossal rock wall of the Terlingua Fault,
cut through on the right by Santa Elena Canyon.

East of Big Bend National Park, other huge tracts are used for wildlife management or belong to The Nature Conservancy. The northern half of the Big Bend country consists primarily of private ranches and is inaccessible. With the exception of some yet-to-be-opened single-track trails in Big Bend Ranch State Natural Area, single-track bike trails are nonexistent. Additionally, a series of paved roads takes you through the heart of this wild border region, including a 50-mile ride beside the Rio Grande on one of America's most spectacular river roads.

Since temperatures may reach 110 degrees or more from May through September, cycling is not recommended in the Big Bend region during these months. Early spring and late fall are ideal, and I've spent entire weeks here in December and January, bicycling all day, every day, in generally ideal weather and at a time of year when few tourists visit. All over West Texas water is more precious than titanium, and for any ride of 3–5 hours you should carry at least two 24-ounce water bottles or the equivalent in a camelback. For rides exceeding 5 hours, or in warmer weather, three water bottles are recommended; in hotter weather, four bottles. Few bikers carry rain gear, yet when it does rain in West Texas, it often comes in torrents. It's not unknown for the entire annual rainfall of 8 inches to fall in a single afternoon.

It's best to avoid Terlingua Ranch during the short hunting season, usually from Thanksgiving to mid-December. Big Bend National Park is also filled with students during spring break, as, undoubtedly, will be Big Bend Ranch State Natural Area when it opens.

Wildlife is abundant in West Texas though not always visible, since many animals are nocturnal. Black bear and mountain lion are making a comeback. But the animals you're most likely to see while bicycling include herds of *javelina* or black wild pigs (usually in mountains), herds of fawn-and-white pronghorn antelope, which always have a sentinel on lookout, and mule deer, if you're out riding early. Commonly seen crossing roads in daylight are bushy-tailed coyotes and the comical *paisano,* or roadrunner, the state bird of Texas. Also common along roads are large raptors like red-tailed and Harris hawks, which perch atop utility poles. On Tours 14 or 19 you may also spot a golden eagle or peregrine falcon.

Immense cliffs and canyon walls near highways make the Big Bend area a geological showplace. A hundred million years ago, this area lay beneath the ocean. But 35 million years later it was home to the Big Bend pterodactyl, with a wing span of more than 50 feet the largest creature ever known to fly. Dinosaurs also roamed here then. Erosion and time shaped the land into the mountainous Chihuahua Desert that you pedal through today. Among local names for natural features are *tinaja* or *hueco,* which means a natural water tank, and "pouroff," a waterfall that exists for an hour or two after a rain.

While a few shoulderless two-lane roads must be ridden with care, most West Texas highways have wide shoulders and are lightly traveled. For the fit, experienced cyclist, the entire area offers superb cycling at a time of year when much of the US is buried in snow.

For more information on the Big Bend parks, call or write Big Bend Ranch State Natural Area, PO Box 1180, Presidio, TX 79843 (915-229-3613); or Big Bend National Park, TX 79843 (915-477-2251).

12

Sawmill Mountain Loop (mountain bike)

Distance: *20.4 miles*
Terrain: *A fairly strenuous and hilly cross-country loop through scenic mountains and canyons; an optional extension adds 10.8 miles, making a grand total of 31.2*
Nearest city: *Study Butte*

From colorful Terlingua ghost town, you ride a roller-coaster loop on unmarked roads across a rugged section of West Terlingua Ranch. Terlingua Ranch is an association of the owners of small hunting preserves, and the roads you'll be riding were bulldozed to provide access to these properties. The roads are open to all, but the land is private, so, please, stay on the roads and off the land.

The road you'll be following is not the only road. A score of lesser side roads lead off it. Most are obviously side roads, or you can see that they lead to a cabin. But finding your way can be mildly challenging. No signs exist until you've ridden 11 miles, and you must navigate by landmarks. It may help to have a set of topo maps. In the 7.5 series, these are Terlingua, Amarillo Mountain, Yellow Hill, and Hen Egg Mountain quads. While these four maps show some of the roads you will ride, they do not show them all. Thus topo maps are mainly useful for identifying mountains, creeks, and other landmarks. Actually, the map in this book should prove more helpful than most others.

I recommend avoiding this area during the Thanksgiving-to-mid-December hunting season. The rest of the year, once you're a mile or two away from RR 170, you may not see another human or vehicle all day. You and your bike are simply swallowed up in the silence. No shelter, trees, or water exist either, so come prepared. To avoid getting lost, if you don't sight the landmarks I mention fairly close to the mileage I give, you may be on

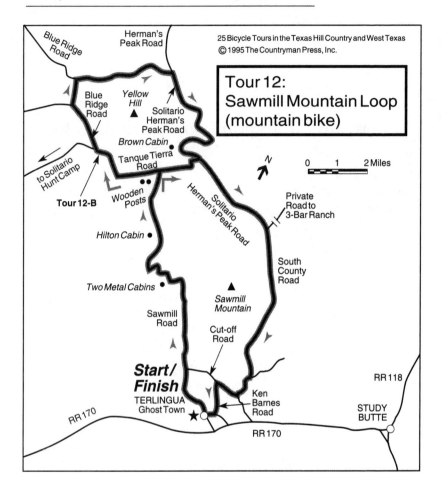

Tour 12: Sawmill Mountain Loop (mountain bike)

the wrong road. While your cyclocomputer or mine might be off by a few percent, consider turning back if you fail to find these identifying landmarks within a reasonable time. To guide you back, I suggest marking the return route with a small stone cairn at each intersection. I took 4.5 hours to complete this loop. It could take longer if you take a wrong turn or if you take the optional extension around Yellow Hill. This extension, which adds 10.8 miles, is described in the road log that follows.

The ride begins in the center of Terlingua ghost town, reached by a signed but unpaved spur road (0.5 mile long) that branches north off RR 170 four miles west of Study Butte. Park near, but not in front of, the Terlingua Trading Company store and the Starlight Theater. A café on the left serves breakfast (but check the opening time beforehand).

Until 1942, Terlingua's quicksilver mines employed several hundred miners, and this was a thriving community. Today it's a place of rambling adobe ruins. Some have been rebuilt and are occupied. The large trading post is still intact and sells Native American jewelry and handicrafts as well as guidebooks, maps, soft drinks, and beer. There's also an old cemetery. I suggest postponing any exploration until after you return.

To get started, face north. You will see a dirt road climb out of Terlingua and head north up a steep hill. This is Sawmill Road, the one you will ride.

0.0 *From outside Terlingua's Trading Company store, ride east on a dirt road for 50 yards, then turn left and walk or ride up Sawmill Road.*

As you ride over rock slabs and follow the road around to the left, panoramas of Terlingua are revealed on your left. At Mile 1.2, at the top of the hill, is a stone cottage on the left side of the road.

1.75 *Turn right at the Y-fork here.*

1.8 *Turn left at this Y-junction.*

The road to the right is a cut-off road leading 0.5 mile east to a county road that you will ride today and also on Tour 20. Ignore obvious side roads, roads that lead to cabins, or that have grass or weeds.

You can now see Sawmill Mountain, 3797 feet high and about 2.5 miles north. Weaving a tortuous roller-coaster route, Sawmill Road crosses a wide patch of bare ground at Mile 3.3. Ignore the turnoff here on the right. Sawmill Road is now plainly visible hugging a hillside as it climbs up Sawmill Canyon about a mile to the north. Sawmill Mountain, with its rocky south face, is now on your right (east).

At Mile 4.2 you climb out of Sawmill Canyon onto a hilltop. Stunning vistas reach away north across eroded badlands to the huge bulk of Hen Egg Mountain (shaped like a single camel hump), and the high peaks of the Chisos are clearly visible on the right. Sawmill Mountain is just 0.5 mile to the east. The road now descends.

4.5 *A road forks left. At the apex of this Y is a small grass triangle with a bush growing in the center. Turn left.*

Sawmill Road now drops steeply downhill, angles 90 degrees to the right, and climbs another hill for almost a mile. To your left is a pointed, conical hill, and behind it is Hen Egg Mountain. Splendid views of distant mountains reach away on all sides, while spindly ocotillo and prickly pear cactus border the road.

At 5.5 miles, as the hill tops out, you see two metal cabins close together about 200 yards from the road on the left. This is a key landmark you cannot miss.

5.7 *Turn left at this unmarked Y-junction.*

The road then descends 0.3 mile to another junction.

6.0 *Turn right at this unmarked Y-fork. You can identify it because Sawmill Road makes a U-turn to the right here.*

Your road then immediately begins to switchback down a mountainside. This is a long but mostly smooth descent. At Mile 6.5 you reach the bottom. Sawmill Road then crosses a creek bed on a rock slab and winds through more foothills. On your left at Mile 7.2 is another unmistakable landmark: an old stone cabin with porch about 25 yards from the road and marked Hilton with a reversed N. Please, do not leave the road to go to this or any other cabin. Sawmill Road then winds through a canyon.

8.0 *Fork left at this unmarked T-junction. At Mile 8.35 do not take the side road that branches right and heads up a canyon.*

9.6 *At this T-junction Sawmill Road meets Tanque Tierra Road. No signs exist, but a pair of wooden posts on the west side of the intersection once held a sign, and they clearly identify this road junction. Fork right here, and head east on Tanque Tierra Road.*

OPTIONAL EXTENSION AROUND YELLOW HILL: At the junction at Mile 9.6 you may extend this ride by adding an additional 10.8-mile loop around Yellow Hill. To do so, turn left instead of right. The routing for this extra loop, designated as Tour 12-B, is described at the end of Tour 12. Road log mileages in parentheses indicate the total distance via the Yellow Hill extension.

9.6 *To resume Tour 12: Head east on unmarked Tanque Tierra Road. This*

The Terlingua Trading Company store and the Starlight Theater in the center of Terlingua ghost town, the starting point of Tour 12.

smooth road soon drops into a deep, eroded canyon. As you start up the other side, a road branches left and heads north along the canyon bottom. Do not take it. Stay right and climb up out of the canyon to a T-shaped junction at the top.

11.0 (21.8) Intersection of Tanque Tierra Road and Solitario Herman's Peak Road, also known as the County Road. A wooden sign here identifies both roads. Turn right onto Solitario Herman's Peak (the county) Road. (Tour 12-B, the Yellow Hill extension, rejoins the main itinerary here.)

Wider now, the county road winds along a high ridge between a deep, eroded badlands area on the right and an eroded wash on the left.

14.2 (25.0) At this T-intersection a private road branches left to the 3-Bar Ranch. A wooden sign here identifies the road you came on as Solitario Salt Grass Draw Road and the road on your right as South County Road. It seems the county road has many other names. Turn

right onto South County Road.

Riding is easier now, and Sawmill Mountain is clearly visible 1.5 miles on the right.

17.0 (27.8) *Fork right at this unmarked T-shaped junction.*

The roofs of several ranch houses are visible on the left.

18.8 (29.6) *Fork right at this unmarked junction, and ride 0.5 mile to the west.*

You're now riding a cutoff road that links the county road with Sawmill Road. Before reaching Sawmill Road, however, make the following turn.

19.6 (30.4) *Fork left at this T-junction onto Ken Barnes Road.*

Ken Barnes Road is not marked until farther on, but you can see some of the houses of Terlingua below on the left. Follow Ken Barnes Road downhill for about 0.6 mile and past several houses.

20.2 (31.0) *Here Ken Barnes Road meets the dirt spur road leading from RR 170 to Terlingua. The ghost town is visible 0.2 mile on the right.*

20.4 (31.2) *Terlingua ghost town.*

And you deserve a well-earned cold drink on the porch of the Trading Company store.

12-B

The Yellow Hill Extension, 10.8 miles

This loop around Yellow Hill adds 10.8 miles of exciting scenery to Tour 12, making a total of 31.2 miles. To ride it, follow Tour 12 as far as Mile 9.6, then continue as follows:

9.6 *Junction of Sawmill Road and Tanque Tierra Road. Turn left.*

From here, Tanque Tierra Road climbs steeply west through eroded foothills for almost a mile, then drops into a draw. You ride across a canyon and climb steeply up the other side. The road is now circling Yellow Hill, named for the eroded yellow foothills that surround it, and you're about a mile away from Yellow Hill summit.

12.2 *At this Y-junction are three wooden signs. One points left to Solitario*

Hunt Camp, another points right to Blue Ridge Road, and a third also points right to Solitario Hunt Sections E, F, G, and H. Turn right onto Blue Ridge Road.

13.5 *At this T-junction signs indicate that Blue Ridge Road is to the right, while Solitario Hunt Camp and Hunt Sections E, F, G, and H are to the left. Turn right onto Blue Ridge Road.*

The mountain ridge to the west is the outer rim of the huge Solitario caldera, which lies within Big Bend Ranch State Natural Area. You now head north across a wide, level area with Hen Egg Mountain looming to the east.

14.4 *At this T-junction signs indicate that Blue Ridge Road forks left, while Herman's Peak Road is to the right. Turn right toward Herman's Peak Road.*

As you head gradually downhill, a deep canyon appears below on your left, and the road plunges steeply to the canyon floor. At Mile 16 you cross a narrow wash on the canyon bottom, and climb steeply up the other side.

17.4 *T-junction with Herman's Peak Road, also known as the county road. Turn right here and head south.*

Below on your right you see another wide, deep canyon with a brown cabin on the canyon floor. The road you see crossing the canyon floor is the same one on which you are riding. At Mile 19.7 your road switchbacks abruptly down into the canyon, crosses the canyon floor on a wide slab of slickrock, and heads past the lone cabin, which is off to your right. All around are walls of stratified rock tinted with muted tones of yellow and gray. Your road then climbs up out of the canyon and crosses the shoulder of a hill on your right.

20.7 *Here a side road forks right up the hill. A single sign points back the way you came and reads: Herman's Peak Road. Bear left.*

As you gradually descend for the next mile, a deep canyon parallels your route on the right. Far below you see green mesquite trees along the canyon floor.

21.8 *Junction of Herman's Peak Road and Tanque Tierra Road. A wooden*

sign identifies both roads but names Herman's Peak Road as Solitario Herman's Peak Road. At this point rejoin Tour 12 at Mile 11. In the description of Tour 12, mileages via the Yellow Hill extension are given in parentheses from this point on.

13
Old Maverick Road–Santa Elena
(mountain bike)

Distance: *26.5 miles*
Terrain: *A moderately easy dirt-road ride without major hills; optional side trips and extensions*
Nearest city: *Study Butte*
Map: *Trails Illustrated Big Bend National Park, 1:100,000*

Old Maverick Road begins near the west entrance to Big Bend National Park and runs gradually downhill for 13.25 miles to emerge near the mouth of immensely deep Santa Elena Canyon. Though the landscape appears harsh and barren, a century ago the foothills were covered with native grasses, and tall cottonwoods grew along the creeks. Sufficient water existed for pioneer farmers to raise grains and vegetables in the floodplains of streams. But overgrazing by early ranchers, followed by the appearance of sheep and goats, destroyed the vegetation, and nowadays the creeks flow only after heavy rains. Yet relics of pioneer-day agriculture and early homesteads provide interest along the way, and the views of distant mountains are dramatic.

Although Old Maverick Road lies completely within Big Bend National Park, it is seldom patrolled. It is also badly washboarded and after rains may be impassable to cars. Even in dry weather relatively few cars use it. All of which makes it attractive for bicycling, and bikers can avoid the washboard ripples by riding at the edge of the road. Only a single turnoff exists, and it is clearly marked. However, no water is available the length of the road.

Even with some sightseeing and a short side trip to a ruined village, you can ride the length of Old Maverick Road in 3 hours, and you should easily return in 2. With a couple of extra hours to spare, consider the following options:

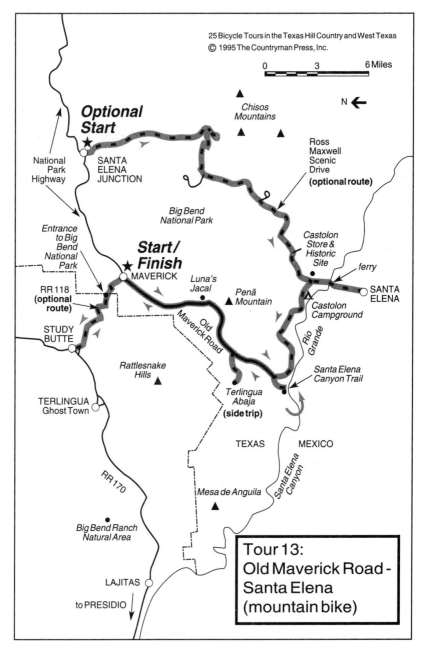

25 Bicycle Tours in the Texas Hill Country and West Texas
© 1995 The Countryman Press, Inc.

0   3   6 Miles

N ←

Optional Start

National Park Highway

SANTA ELENA JUNCTION

Chisos Mountains

Ross Maxwell Scenic Drive **(optional route)**

Big Bend National Park

Entrance to Big Bend National Park

RR 118 **(optional route)**

Start / Finish
MAVERICK

Luna's Jacal

Castolon Store & Historic Site

ferry

SANTA ELENA

Penā Mountain

Castolon Campground

STUDY BUTTE

Old Maverick Road

Rattlesnake Hills

Rio Grande

Santa Elena Canyon Trail

TERLINGUA Ghost Town

Terlingua Abaja **(side trip)**

TEXAS   MEXICO

RR 170

Santa Elena Canyon

Mesa de Anguila

Big Bend Ranch Natural Area

LAJITAS

to PRESIDIO ↓

Tour 13: Old Maverick Road - Santa Elena (mountain bike)

1. At the south end of Old Maverick Road, turn right onto the paved park road, and ride 0.5 mile to the parking area for Santa Elena Canyon. It's a hike of 0.3 mile to the canyon mouth, and, if you like, you can hike another 0.5 mile into the canyon.

2. At the south end of Old Maverick Road, turn left onto the paved park road, and ride a flat 7 miles east to Castolon Campground (water). It's another mile up the same road to Castolon Historic Site, where you'll find a historic store (water, soft drinks) plus some pioneer-day agricultural machinery. Alternatively, from the campground you can ride 0.5 mile east on the paved road, then turn right onto a dirt road that leads for 1 mile to Santa Elena ferry. Here you can cross with your bike on the rowboat ferry to the Mexican village of Santa Elena, and, if you like, you can lunch at one of two restaurants.

3. For anyone with a car shuttle available, a third option exists, starting from the junction of the park highway and the Castolon–Santa Elena Road, which is located 13 miles west of Panther Junction (park headquarters). The Castolon–Santa Elena Road is also known as Ross Maxwell Scenic Drive. Though this paved road has no shoulders, it runs generally downhill for over 20 miles through some of the grandest mountain scenery in Big Bend. Even with a fat-tired bike you should make it to Castolon store in 2 hours. I suggest starting to ride early in the morning and moving along briskly because car and camper traffic builds up by midmorning, and the road has many blind curves. Once at Castolon store you can follow our road log in reverse back up Old Maverick Road to the park highway. Your car shuttle should meet you here. Or, with care, you could ride the narrow paved road (RR 118) for 5 mostly downhill miles to Study Butte. (Eventually RR 118 may be widened.)

   To reach the start of this ride, drive to the junction of Old Maverick Road located approximately 5 miles east of Study Butte on the park highway. The trailhead is well marked and has parking space for several cars.

0.0   Old Maverick Road Trailhead.

This two-lane road starts off gradually downhill and heads across a treeless expanse of creosote bush toward the low Rattlesnake Hills. At Mile 4 the road dips down through the Rattlesnake range. Off to the left the sharp peak of Elephant Tusk soars above the horizon, and next to it is the unmistakable outline of Mule Ears Mountain. Ahead, the deep cleft of Santa Elena Canyon is clearly visible in the immense rock wall that runs for miles along the Mexican side of the Rio Grande River.

Soon you see a rocky mountain and a line of cliffs bordering the road on the left. Just before reaching the cliffs, at Mile 6.9, the *jacal* of Gilberto Luna appears low down beside the road on the left. *Jacals* are primitive, low-ceilinged dwellings built years ago by Mexicans in the Chihuahua Desert. Although Luna's *jacal* has been restored by the National Park Service, a marker tells how the intrepid farmer Luna lived here—astride the Comanche War Trail—and successfully raised a large family while farming the adjacent flood plain for many decades. Luna finally died here in 1947 at age 109. Ravens wheel overhead as, for the next mile, the road runs along the foot of the high cliffs of Peña Mountain on your left.

10.35 Here a side road forks right to Terlingua Abaja.

SIDE TRIP TO TERLINGUA ABAJA: The one-lane side road winds down through low, eroded hills for 1.25 miles to a primitive park campground. A permit is needed to camp, and no water is available. At the campground is a ruined adobe house, and a marker beside it tells how the now-abandoned village of Terlingua Abaja was once located on the floodplain here. From 1900 to the early 1930s, it supplied grains and produce for miners and ranchers throughout the Big Bend area. The main group of ruins is a 0.5-mile walk across dry Terlingua Creek, and you can walk your bicycle there if you like (bicycles may not be ridden on single-track trails in national parks). You return the same way to Old Maverick Road.

10.35 Junction of Old Maverick Road and the Terlingua Abaja side road.

As you pedal on down toward the river, the wild crags of the Chisos Mountains reach skyward on your left while straight ahead the colossal rock wall of the Terlingua Fault reaches for miles along the Mexican side of the Rio Grande. While this massive cliff towers 1500 sheer feet above the river today, geologists report that when formed 50 million years ago, it was twice as high. Today the lower half lies buried below the surface, covered by deposits of silt brought down by the river. On this same silt, the residents of the Mexican village of Santa Elena, 8 miles downstream, live by cultivating crops. The huge gash visible in the rock wall is the mouth of Santa Elena Canyon,

The *jacal*, or Mexican-style house, of Gilberto Luna, who farmed a flood plain near Old Maverick Road in Big Bend National Park. He died in 1947 at age 109.

through which the Rio Grande flows for 17 miles. At one point the canyon walls rise 1700 sheer feet above the river.

13.25 Old Maverick Road meets the paved park road.

You can turn around here and go back, making a total distance of 26.5 miles. Or you can turn right and ride 0.5 mile on the paved road to the Santa Elena Canyon parking lot and return, making a round-trip distance of 27.5 miles. Or you can turn left and ride 7 miles east on the paved park road to Castolon Campground, or 1 mile beyond to Castolon store, or you can branch off right to the Santa Elena ferry as outlined earlier. From the end of Maverick Road, riding to Santa Elena and back could add 19 miles—generally flat, easy, paved-road miles, I might add. By starting this ride early in the morning, you'd probably have time to ride all the options and still be back at the car by 5 PM.

Since all roads and trails in the park are clearly marked, you should have no difficulty finding these optional rides. I located a metal bike rack at Santa Elena Canyon parking lot to which bikes could be locked, but if you're with a group, it's best to have one member stay and guard the bikes while the others see the canyon. The ride east along the paved park road to Castolon Campground affords magnificent views of the Terlingua Fault towering high on your right, and it provides occasional glimpses of the river. You won't see many RVs here, but car traffic builds up after noon.

If you cross on the ferry to Santa Elena, pay the ferryman on the return trip. Santa Elena village is just 0.25 mile from the ferry. I found two restaurants here: Maria Elena's in a house on the right and a second restaurant near the plaza with a menu displayed outside in English. Fast food is unknown here, so you may have to wait half an hour for your tacos to be prepared. While waiting, you could ride for a mile down the main street of Santa Elena to the end of the village and return. Most houses are of adobe, and you'll see numerous vignettes of a culture that seems to lag ours by almost a century.

14
Old Ore Road (mountain bike)

Distance: 29–41 miles
Terrain: A moderately strenuous out-and-back ride through the high
  desert, canyons, and mountains of Big Bend National Park
Nearest city: Study Butte
Map: Trails Illustrated Big Bend National Park, 1:100,000

Once used by wagons to haul ore from a mine near Boquillas Canyon to
Marathon, Old Ore Road today spans 27 miles of waterless and uninhabited desert and mountains on the east side of Big Bend National Park. So
far, it is free of the deep gravel used on some other park back roads to prevent washboarding. Thus, despite some long, gradual upgrades and a few
rough and rocky sections, this is an excellent road for mountain-bike touring. All turns and side roads to points of interest are clearly marked. Along
the way you enjoy splendid views of the towering Chisos peaks, and you
ride the length of a rugged canyon, then double back through it.

Only the strongest, advanced-level rider should consider riding the
length of Old Ore Road and back to the starting point in a single day. I suggest riding the full length of this road only if you have a car shuttle waiting
to meet you at the other end. Otherwise you should ride only as far as your
capability will allow before turning around and returning to the starting
point. For most intermediate-level riders, the halfway point will probably
be between Mile 14.7 and Mile 20 (between Telephone Canyon and
McKinney Canyon). This makes a round trip of 29.4 to 41 miles.

When I surveyed this route, I rode one day from the south end of Old
Ore Road to Telephone Canyon and back again. The following day I rode
from the north end of Old Ore Road to Telephone Canyon and back.
However, if you have only 1 day for Old Ore Road, you may want to go
farther as outlined above. No potable water exists en route, so even in cool

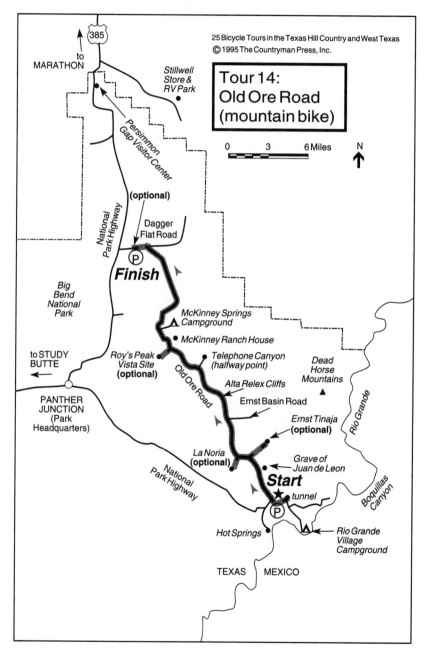

25 Bicycle Tours in the Texas Hill Country and West Texas
© 1995 The Countryman Press, Inc.

**Tour 14:
Old Ore Road
(mountain bike)**

weather carry three 24-ounce water bottles and plenty of food. Few cars seem to go more than 5 miles up Old Ore Road, and I met only two vehicles all day while riding the northern half of the road.

You can drive to either end of Old Ore Road in about an hour from Study Butte's motels. But the south end of Old Ore Road is just 3.5 miles from Rio Grande Village Campground. The routing below starts at the south end of Old Ore Road and proceeds north. Old Ore Road branches north off the paved park highway roughly 3.5 miles northwest of Rio Grande Village and 16.5 miles east of park headquarters at Panther Junction. Park at the parking area located immediately west of the tunnel on the park highway. The highway tunnel is approximately 3 miles northwest of Rio Grande Village. From here, ride your bike 0.6 mile west on the park highway to the start of Old Ore Road.

0.0   Head north on Old Ore Road.

One lane wide throughout its length, Old Ore Road heads north into a vast region of Chihuahua Desert covered with low creosote bush. At Mile 4.25, on the right near a low hill, a white cross marks the grave of Juan de Leon, who was killed nearby in 1932 during an argument with Joe Loftin. Loftin farmed part of the Tornillo Creek wash, visible on the left from the nearby hilltop. He was later tried for the murder and imprisoned. Juan de Leon's grave is often covered with loose change left here for "good luck" and to help pay for its preservation.

4.75 A side road branches right to Ernst Tinaja.

Tinaja is Spanish for water jar and the side trip to this natural rock water tank in a canyon is well worthwhile. So turn right and ride 0.4 mile east on a dirt road, and continue up a dry riverbed into a canyon. You can ride on the riverbed for 0.25 mile until a series of huge rocks blocks the way. Leave your bike here and walk 0.25 mile through the canyon to the water-filled hole in the bed of the canyon, which is Ernst Tinaja. It's worth coming to see the unique stratification, or layering, of multicolored rock in the canyon walls. When you're ready, return to Old Ore Road.

5.1   A side road branches left here to La Noria.

Max Ernst, for whom the *tinaja* was named, operated a general store at La Noria, a farming community that endured until the mid-1930s.

It's a side trip of 0.5 mile each way, and there isn't a lot left to see.

At Mile 7, Old Ore Road winds through a long, narrow, and scenic canyon, then makes an abrupt U-turn, doubles back, and hugs the opposite side of the same canyon, finally to emerge on top. An overlook in the canyon provides a view of several more *tinajas,* including the largest called Carlota's Tinaja. Extensive views of the Tornillo Creek wash reach away on your left as you continue riding north.

10.5   At a wooden sign, a side road branches right to Ernst Basin Road.

This was the original ore road, and it led several miles south to meet an aerial tramway that hauled ore from a mine near Boquillas Canyon. A short side road also branches left off Old Ore Road and leads to Willow Tank, an earthen stock tank built by early-day ranchers around a spring now buried in a dense clump of trees.

At Mile 11.7 Old Ore Road approaches a long line of limestone cliffs towering high on the right above the road. Called Alta Relex, the cliffs line the road for several miles. Huge boulders that have fallen from the cliffs lie scattered near the road. Some are larger than automobiles. Plainly visible in the cliff wall is a canyon with a pour-off (waterfall) immediately below it. You can hike up to the pour-off across a hillside covered with cactus and candelilla (wax) plants.

Climbing gradually but steadily, the road traverses several rough, rocky sections before coming to a Y-fork.

14.75 A wooden signpost points right to Telephone Canyon.

You can ride about 0.25 mile into Telephone Canyon, but beyond there the trail is blocked by undergrowth.

To get this far will take the average rider 2.5–3 hours and perhaps longer with sightseeing en route. Unless you have a car shuttle at the north end of Old Ore Road, I suggest turning back somewhere in the next 4 miles. If you plan later to spend another day riding Old Ore Road from the north end, this is roughly the halfway point. If you do not intend to ride the north end of Old Ore Road, and assuming you have ample time and water, you might continue on to Mile 18 or 20 before turning back. The return ride is generally downhill, and you may make slightly better time than you have so far (you could also be more tired). Try to use good judgment in deciding when to turn back.

This wooden sign marks the turnoff to Telephone Canyon, located midway along Old Ore Road in Big Bend National Park.

For the next 1.2 miles Old Ore Road becomes quite rough as it climbs uphill past Roy's Peak, a mountain high on the left. Old Ore Road then flattens out and brings you quickly to Mile 18.

18.0 *A narrow side road branches left to Roy's Peak Vista.*

It's a 0.2-mile side trip down a narrow road to Roy's Peak Vista Backcountry Site. Here you'll find the remains of a corrugated iron shack, a toppled metal windmill, and an assortment of rusted pipes, food cans, and other paraphernalia. All were used by the McKinney family when they had a corral and a small wax operation here sometime in the early 1900s.

Back on Old Ore Road, and just 0.1 mile north, the still-substantial stone walls of the McKinney ranch house stand on the right side of the road. The chimneys are still intact, and some of the walls are over 6 feet high. Piles of rock nearby indicate the remains of other buildings.

For another 2 miles Old Ore Road winds on through the McKinney Hills, then drops steeply into McKinney Canyon.

20.4 *A short side road leads right into McKinney Springs Backcountry Campground.*

Green grass and trees indicate the presence of water at a spring in the canyon, but the water isn't safe to drink. From the campground Old Ore Road climbs up a hillside and curves to the right to the top of McKinney Canyon. For over a mile you ride along the rim of a valley that drops abruptly away on the left side of the road. Then Old Ore Road crosses a series of dry, and often rocky, arroyos. You can make good time on the final 3 miles, which cross a flat plain.

27.0 *At this T-junction, Old Ore Road meets Dagger Flat Road and ends.*

For car shuttle drivers, or for anyone else driving to the north end of Old Ore Road, there is parking for a single car on the gravel on the north side of the junction. Most people prefer to park in a parking area 1.7 miles west on unpaved Dagger Flat Road. True to its name, Dagger Flat Road is dead flat. From this parking area it's 2 more miles to the paved park highway and an additional drive of 12 miles south to park headquarters at Panther Junction.

15
Pinto Canyon (mountain bike)

Distance: *36 miles*
Terrain: *A strenuous out-and-back ride in a steep mountain canyon*
Nearest cities: *Presidio, Marfa*
County map: *Presidio*

Though requiring little or no technical skill, Pinto Canyon is not for the fainthearted. Starting from the remote adobe hamlet of Ruidosa beside the Rio Grande, unpaved Pinto Canyon road heads immediately uphill and in the next 18 miles threads its way through the rugged Sierra Vieja Mountains to finally climb up and over an escarpment called the Rimrock. After gaining an estimated 2000 feet in elevation while climbing Pinto Canyon, the road tops out on a flat grassland plateau known as the Marfa Highlands. Once on this plateau the road is paved and signed as FM 2810. It then continues for 32 miles north to Marfa. However, via our recommended itinerary, you turn around at the top of the Rimrock and enjoy an exhilarating 18-mile downhill run back through Pinto Canyon to Ruidosa.

Despite the long climb, almost any intermediate rider can pedal virtually all the way up Pinto Canyon. You may walk two short, steep stretches near the top, as I did. But any moderately experienced rider with low gears should be able to ride up the rest of the way. Descending may require some care because you must brake, and there are loose stones and gravel on the road. If you're new to mountain biking, consider lowering your saddle for the descent. This lowers your center of gravity and brings your feet closer to the ground.

Come prepared with at least two 24-ounce water bottles—three in warm weather—and plenty of food. There is no water, food, or shelter in Pinto Canyon. A high wind could spring up at any time, and I recommend bringing rain gear. You will probably see deer and *javelina* in the canyon,

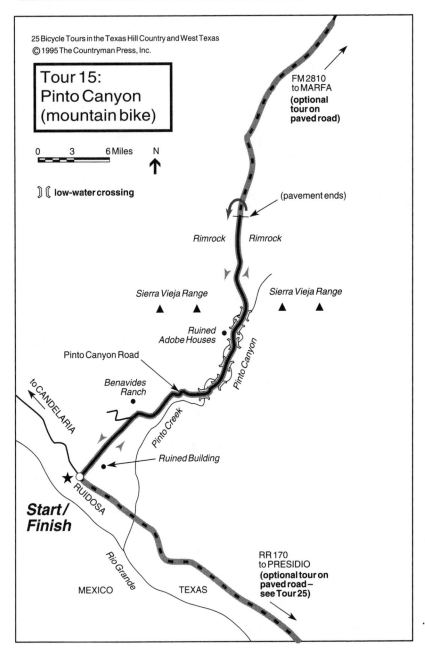

25 Bicycle Tours in the Texas Hill Country and West Texas
© 1995 The Countryman Press, Inc.

Tour 15:
Pinto Canyon
(mountain bike)

0   3   6 Miles   N

)[(low-water crossing

FM 2810
to MARFA
**(optional
tour on
paved road)**

(pavement ends)

Rimrock   *Rimrock*

Sierra Vieja Range   *Sierra Vieja Range*

Ruined
Adobe Houses

Pinto Canyon

Pinto Canyon Road

*Benavides
Ranch*

to CANDELARIA

Pinto Creek

Ruined Building

★ RUIDOSA

*Start/
Finish*

Rio Grande

MEXICO   TEXAS

RR 170
to PRESIDIO
**(optional tour on
paved road –
see Tour 25)**

and ranchers have problems with poachers. So stay on the road, and do not venture onto land on either side.

There are lots of washboard ripples on the road, but a biker can avoid most of these by riding at the road's edge. You should avoid riding this road if it has recently rained or if rain appears imminent. And do start early. I took 5 hours to go up and 2.5 to come down. Add an hour each way for driving to Ruidosa and back, and the entire trip could easily take 9.5 hours.

An occasional green border-patrol car or a rancher's pickup is about the only traffic you're likely to see. During my ride, I passed an average of two vehicles per hour. The mountains are monumental, the scenery is awesome, and the views are breathtaking. This is a ride that every mountain biker should make at least once. But Pinto Canyon remains almost unknown to bicyclists, and even in Texas few people are aware of its existence.

Since the closest motel is in Presidio, we'll use that as our starting point (look up Presidio in the City and Resource Directory). Drive 37 miles northwest on paved RR 170 (this route is described in Tour 25) to Ruidosa, a picturesque hamlet of scattered adobe homes. A small store carries soft drinks and staples. Park on the shoulder at the junction of RR 170 and Pinto Canyon Road. No signs exist, but you'll have no difficulty recognizing the Pinto Canyon road.

While I believe it is best to ride up from Ruidosa and coast back down, I *have* driven out from Marfa on paved FM 2810 to the top of Pinto Canyon, parked the car there, bicycled down to Ruidosa, then pedaled back up to the car and driven back to Marfa. This strategy is entirely possible but has two drawbacks: It leaves the hard part until the end, and it has you climbing late in the day when, even in winter, the temperature in the canyon may reach 90 degrees.

How about starting from Marfa and riding 32 paved miles on FM 2810 to Pinto Canyon, continuing on down to Ruidosa, and pedalling 37 more miles on paved RR 170 into Presidio for overnight? Although this 88-mile ride is generally downhill, only the fittest, strongest, and most experienced rider should attempt it. Water or drinks are available only in Ruidosa. If you do decide to try it, I recommend using a hybrid bike, or fitting your mountain bike with 1.5-inch tires. Despite the stones and gravel in Pinto Canyon, you'll make better time on the 69 miles of paved road. I also recommend that you have a backup vehicle.

A variety of other options are available to anyone who has a car shuttle available. For example, you could ride out for 32 miles from Marfa on paved FM 2810, drop down Pinto Canyon to Ruidosa, then return by car to Marfa. Almost any car in good condition can make it up or down Pinto Canyon. If you ride FM 2810 from Marfa, the first 15 miles are flat and monotonous. The road then becomes increasingly hilly before dropping down a long hill to the top of Pinto Canyon. Don't be put off by an arch across the road at the top of the canyon that proclaims: A.J. Rod, Pinto Canyon Ranch. Sure, the land belongs to the ranch, but the road is open to public travel.

The following itinerary assumes you will start bicycling from Ruidosa, ride to the top of the canyon and cycle back down to Ruidosa.

0.0 *From the center of Ruidosa, head northeast up the unpaved road to Pinto Canyon.*

The road climbs steadily for the first 1.5 miles. About a mile past Ruidosa you'll see a large, ruined building 0.5 mile off to the right with chimneys intact. Ahead, the ramparts of the Sierra Vieja thrust skyward. Stretches of hard dirt road alternate with shorter stretches of thin gravel.

4.3 *Ignore the graded road that forks left here and stay right.*

A mile beyond is a parking area on the left. Probably no one would object if you drove this far and left your car here. Steadily climbing through scrub-covered foothills, the road crosses two cattle guards. At the second, a side road leads west to the Benavides Ranch, visible about a mile away on your left in the foothills. From here on, the road is fenced on both sides, a precaution against poachers.

At Mile 9, the road climbs over the shoulder of a mountain, then makes a spectacular descent into Pinto Canyon. Once in the canyon, the road is narrow and rocky, but the surface is still smooth and easily traversable by cars. As you pedal up brushy Pinto Canyon, you cross Pinto Creek six times on shallow low-water crossings. Some are paved and can be slippery. Mountains tower on both sides, and just about here I saw a herd of 15 wild *javelina* pigs a bare 30 yards from the side of the road.

As the canyon narrows, the road hugs the mountainside. At Mile 12.3 some logs beside the road invite a rest stop. On again, the road snakes through a narrow cut between rugged mountain walls, and

Pinto Canyon Road as it runs through a wide section of the canyon.

at Mile 13.4 you pass several ruined adobe houses on the left. More towering peaks surround the buildings of a small mine on the right side of the road. Just beyond, also on the right, are two mobile homes and a large corral.

At Mile 17, the road heads steeply up the Rimrock. For the next mile it serpentines and switchbacks up the mountainside with unfenced drop-offs on one side or the other. Then come two very steep stretches, each about 200 yards in length.

18.0 *Top of the climb.*

The grade becomes easier, and you ride under an arch marked: Exit. This is the same arch that on the other side reads: A.J. Rod, Pinto Canyon Ranch. It's about a mile from here to the beginning of the pavement and to where the road is signed FM 2810. It's not worth riding more than 100 yards beyond the arch.

That's far enough to see the tawny grasslands of the Marfa Highlands reaching away to the north. The grass here is a nutritious native gamma grass on which Herefords and other cattle thrive. Even so, the area is so dry that ranchers graze only as many cattle per square mile as there are inches of rain per year. To be economically feasible, a ranch must cover at least 200,000 acres. Huge ranches like these border the road to Marfa.

18.0 *Turn around and start back down Pinto Canyon.*

Stunning views of the canyon and the road below open up as you retrace the route you just ascended. This is a steep descent, and you have to brake. Since you see mountains and canyon from a fresh perspective, the return trip is like an entirely new ride. As you work your way down, the tiny white specks of Ruidosa's houses dot the foot of the mighty mountain wall that borders the Rio Grande on the Mexican side.

Extravagant panoramas reach away on all sides. Then suddenly you're back in Ruidosa, and you're riding on pavement.

36.0 *Junction with RR 170, the end of your ride.*

Turn right here, and it's just a 1-minute ride to the general store for a refreshing cold drink.

16

Terlingua Ranch–Lake Ament Loop (mountain bike)

Distance: *36 miles*
Terrain: *A moderately strenuous, all-day loop tour on mostly unpaved roads that begins with 16 miles across a high, mountain-rimmed desert and ends with 12 miles through the rugged Christmas Mountains*
Nearest city: *Study Butte*

The ride begins at Longhorn Ranch Motel, located 12 miles north of Study Butte on RR 118. Park outside the motel and, if you like, have breakfast at its Matterhorn Restaurant (915-371-2541). You then ride east across the high desert on a graded two-lane road to Terlingua Ranch Lodge. At this quiet retreat in the Christmas Mountains, you can lunch at the café and perhaps even have a dip in the pool. You then return on a spectacular one-lane dirt road that winds through sawtoothed mountain peaks to Ament Lake and descends down a series of switchbacks onto RR 118 and so back to Longhorn Ranch Motel.

The preceding scenario assumes you will spend the previous night at Study Butte or, perhaps, at Longhorn Ranch Motel. A worthwhile alternative is to drive out the previous day to Terlingua Ranch and stay overnight there. You would then commence our itinerary at Mile 19.8 and follow it around to Longhorn Ranch Motel. Your return route then starts at Mile 0.0 and takes you back to Terlingua Ranch. (This is also the automobile route to Terlingua Ranch; do not drive via Lake Ament.)

Terlingua Ranch and Lodge is headquarters of an association of owners of hunting tracts subdivided out of the huge 435-square-mile expanse of Terlingua Ranch. A total of 1100 miles of bulldozed roads provides access to these tracts. The roads are open to all, but the land is private. Except at the lodge and at Lake Ament picnic area (which you pass), stay

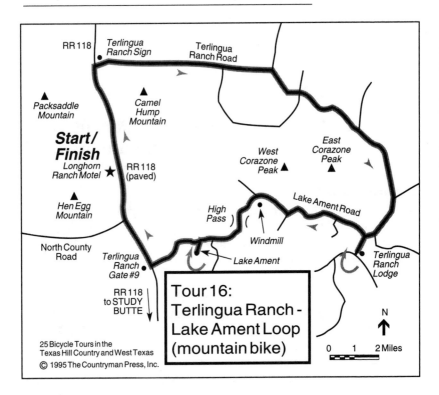

on the road and do not venture onto the land. Some tracts have cabins or houses, and all are strictly private. In addition to a café and swimming pool, the lodge has comfortable motel units, tent sites, RV hookups, and a bunkhouse (915-371-2416). If you care to spend an extra night or two here, other ride possibilities exist, as well as a hike up Old Mine Road to the top of a mountain.

Before starting, I strongly advise reading the preliminary advice for Tour 12, a similar tour through Terlingua Ranch property. Start out early, carry plenty of water and snacks, and on the 12-mile stretch through Ament Lake leave small stone cairns in case you must retrace your route. Terlingua Ranch usually has a small outline map available showing this and other ranch routes.

0.0   *At Longhorn Ranch Motel, head north (left) on paved highway RR 118.*

Ride on the wide shoulder for 3.8 flat miles until you reach a large display sign on the right directing you east to Terlingua Ranch.

3.8 *Turn right at the Terlingua Ranch sign onto a two-lane graded road.*

Scattered trailers and cabins poke up above the sagebrush, creosote bush, and cactus that cover the high desert. Every half mile a Terlingua Ranch sign offers such encouragement as:

"Don't give up!"

"Don't be fooled, we have a pool."

"Lodge 10 miles, persevere."

Other signs indicate feeder roads and cabins. Although the road is badly washboarded, I was able to avoid the ripples by riding at the road edge. There are long, gradual downgrades and upgrades but no real hills.

Soon the jagged peaks of the Christmas Mountains are gliding past on the right, and a sign announces: Miles of Roads with No Toads. Another reads: Lodge 3 Miles, and still another: This Is Where the Stories Are Told. At this point the road turns south into a mountain-rimmed basin. Ranch buildings and cabins appear ahead, and you pass an adobe church off to the left.

19.8 **Terlingua Ranch.**

Ride past the registration office and up to the café. Right outside the café door is a wide, shady patio and an inviting swimming pool. The elevation of 3700 feet here is high enough to guarantee cool nights, but it can still heat up during the day. When you're ready, return by the following route.

19.8 *From Terlingua Ranch, retrace your route for 1 mile on the two-lane dirt road you just arrived on.*

20.8 *At the Lake Ament sign turn left onto a two-lane graded road.*

From here you climb gradually uphill for the next 7 miles. At Mile 21.1 you pass close to a white house on the right. Trailers and cabins are scattered across the landscape. Avoid any obvious side roads. At Mile 23 you should pass a tan stucco house with a red roof close to the road on your right. At Mile 23.8, you're in the heart of the Christmas Mountains with the giant crags of East and West Corazone Peaks towering above the road on your right. These steep-sided mountains were formed by volcanic intrusion into a limestone formation. They are the only mountains in Texas to contain fluor-spar.

At Mile 24.5, still gradually climbing, you should pass close to a house with a light-gray roof on the right side of the road. If you don't sight these houses reasonably close to the mileages I give, you could have taken a wrong turn. By now the road is just one lane wide.

25.6 *A sign pointing to Lake Ament indicates that you turn left at the Y-junction here. A windmill further identifies this junction.*

Up ahead you see your road twisting and climbing up a mountain-side. The road itself is quite smooth with little gravel, but it is full of short dips and climbs. At Mile 28 you finally reach the top of a pass. I estimated this pass as 4700 feet high. Stop and take in the breath-taking panoramas. On both sides of the pass range after range of mountains reach away to the horizon. From the pass the narrow road descends steeply in a series of sweeping curves and passes between hundreds of huge boulders.

Ignore the sign at Mile 28.8 that points left and reads: Section N. Stay right instead, and at Mile 30.2 the road leads down into a wide basin with two houses and six sheltered picnic tables. These also serve as tent or RV campsites. Lake Ament is on your left behind a dam wall and is invisible from the road. If you register at ranch head-quarters you may camp here overnight. However, most bikers are content to stop for a few minutes in the shade of a picnic table and ride on. No other shelter exists the length of this ride.

From the far side of Lake Ament basin the road climbs steeply to cross another pass at Mile 30.8. A sheer mountain wall lies straight ahead. Immediately the road angles sharply right and begins to switchback steeply down. Off to the west you sight a thin ribbon of concrete that is RR 118.

32.0 *The road emerges between the rock gateposts of Terlingua Ranch entrance #9 onto RR 118. Turn right.*

For the next mile you climb steadily on the wide highway shoulder. Then you top a rise, and clearly visible ahead are the red roofs and white water tank of Longhorn Ranch Motel. Expect some traffic and an occasional truck or RV to roll by as you ride the wide shoulder. But it should take only 15 minutes to reach the motel.

Lake Ament Road takes mountain bikers close to
the rugged peak of West Corazone Mountain.

36.0 *Longhorn Ranch Motel and end of the ride.*

The motel restaurant will probably be closed, but a soft-drink machine is usually accessible to nonguests. Now, here's a final tip: If you're staying overnight at Terlingua Ranch, consider riding back there via the scenically superior Lake Ament Road. I guarantee you'll find it a more pulse-quickening experience.

17
Lajitas to San Carlos, Mexico (mountain bike)

Distance: *39 miles*
Terrain: *A fairly strenuous out-and-back ride on a rough dirt road with several steep climbs*
Nearest city: *Lajitas*

From the creature comforts of Lajitas, you cross the Rio Grande by row-boat into Mexico and ride for 18.6 miles through the arid backcountry of Chihuahua State to the surprisingly neat and well-kept village of San Carlos. You return the same way. I've made this trip once on my own and once with 50 other mountain bikers attending the Chihuahua Desert Rally. On both occasions I met cowboys on horseback and saw a train of burros carrying packloads. You may pass two or three pickup trucks per hour, but other traffic on this road is almost nil. The ride is dusty, and the return trip can be hot, so carry two 24-ounce water bottles and some high-energy snacks. Fruit and soft drinks are available at San Carlos, as is water. But is the water safe to drink? To be safe, you might bring some water-purifying tablets. Proof of citizenship is not normally needed to reenter the US.

Do start early. By the time you've ferried across the river twice, ridden both ways, and spent an hour or so in San Carlos, it can total 9 hours. The ferry runs from daylight to dusk. In case you don't make it back to Paso Lajitas in daylight, ask for *el chalupero* (the ferryman). You may have to pay extra, but he'll usually take you across.

0.0   *From the center of Lajitas, ride west on paved RR 170 for 0.75 mile to the second dirt road on the left. Turn left here and ride about 150 yards to the riverbank.*

Hail the ferryman if he is on the other bank. You must wheel or carry

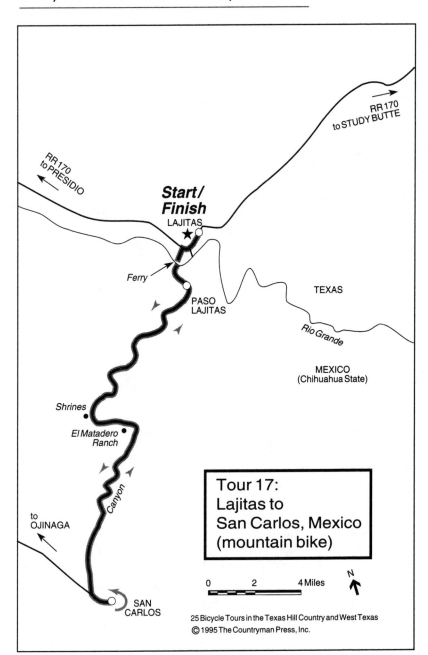

RR 170
to STUDY BUTTE

RR 170
to PRESIDIO

***Start/
Finish***
LAJITAS

Ferry

PASO
LAJITAS

TEXAS

Rio Grande

MEXICO
(Chihuahua State)

Shrines

*El Matadero
Ranch*

Canyon

to
OJINAGA

SAN
CARLOS

Tour 17:
Lajitas to
San Carlos, Mexico
(mountain bike)

0   2   4 Miles

N

25 Bicycle Tours in the Texas Hill Country and West Texas
© 1995 The Countryman Press, Inc.

your bike down the steep bank to the rowboat ferry. The crossing takes about 2 minutes. Getting out on the Mexican side is easier. You pay the ferryman on the return trip.

0.9 *Take the dirt road leading up from the ferry landing. This is the road to San Carlos, and there are no turnoffs for the next 18 miles.*

Almost immediately you ride through the dozen or so rambling adobe houses of Paso Lajitas. One of these is Garcia's Restaurant. Pedal on out of the village. The one-lane dirt road climbs into tree-less foothills and heads south. The road is rough and washboarded with a wide ridge of gravel down the center. Despite this, you can average 8 MPH or more.

On across dry washes and through more scrub-covered foothills, the road gradually gains elevation. At Mile 10.6 you pass two shrines: One is in a small white building on a hilltop on your right, and the other is close to the road on the same side. The road then makes an abrupt U-turn and passes a ranch and corral on the right. A sign identifies it as El Matadero or The Slaughterhouse. Next, the road climbs a long, steep hill, then plunges into a low canyon. It snakes through the canyon for 2 miles only to climb up another long, steep hill. Small stones, pea-sized gravel, and pulverized dust alternate as the road heads down a long, straight stretch toward a patch of green at the foot of a mountain.

At Mile 17 the green patch becomes trees and fields, and among them the roofs of San Carlos are clearly visible.

17.9 *Here a dirt road branches right and heads west to Ojinaga. Ignore it and keep straight on toward San Carlos.*

Wider now, the road drops down through a cut, crosses a shallow river on a concrete bridge, curves to the left, and enters San Carlos.

18.9 *San Carlos.*

Cobblestones begin at the city limit and every 100 meters you ride over a speed bump. Alternatively, you can ride on a smooth sidewalk on the right. As you enter the pueblo you pass a children's play-ground on the left. Low, one-story adobe houses appear on both sides of the street. It's 0.5 mile to the central plaza.

19.5 *San Carlos plaza.*

Relax on a seat on the plaza, and enjoy a cold soft drink with some

This rowboat ferry carries bikers and their bikes across the Rio Grande between Lajitas, Texas and Paso Lajitas, Mexico.

fruit. Both are sold by a small store here. Also here are a couple of restaurants, but service is slow, and it can take an hour or more before your tacos are ready. After you've rested, ride around and see the rest of San Carlos. It's only 4 blocks wide, but there are two churches. The streets are swept clean—San Carlos is cleaner than many small American towns—and there's a litter barrel on every block. It also appears quite prosperous. Half of the 600 residents are children, and most of the men work on nearby farms and ranches. No overnight accommodation exists.

19.5 *Return to Lajitas the same way you came, encountering about as many hills as you did coming. One is particularly long and steep, and most riders walk up.*

39.0 *Lajitas.*

Back in Lajitas, head for the historic trading post store, and enjoy a cool beer or soft drink in the shade of the traditional cane-canopied porch.

18

Mariscal Mine via River Road
(mountain bike)

Distance: *40.6 miles*
Terrain: *A moderately strenuous out-and-back ride through an isolated frontier desert region*
Nearest city: *Study Butte*
Map: *Trails Illustrated Big Bend National Park, 1:100,000*

For over 50 miles River Road runs east and west across Big Bend National Park, always close to the river but seldom within sight of it. Starting at the eastern end of River Road, this ride takes you west along the road for 20.3 miles, as far as Mariscal Mine, and returns the same way. Once a major producer of quicksilver, Mariscal Mine hasn't operated since World War II. But many of the buildings are still intact, and you're welcome to explore this historic mine and smelter area.

While the scenery isn't dramatic, a brief rain can turn the desert into a vivid palette of yellow, purple, and scarlet wildflowers. Rock formations reveal aeons of geological time. And endless panoramas of mountain peaks and ranges glide past as you pedal.

I took 7 hours to complete this round-trip ride, plus another hour spent exploring the mine. For about three-quarters of the way the surface is smooth, hard-packed dirt, but the final 4.5 miles gradually climb through riverbed gravel. For superior flotation, I recommend using 2.35-inch or 2.5-inch tires both front and rear, or at least in front. Carry three 24-ounce water bottles regardless of the season. Though a car with moderately high clearance can be driven to Mariscal Mine in dry weather, relatively few motorists attempt it. During the survey ride for this write-up, I met only three vehicles all day. The entire ride lies within Big Bend National

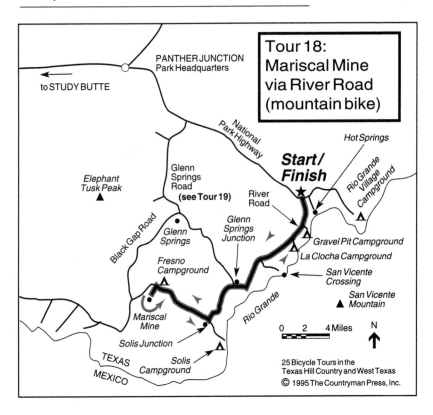

**Tour 18:
Mariscal Mine
via River Road
(mountain bike)**

Park, it is infrequently patrolled, and water is available only by riding one of the side roads down to the Rio Grande. But the river water is considered impure and may contain toxic agricultural chemicals.

The ride start is about an hour's drive from Study Butte's motels, but Rio Grande Village Campground is much closer. The ride begins where River Road branches south from the paved park highway, 5 miles north of Rio Grande Village or 15 miles west of park headquarters at Panther Junction. This intersection is clearly marked by park signs. Drive 200 yards down River Road to a parking area on the left. A sign warns against leaving anything of value in cars. It advises locking any possessions in the trunk and locking the car securely.

0.0   The ride begins at the east end of River Road.

Loose gravel covers River Road for the first mile, but the road then becomes smooth dirt with occasional washboard. At Mile 1.8 a pink marker points left and reads Gravel Pit, and at Mile 2.8 another points left and reads: La Clocha. La Clocha is the Mexican name for a rock crusher that once operated here. Both side roads lead to backcountry campgrounds. At Mile 5.5 a wooden sign points left to San Vicente Crossing and the white houses visible some 3 miles on the left are the village of San Vicente in Mexico. Ahead, a massive rock wall reaches almost to the 3600-foot summit of San Vicente Mountain just across the river in Mexico. A deep canyon is clearly visible on the mountain's steep north face.

Save for a couple of deep mudholes created by motor vehicles, the riding is flat and easy. You pedal on across a wide salt flat to a desolate fork in the road.

10.3 *A pink stone marker identifies this as the junction of River Road and Glenn Springs Road (Glenn Springs Road is described in Tour 19). Turn left here.*

In quick succession River Road winds up a low canyon, passes under a series of eroded earth cliffs, then travels on a slickrock surface cut by a series of dry arroyos. Finally it crosses a wide salt flat to a junction with a side road.

14.7 *Solis Junction. Here a side road branches left for 1.5 miles to Solis Backcountry Campground and the Rio Grande.*

For the next mile River Road crosses another wide salt flat, and patches of white salt coat the road's sandy surface. Then at Mile 15.8 the road surface becomes deep gravel. For the next 4.5 miles River Road climbs gradually up to Mariscal Mine, and the gravel continues the entire distance. Whether going uphill or down, the gravel makes pedaling harder, and it's almost impossible to coast when going back downhill.

At Mile 18 Mariscal Mine comes into view, poised on the northern tip of Mariscal Mountain. And by Mile 19 the smelter and mine buildings are clearly visible. At Mile 20 a pink stone marker points right to Fresno Campground. And 200 yards beyond another sign indicates the trail on the left that leads to Mariscal Mine. Ride up the short side road to the parking area below the mine.

Bicyclists on Tours 18 and 19 can explore Mariscal Mine, a former quicksilver mine and smelter located in a remote corner of Big Bend National Park.

20.3 Mariscal Mine.

A foot trail leads up past the ruins of the superintendent's frame house and the adobe homes of Mexican workers to the complex of four condensers and the Scott Furnace. All are built of locally produced glazed brick. Much of the plant is still intact, and it isn't hard to figure out how, once it was roasted in the furnace, the ore slid down the flat tile chutes through each condenser in turn until pure vaporized mercury finally poured from the fourth condenser. Still standing are some of the scaffolds from which workmen looked through peepholes into the condensers. Other buildings are scattered across the hillside mine area, while rubble and bits of old machinery are everywhere. Avoid touching any bricks or tile since they may still contain dangerously high levels of mercury.

Mariscal Mine began operating in 1909. Depressed mercury prices forced it to close in 1923. It operated briefly once more during World War II but has been inactive since.

20.3 Ride back from Mariscal Mine to River Road and turn right.

Though you ride back the same way to your car, bicycling in the opposite direction is like taking an altogether different route.

25.9 Solis Junction.

With time to spare, you could fork right here and take an optional 1.5-mile side trip to Solis Backcountry Campsite and the Rio Grande. Among the trees that border the road, you may glimpse the ruins of a stone ranch house built by the Solis family, who first settled here.

Via River Road you continue 4.4 miles northeast to Glenn Springs Junction. Horses and cattle—strays from ranches across the river in Mexico—often graze among the cactus and mesquite trees that border the road. It's another 10.3 miles from here back to the parking lot.

40.6 Junction of River Road and the paved park highway.

Back in the car, most bikers drive 5 miles downhill to the store at Rio Grande Village for a cold drink. Hot showers are also available here. Afterward, you might consider driving 4 miles back up the park highway to the Hot Springs turnoff on the left. (Actually, the Hot Springs turnoff is only a mile from River Road where this ride ends.) A brief 1.5-mile drive on a narrow dirt road brings you to a parking lot beside the remains of a former hot springs resort. It's a 0.5-mile walk from here along the river to a series of river-edge pools, where you can sit and relax in hot-spring water.

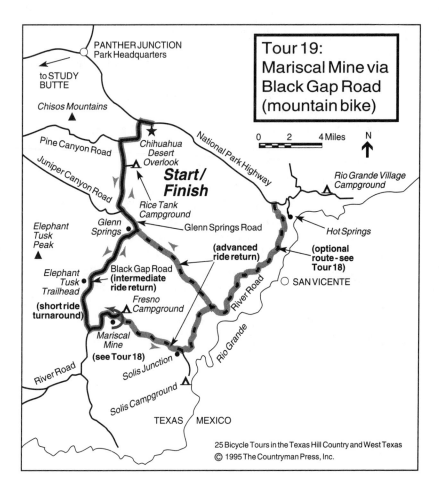

PANTHER JUNCTION
Park Headquarters

to STUDY
BUTTE

Chisos Mountains ▲

Pine Canyon Road

Juniper Canyon Road

Chihuahua
Desert
Overlook

**Start/
Finish**

Rice Tank
Campground

National Park Highway

**Tour 19:
Mariscal Mine via
Black Gap Road
(mountain bike)**

0   2   4 Miles   N
↑

Rio Grande Village
Campground ⛺

Glenn
Springs

Glenn Springs Road

Hot Springs

Elephant
Tusk
Peak ▲

Elephant
Tusk
Trailhead ●

**(short ride
turnaround)**

Black Gap Road
**(intermediate
ride return)**

Fresno
⛺ Campground

Mariscal
Mine

(see Tour 18)

**(advanced
ride return)**

River Road

**(optional
route-see
Tour 18)**

○ SAN VICENTE

Solis Junction ●

Solis Campground ⛺

Rio Grande

River Road

TEXAS   MEXICO

25 Bicycle Tours in the Texas Hill Country and West Texas
© 1995 The Countryman Press, Inc.

19
Mariscal Mine via Black Gap Road (mountain bike)

Distance: *42 miles*
Terrain: *A strenuous out-and-back ride through hilly desert with some moderately technical rocks and ledges and an elevation gain of 1100 feet. Options allow a shorter ride of 29.6 miles or a longer, very strenuous loop ride of 47.4 miles with an elevation gain of 1470 feet.*
Nearest city: *Study Butte*
Map: *Trails Illustrated Big Bend National Park, 1:100,000*

For anyone who enjoys a long, all-day ride, this tour takes you over primitive roads into a remote but starkly beautiful corner of Big Bend National Park. You'll see relics of early ranching days, and you can wander through the ruins of a once-thriving wax-making community that was raided in 1916 by some 70 gun-toting Mexican bandits. You can also explore the well-preserved ruins of one of America's largest quicksilver mines and smelters. The entire ride lies within Big Bend National Park, a waterless and uninhabited region of mountains and desert.

The goal of this ride is Mariscal Mine, located 21 miles from the starting point. In the first 9 miles, the road drops nearly 1000 feet in elevation plus another 200 feet by the time you reach the mine. Speed is also reduced by stretches of deep, river-bottom gravel spread on the road to prevent washboarding. Thus, the return ride from Mariscal Mine by this same route is a rather slow 21-mile climb with an elevation gain of more than 1100 feet. For most intermediate riders, biking to Mariscal Mine and back is a full day's ride.

However, advanced riders in excellent condition might consider returning from Mariscal Mine by heading east on River Road for 10 miles to the junction of Glenn Springs Road. From here back to the starting point via Glenn Springs Road is a steady uphill grind of 16.4 miles with an elevation gain of 1470 feet. But this long climb may not be necessary. Anyone with a car shuttle available could simply continue east on River Road for another 10.3 miles to its junction with the paved park highway and a rendezvous with the shuttle car. Since River Road is almost level, this avoids the long climb back up Glenn Springs Road. The total distance this way is 41.3 miles with an elevation drop of roughly 1500 feet, a ride well within the capabilities of most intermediate bikers.

Meanwhile, a shorter alternative is this: From the starting point, follow our route down Glenn Springs and Black Gap Roads to Mile 14.8 where Elephant Tusk Trail intersects with Black Gap Road. Simply turn around here and return the same way. It's an uphill climb back, of course—with an elevation gain of about 1000 feet—but the total distance is only 29.6 miles.

While this route passes several backcountry campsites, lack of water renders them impractical for bicyclists without a backup vehicle to carry water. However, a biker with a pump filter could camp at Solis Campground, about 6 miles east of Mariscal Mine, and purify water from the Rio Grande. Better check with a ranger at headquarters first, though. Camping permits are available at park headquarters.

Even in winter, I recommend carrying three 24-ounce water bottles and turning back when only two are left. I also recommend starting as early as possible; certainly you should be riding by 8 AM. I also suggest turning back if you haven't reached the midpoint of your ride by 11:30 AM. Another recommendation is to use 2.3- or 2.5-inch tires on both front and rear wheels, or at least on the front. Any tire smaller than a 1.95-inch will have a hard time negotiating the drift sand, deep gravel, dry creek beds, rocks, and stairstep ledges you will meet on this trip. Although easily negotiated by mountain bikes, Black Gap Road has become so rough that few four-wheel-drive vehicles attempt it anymore. While a car with moderately high clearance can usually make it to Mariscal Mine via River Road, Glenn Springs Road is too rough for most passenger cars.

To start this ride, head first for Big Bend National Park headquarters at Panther Junction, 24 miles east of Study Butte via paved park highway or 68 miles south of Marathon via US 385. From Panther Junction drive southeast on the paved park road toward Rio Grande Village until, at Mile 5.5, a sign points right to Glenn Springs Road. You *can* drive down Glenn Springs Road for 0.4 mile to a small parking area, but most bikers prefer to leave their cars parked within sight of the highway. To do this, continue another 0.6 mile on the highway, and park on a paved lot on the right marked: Chihuahua Desert Overlook. (There is room here for only two cars.) Then ride back to Glenn Springs Road. This starting point is also within convenient driving distance of Chisos Basin or Rio Grand Village National Park campgrounds. All turns and junctions in the park are clearly marked.

0.0 *Start of Glenn Springs Road, a rough one-lane road for high-clearance vehicles only.*

Winding across several draws and crossing a mile of sotol grasslands, this primitive dirt road climbs over the shoulder of Nugent Mountain.

2.65 *Pine Canyon Road forks right. Turn left here.*

As Glenn Springs Road heads downhill, the great crags of the Chisos Mountains loom high on the right while a vast panorama of Mexico's Sierra del Carmen Range spans the horizon far ahead. At Mile 4.5 is Rice Tank Campground with the remains of an earthen stock pond and a wooden corral built in 1920 by a rancher named Rice.

7.4 *Juniper Canyon Road forks right. Stay left.*

For the next 2 miles Glenn Springs Road makes a rough descent over a series of rock slabs and ledges. At Mile 8.8 begin to look for a white metal gate on the right. Twenty yards beyond it, on the left, is a gate of metal pipe used to close the road. Ten yards past this a wooden sign, difficult to see, reads: Black Gap Primitive Road.

9.0 *Black Gap Road forks right. Turn right.*

Black Gap Road is a rough, badly eroded jeep road that is no longer maintained and is recommended only for four-wheel-drive vehicles. Fifty yards down it you cross a shallow creek fed by Glenn Spring. Stop and rest at this cool desert oasis if you like—but don't drink the water. On the left, 100 yards beyond, is the ghost town of Glenn Springs. Blackened posts and a few foundations are all that remain of a once-flourishing wax factory and the homes of some 80 residents that existed in 1916. Despite a small force of nine US troopers stationed here, on the night of May 5, 1916, an estimated 70 or more mounted Mexican bandits stormed and looted the village, burning the houses and factory. Crude wooden crosses can be seen in a primitive cemetery on the left side of Black Gap Road just past the village. The village was rebuilt after the raid but was abandoned altogether after World War I.

From here the road climbs a hill, then plummets down a rock-strewn incline into Black Gap. Erosion has almost destroyed the road in many places; in others, huge rocks have been used to fill gaps. Even so, it's nearly all rideable. From the bottom of the gap, at 10.8 miles, the road winds on through foothills covered with pungent creosote bush and heads toward the sheer-sided mass of Elephant Tusk Mountain. At Mile 13, the road traverses a low canyon paved with concrete studded with large rocks. Most bikers prefer to walk this 50-yard stretch.

At Mile 14.8, you reach Elephant Tusk Trailhead, start of a hiking trail to the mountain. Depending on your remaining water and energy levels, and on the heat and wind, you may wish to have lunch here and then start back.

Tall flowering stalks of spiny century plants and yuccas line the road as you pedal downhill through a deep layer of gravel.

18.0 *Junction of Black Gap Road and River Road. Turn left here and ride east on River Road.*

For the next 1.5 miles, River Road skirts the western edge of a geological formation called a graben (German for grave) because of its resemblance to a huge, shallow grave. Some of the road consists of rough bedrock. Soon you see the gray stone buildings of Mariscal Mine poised on a hillside overlooking the graben.

21.0 *A sign here points right to Mariscal Mine turnout. Ride the short dirt road to the parking area. (For a description of Mariscal Mine, see Tour 18.)*

From the mine, it's shorter and easier to ride back the way you came than to continue east along River Road and loop back via Glenn Springs Road. For those determined to return the long way around, the road log continues.

21.0 *Mariscal Mine and River Road.*

Turn right and commence a gradual descent of 5.6 miles through flat desert scrub and across a wide salt flat to a fork in the road.

26.6 *A pink stone marker points right to Solis Campground. Turn left.*

On across flat slabs of rock and past low cliffs, River Road winds through a low canyon to emerge at a desolate road junction.

31.0 *Junction of River Road and Glenn Springs Road. Riders returning up Glenn Springs Road to the starting point, turn left. Riders heading east on River Road to rendezvous with a car shuttle, turn right. (River Road east of here is described in Tour 18.)*

From here, Glenn Springs Road climbs steadily uphill on deep gravel through a wild and rugged badlands area. As you gain altitude you see behind you the white houses of San Vicente, a village in Mexico. Meanwhile, on your right are the badlands through which the Mexican bandits are believed to have ridden to attack Glenn Springs in 1916. At Mile 38 Glenn Springs ghost town appears on the left.

38.4 *Black Gap Road forks left here. Keep right.*

At this point you have already gained 540 feet in elevation from River Road. In the next 6.5 miles you ascend another 933 feet, climbing back up over the rock slabs and ledges that you descended on the way out. Occasionally a truck or jeep may go by, but you're far more likely to glimpse a coyote or a *javelina,* or perhaps a peregrine falcon or a golden eagle.

47.4 *Junction of Glenn Springs Road and the park highway—and end of the ride.*

Once back in your car, it's a drive of 6 miles west to a gas station that sells cold drinks.

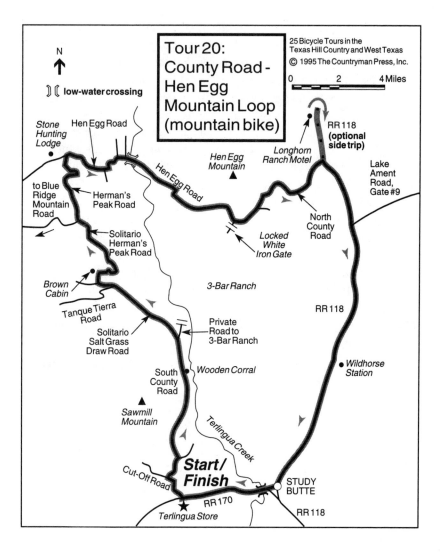

**Tour 20:
County Road -
Hen Egg
Mountain Loop
(mountain bike)**

25 Bicycle Tours in the
Texas Hill Country and West Texas
© 1995 The Countryman Press, Inc.

0   2   4 Miles

N

) (**low-water crossing**

Stone
Hunting
Lodge

Hen Egg Road

Hen Egg
Mountain

Longhorn
Ranch Motel

RR 118
**(optional
side trip)**

Lake
Ament
Road,
Gate #9

Hen Egg Road

to Blue
Ridge
Mountain
Road

Herman's
Peak Road

Solitario
Herman's
Peak Road

North
County
Road

Locked
White
Iron Gate

3-Bar Ranch

RR 118

Brown
Cabin

Tanque Tierra
Road

Solitario
Salt Grass
Draw Road

Private
Road to
3-Bar Ranch

South
County
Road

Wooden Corral

Wildhorse
Station

Sawmill
Mountain

Terlingua Creek

**Start/
Finish**

Cut-Off Road

STUDY
BUTTE

RR 170

Terlingua Store

RR 118

20
County Road–Hen Egg Mountain Loop (mountain bike)

Distance: *43 miles*
Terrain: *A moderately strenuous loop consisting of 29.5 miles of gradual uphill on an unpaved road, followed by a paved road descent of 13.5 miles*
Nearest city: *Study Butte*

Traversing a rugged corner of West Terlingua Ranch, this all-day loop tour takes you on an exciting roller-coaster ride across a far-flung expanse of mountains, canyons, washes, draws, and salt flats and past miles of eroded foothills and cliffs. Since this ride crosses much the same territory as Tour 12, I suggest carefully reading the advice given for that ride.

This tour consists of two stages. First: Starting on RR 170, 3 miles east of Study Butte, you ride for 29.5 miles generally uphill and northwest on an unpaved county road to finally emerge onto RR 118, 11 miles north of Study Butte. Second: You then head south and downhill for 10.5 miles on paved RR 118 to Study Butte, and you pedal 3 more miles west on RR 170 back to your starting point.

Chances are that once you're well clear of highway RR 170, you won't see another human or vehicle, or an inhabited building, until you emerge again onto RR 118. Despite this, I have never seen much wild game here. A few deer, to be sure, but most wildlife seems to consist of hawks and ravens circling overhead. Ask anyone who lives here, though, and they'll confirm that this is one of the most rewarding backcountry trips in the area.

You must have a reasonably accurate computer on your bike to be able to navigate reliably. As you travel the county road, you will find it is referred to on signposts by a variety of other names. These different names help to identify each intersection and keep track of your progress. Do heed the advice in Tour 12 to mark your return route with cairns. Then if you stray off the route, you can find your way back.

The ride begins at Terlingua Store, located on the south side of RR 170 approximately 3 miles west of Study Butte and 1 mile east of Terlingua. If you're staying at a motel or trailer park in Study Butte, you could easily ride along RR 170 to Terlingua Store. Use care, however, since local people use this road each morning to drive to work. If you drive here, park your car on the same side as the store but on the wide shoulder west of, and well clear of, the store itself. Pedal east and ride out of the store driveway onto RR 170. South County Road is across the highway from the store and is identified by a wooden sign reading: Solitario South County Road.

0.0   *Ride north on this graded two-lane dirt road.*

1.35   *At this unmarked Y-intersection, turn right.*

The county road snakes downhill and passes two rustic houses on the right.

2.0   *At this unmarked Y-intersection, turn left.*

Ten miles ahead, the dome-shaped peak of Hen Egg Mountain is clearly visible on the horizon. Disregard any obvious side roads that lead off to cabins or ranches. At Mile 4.4 the 3797-foot peak of Sawmill Mountain is on your left, and at Mile 5 you cross a cattle guard with a wooden corral on the right side of the road.

6.25   *At this Y-intersection a sign reading South County Road points back the way you just came, while another reading Solitario Salt Grass Draw Road identifies the fork on your left, and a third sign, 3-Bar Ranch, marks the fork on your right and also states that the road is private. Turn left here toward Solitario Salt Grass Draw Road, another name for the county road.*

The county road then heads up a ridge with a deep canyon below on your left and a wide eroded valley on your right.

9.5   *At this Y-fork a sign points left and reads: Tanque Tierra Road, while another points right and reads: Solitario Herman's Peak Road. Bear right.*

For the next 0.5 mile you ride along the brink of a canyon that drops abruptly on your left. Green mesquite trees line the canyon floor.

10.6 *At this hilltop junction a side road branches left and heads steeply uphill. A sign reading Herman's Peak Road points right. Bear right.*

From this vantage point the county road drops into a wide canyon, its sides tinted in yellow and gray. Halfway across the canyon floor you pass a brown cabin 0.25 mile off to your left. Next, you ride a rock slab for 60 feet across a dried-up riverbed. The road then swings right and climbs out of the canyon on a series of switchbacks. Disregard a side road on the right at Mile 12.7.

13.9 *At this Y-fork a sign points left and reads: To Blue Ridge Mountain Road. Another points right and reads: Herman's Peak Road. Turn right.*

Look up ahead; slightly on your left and about 2 miles away you should see a stone hunting lodge perched on a hillside. You ride toward it across a series of steep hills and dips.

16.1 *At this Y-fork a sign pointing back the way you came reads: Solitario Herman's Peak. (This junction has a triangle of vegetation at its apex, and the sign is on this triangle.) The left fork leads uphill to the lodge you sighted earlier. Now about 0.5 mile away, this lodge is a key landmark. It has six windows and a red water tank at the right side of the house. Turn right at this intersection.*

Your road is visible ahead, winding up a hill and heading toward a low, flat-topped mountain ringed by low cliffs. The road, now somewhat rough and rocky, heads around the right side of this mountain. As it works around the foot of the mountain you pass a hunting cabin about 200 yards on the right.   .

17.8 *This Y-intersection is marked by a sign reading Hen Egg Road that points back the way you came and also points to the left fork. Turn left.*

While all this route information may sound overly detailed, in an expanse of country this wild it's important to keep track of your position by identifying the various landmarks as you go along. The road now is only one lane wide but easily negotiable by a light truck or any vehicle with sufficient clearance.

18.35 *At this unmarked Y-junction turn right.*

The road curves uphill to the right and heads toward the massive bulk of Hen Egg Mountain. It then plunges down a steep, loose descent to the floor of a canyon.

19.0 *At the foot of the hill, on the canyon floor, is a T-intersection. On the ground I found a sign reading Hen Egg Road and pointing back up the hill I'd just descended. Turn right.*

The road heads east through a flat, wide canyon between steeply eroded cliffs. At Mile 19.9 you ford a shallow, muddy creek about 5 yards across. The steep, rocky mass of Hen Egg Mountain now thrusts skyward close on your left. Occasionally your tires may sink into sections of pulverized dust. At Mile 20.1 you pass through a fence and emerge onto a salt flat. As you pedal across the flat, you gradually draw away from Hen Egg Mountain. On your right at Mile 23.8 is a white, locked, iron gate with a 3-Bar Ranch sign on or near it. The road gradually climbs out of the salt flat and heads northeast.

25.1 *At this unmarked fork stay left.*

The road then winds up into a low eroded canyon. As you pedal uphill you pass a wall of rock on your left, and at Mile 26.5 a ridge of rock crags appears on the right topped by a spectacular free-standing rock chimney. Then at Mile 26.7 you pass two metal gates on the right. More rugged mountains appear as you continue to climb, and at Mile 27.1 you cross a cattle guard with a rusty iron gate.

29.5 *The county road meets paved RR 118.*

OPTIONAL SIDE TRIP: At this point you can turn left and ride an easy 1.6 miles north on the wide shoulder of paved RR 118 to Longhorn Ranch Motel, which has a soft-drink machine. As this was written, however, the motel's Matterhorn Restaurant served only breakfast and dinner. Return south on RR 118 and continue with the itinerary below.

29.5 *Turn right and ride south on the wide shoulder of paved RR 118 and climb a 0.5-mile hill.*

You then commence a long, fast, downhill run that winds between mountain peaks into Study Butte. The pairs of stone gateposts that you pass are entrances to various dirt roads leading to hunting tracts on Terlingua Ranch, which borders both sides of the highway. Entrance gate #9 on the left at Mile 31 is part of the route of Tour 16.

On the left at Mile 35 is Wildhorse Station, a roadside curio store with a soft-drink machine and a public phone. Although your ride continues downhill, the shoulder currently ends here, and the road becomes quite narrow. (It might have been widened by now.) Meanwhile, watch for RVs or other large vehicles. At Mile 10 the highway squeezes between a pair of mountains, and you fly down a steep hill into Study Butte.

40.0 *Study Butte. Fork right at the Y-junction outside the Big Bend Motor Inn.*

Or stop and have a cool drink at the café next door. Terlingua Store, where you left your car, is 3 miles west on RR 170. This shoulderless road carries considerable local traffic so use care when riding.

43.0 *Terlingua Store, end of the ride.*

Terlingua Store may or may not have refreshments available, depending on whether it's currently a pizza parlor, a beauty shop, a headquarters for rafting trips, or whatever.

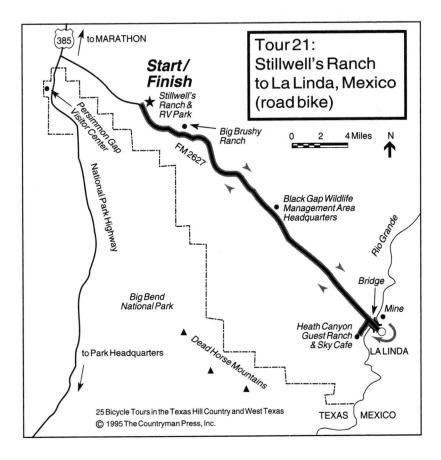

to MARATHON

**Start/
Finish**

Tour 21:
Stillwell's Ranch
to La Linda, Mexico
(road bike)

★ Stillwell's
Ranch &
RV Park

• Big Brushy
Ranch

FM 2627

Persimmon Gap
Visitor Center

National Park Highway

0   2   4 Miles   N

• Black Gap Wildlife
Management Area
Headquarters

Rio Grande

Bridge

Big Bend
National Park

Mine

Heath Canyon
Guest Ranch
& Sky Cafe

LA LINDA

to Park Headquarters

Dead Horse Mountains

25 Bicycle Tours in the Texas Hill Country and West Texas
© 1995 The Countryman Press, Inc.

TEXAS   MEXICO

21
Stillwell's Ranch to La Linda, Mexico (road bike)

Distance: *44 miles*
Terrain: *A moderately strenuous out-and-back ride through desert hills and mountains to a mining town in Mexico*
Nearest city: *Marathon*
County map: *Brewster*

From a museum of pioneer ranching life, FM 2627 runs for 22 paved miles through a series of mountain-rimmed valleys to a guest ranch and café beside the Rio Grande. You can then continue across a narrow bridge over the Rio Grande to a once-busy fluorspar mining community on the Mexican side. At one time, a convoy of four trucks made a twice-daily run to carry ore from the mine to Marathon. But during my recent survey ride, the mine at La Linda was closed, the trucks had ceased to run, and the former mining community was completely deserted. Even when the trucks operated, FM 2627 carried almost negligible traffic. During my most recent there-and-back ride, the only traffic I met during the entire 44-mile distance was an occasional rancher's pickup and a couple of vans hauling canoes from the river.

It's a hilly ride with an elevation gain of around 1000 feet on the way back, and the return ride can be hot. However, water is obtainable at the guest ranch café as are coffee, soft drinks, and tacos or other Mexican-style dishes.

The ride starts at Stillwell's Ranch (915-376-2244), located 38 miles south of Marathon via US 385, then 6 miles south on FM 2627. Stillwell's Ranch has RV and tent camping with hot showers and a small store with basic supplies. Beside the store is Hallie's Hall of Fame Museum, honoring pioneer ranchwoman Hallie Stillwell, who was born in 1897 and was still living at the ranch during my recent ride. "Miss Hallie," as she is affectionately known, spent much of her life at the ranch, and she continued to run it after her husband's death. Borrow a key and visit the museum. On display are relics and memorabilia of pioneer ranch life, including a replica of a house in which Miss Hallie lived in 1918 and historic farming and wax-making equipment.

If you like, you could also stay at Heath Canyon Guest Ranch and Sky Cafe, located at the south end of FM 2627 beside La Linda Bridge. The ranch has rooms, a bunkhouse, RV and tent camping, and a small café serving Mexican food.

A final word: Should the market for fluorspar recover, La Linda mine might reopen, the twice-daily truck convoy might resume, and the community would no longer be a ghost town. Even so, I doubt if it would significantly increase traffic. Meanwhile, though it's a shoulderless two-lane road, FM 2627 offers splendid intermediate-level road-bike riding through a scenic and sparsely populated region.

0.0   *From Stillwell's Ranch, head south on FM 2627.*

    Almost immediately a sign on the left announces that you are entering Black Gap Wildlife Management Area. At Mile 2.5 you pass Big Brushy Ranch over on the left. Then, continually twisting, winding, and plunging, FM 2627 snakes between high hills and mountains with hardly a sign of human habitation.

10.3   *A sign points to Black Gap Wildlife Management Area headquarters, located 0.5 mile left at the end of a narrow dirt road.*

    A historic marker beside FM 2627 describes this 100,000-acre preserve and the work being done to increase food supply for the mule deer, *javelina,* pronghorn antelope, and scaled quail that live here. You are free to enter the area if you register at headquarters. However, chances of seeing wildlife are probably just as good along FM 2627.

    On through several deep cuts, FM 2627 roller coasters down past more mountains and canyons and at Mile 15 a sign indicates a dirt road on the right that leads to Adams Ranch. In top gear, cranks spinning, you fly downhill toward the Rio Grande and the distant mountain ranges of Mexico. At Mile 21 the buildings of La Linda appear, and at Mile 21.5 you see the deep canyon of the Rio Grande close on the left.

Bicyclists on Tour 21 must stop and check with Mexican immigration
before entering La Linda, Mexico.

22.0 *La Linda Bridge.*

Just before the bridge, turn right onto a dirt road and ride 0.25 mile to Heath Canyon Guest Ranch and its Sky Cafe. The café is small with only two tables, but everyone seems to get served.

To continue into La Linda, ride back to the bridge and cross it. Check with the immigration inspector on the Mexican side. Then follow the dirt road around to the left for 0.25 mile into the mine and housing area. You can ride up to the machinery at the mine shaft, and you can pedal past the masonry homes of former mine workers. Be sure to stay on the roads and streets, and do not go into any yards or mine property. I tried to reach a white, twin-towered church visible about 2 miles south, but the road there was closed by a locked gate. Only a single family lived in La Linda.

22.0 *Return to Stillwell's Ranch the same way that you came.*

When you're ready, ride back across the bridge. On your right, on the US side, is a canoe- and raft-launching area. Although water may be obtainable at Black Gap Wildlife Management Area headquarters, it's best to drink your fill before starting back and carry two 24-ounce water bottles (three in hot weather). Even in midwinter the ride back can be thirsty and long.

22
Fort Davis to Balmorhea State Park
(road bike)

Distance: *64 miles*
Terrain: *An intermediate level out-and-back ride through a rugged mountain range*
Nearest cities: *Fort Davis, Balmorhea*
County map: *Jeff Davis*

From the frontier military outpost of Fort Davis, newly widened TX 17 follows the historic Overland Trail, established in the 1840s to link San Antonio with El Paso. For the first dozen miles TX 17 winds up Limpia Creek Canyon to the summit of Wild Rose Pass, then descends just as gradually through the Davis Mountains to Balmorhea State Park. The huge spring-fed pool at the park was a vital water source for wagon trains. Today it forms the world's largest spring-fed natural swimming pool.

So be sure to bring your swimsuit, and enjoy a dip in this cool, refreshing pool. It's 1.75 acres in extent, 30 feet deep, and has a constant temperature of 72–76 degrees. It's also possible to stay overnight at the park (look up Balmorhea State Park in the City and Resource Directory).

For an all-day ride, I suggest cycling from Fort Davis to Balmorhea State Park in the morning and riding back the same way in the afternoon. For a shorter ride, go only as far as Wild Rose Pass and back. Although an adequate shoulder exists the length of this ride, there is less traffic between Labor Day and Memorial Day.

At Balmorhea this ride links with Tour 11, a multiday route connecting Kerrville in the Hill Country with the West Texas cities of Alpine or Fort Davis. For cyclists headed to Fort Davis, Tour 22 forms the last day of this cross-country route.

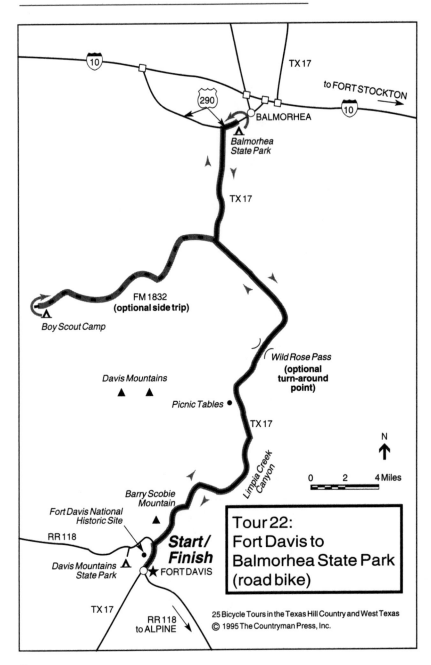

Tour 22:
Fort Davis to
Balmorhea State Park
(road bike)

25 Bicycle Tours in the Texas Hill Country and West Texas
© 1995 The Countryman Press, Inc.

0.0 *Fort Davis. Head north out of this city on wide TX 17.*

Half a mile out you pass on the left the white buildings of Fort Davis National Historic Site.

1.0 *RR 118 forks left at this junction. Stay right and continue north on TX 17.*

At Mile 1.5 a marker identifies nearby Barry Scobie Mountain, 6000 feet high and a lookout post on the Overland Trail. A few odd houses dot the highway to Mile 4; then TX 17 begins to thread its way between the steep, convoluted rock walls of Limpia Creek Canyon. In the next 4 miles the highway crosses the meandering creek on a succession of bridges.

On the left at Mile 11, a picnic site with several tables nestles under shade trees beside the creek. For the next 3 miles the grade is steeper, and at Mile 14 you reach the summit of Wild Rose Pass. Sandwiched between lofty peaks, the pass was a strategic stop on the Overland Trail. Take a break and enjoy the spectacular views of mountains and canyons. From the pass TX 17 runs downhill into a valley rimmed by steep green-and-brown mountains.

25.0 *Paved FM 1832 branches left here and winds through the hills for 11 miles to a Boy Scout camp. Stay right on TX 17.*

However, FM 1832 is open as far as the camp, and if you need an extra side trip to add a few more miles, here's your chance.

Seemingly inexhaustible panoramas of rugged mountain walls, peaks, and buttes open up as TX 17 heads down out of the Davis Mountains. A final flat 3-mile stretch brings you to the junction of US 290.

32.0 *Turn right at the junction of US 290, go 200 yards east on US 290, and turn right into Balmorhea State Park.*

Register at the entrance, and pedal on to the huge swimming pool. Cold drinks and snacks are usually available here in summer at a concession stand. But just to be sure, I'd carry food along. Drinking water is available at all times.

32.0 *Return to Fort Davis the same way that you came.*

The ride back provides a fresh chance to view this grand scenery all over again from the opposite direction.

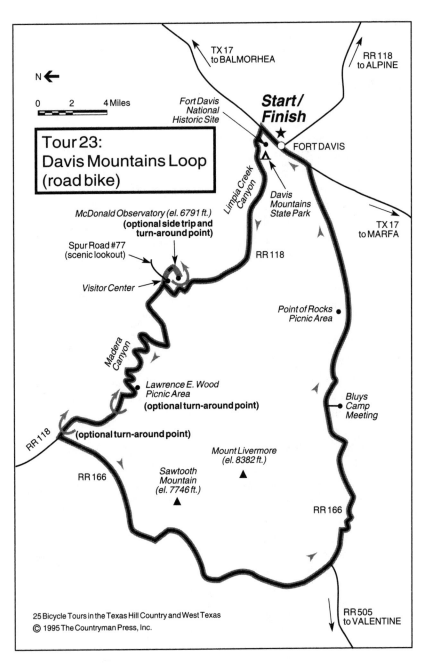

N ←

0   2   4 Miles

TX 17
to BALMORHEA

RR 118
to ALPINE

Fort Davis
National
Historic Site

*Start /
Finish*

★

FORT DAVIS

Tour 23:
Davis Mountains Loop
(road bike)

Limpia Creek Canyon

Davis
Mountains
State Park

TX 17
to MARFA

McDonald Observatory (el. 6791 ft.)
**(optional side trip and
turn-around point)**

Spur Road #77
(scenic lookout)

RR 118

Visitor Center

Point of Rocks
Picnic Area

Madera
Canyon

Lawrence E. Wood
Picnic Area
(optional turn-around point)

Bluys
Camp
Meeting

RR 118

(optional turn-around point)

Mount Livermore
(el. 8382 ft.)

RR 166

Sawtooth
Mountain
(el. 7746 ft.)

▲

RR 166

25 Bicycle Tours in the Texas Hill Country and West Texas
© 1995 The Countryman Press, Inc.

RR 505
to VALENTINE

178

23
Davis Mountains Loop (road bike)

Distance: *75 miles*
Terrain: *Strenuous mountain cycling with numerous hills and long grades*
Nearest city: *Fort Davis*
County map: *Jeff Davis*

One of the most scenic rides in Texas, this all-paved, 75-mile loop winds up through beautiful Limpia Creek Canyon and climbs through pine-clad mountains to McDonald Observatory—poised atop Mount Locke at the highest point on the Texas state highway system. Plunging into deep valleys and soaring up mountainsides, you continue around the loop. The final 30 miles are on level grassland where herds of pronghorn antelope often graze close to the road.

While traffic is usually light, this spectacular loop is also popular with motorists, especially during summer. The shoulder ends just past McDonald Observatory, and there are many blind bends in the mountains. So use a rearview mirror and ride with care. No stores or cafés exist en route, and water is obtainable only at the visitors center below McDonald Observatory. Even in winter you should carry two 24-ounce water bottles (an extra one in warmer weather). An easterly headwind could slow progress on the final 30 miles. During spring, fall, or even winter, this can be a delightful ride. Before riding in winter, check the weather forecast for possible snow.

For a shorter version, consider riding out and back to McDonald Observatory. This makes a round trip of 30 miles with a long downhill run on the way back. Or consider riding as far as Madera Canyon picnic site and back, a round-trip ride of 47 miles. Or you might go as far as the junction with RR 166 and return, a round-trip ride of 58 miles. Each September a road race and a tour is held on the Fort Davis Loop. Participants usually camp or stay at Davis Mountains State Park.

Cycling through the Davis Mountains on RR 166, part of the Davis Mountains Loop.

Our itinerary begins in the center of the town of Fort Davis. For details on Fort Davis and adjacent Fort Davis National Historic Site and Davis Mountains State Park, look up Fort Davis in the City and Resource Directory.

0.0 *From the center of Fort Davis head north on TX 17, a wide road with a 5-foot shoulder.*

Half a mile out you pass on your right the white buildings of Fort Davis National Historic Site.

1.0 *At the junction of TX 17 and RR 118, turn left onto RR 118, which has a 5-foot shoulder.*

Just past the junction on the left are the stone ruins of the Fort's original water-pumping system. RR 118 then threads through the cottonwood trees of steep-sided Limpia Creek Canyon. At Mile 4.0 you pass the entrance to Davis Mountains State Park, and at 5.6 miles Prude Ranch, a popular resort ranch, appears on your right. Traffic diminishes as you pedal up the canyon, and soon you emerge into a wide valley dotted with juniper trees. At 10 miles you pass a Solar Research Project beside the road on your right, and at 11 miles the road begins to really climb. Ahead you glimpse the white domes of McDonald Observatory perched on a mountain far above the road. For 4 miles you climb steadily uphill, pedaling around a series of hairpin bends with breathtaking vistas.

15.0 Turn right off RR 118, and ride 0.25 mile to the W.L. Moody Visitor Information Center for McDonald Observatory (915-426-3640).

Open daily 9–5, the center has water and restrooms and, usually, soft drinks. The center features audiovisual displays depicting the work of the observatory, which is 1.2 miles away by road at the 6800-foot summit of Mount Locke. The dark skies in this unpopulated region are ideal for viewing the star-rich Milky Way and other galaxies. One-hour guided tours that include the 107-inch telescope are conducted daily at 2 PM; you can also bicycle to the observatory and take a self-guided tour, following the itinerary on a map available free at the center.

Since the road to the observatory is one of the steepest and highest paved roads in Texas, most bicyclists shift into their granny gear and ride up. The road is steep but adequately wide, and the views are spectacular. At the top of the road, the elevation is 6791 feet. On the way back down, you can fork right onto Spur Road #77 and ride up another steep hill to a scenic lookout. When you're ready, continue back down past the visitors center onto RR 118.

15.0 Turn right onto RR 118 and head west.

The wide shoulder ends at Mile 16, and the narrow two-lane road alternately hugs steep mountainsides or plunges into deep, forested valleys. Bumping over cattle guards and negotiating hairpin bends, RR 118 enters verdant Madera Canyon. At Mile 23.5 you can turn left into Lawrence E. Wood Picnic Area, where numerous tables are shaded by towering trees. The site is named for the engineer who built this road. Continuing, RR 118 climbs to the top of Elbow Canyon and begins a long 3-mile descent that ends at a triangular road junction.

28.0 At this road junction, turn left onto RR 166.

Narrow and shoulderless but with very light traffic, RR 166 heads south through a wide, hill-bordered valley. Both Mount Livermore and Sawmill Mountain (7746 feet) are clearly visible on the left. At Mile 35 you begin a 2-mile climb to the top of a pass, then commence a long, gradual descent into a green, wooded valley ringed by steep mountain ramparts. You cycle past the craggy peaks and emerge into a wide, grassy plain ringed by distant purple mountains. We found lots of cactus here in spring: white clusters of yucca blooms mingled with yellow-and-pink cholla flowers and the scarlet blossoms of the spidery ocotillo.

50.0 *At this Y-junction RR 505 forks right toward Valentine. Stay left and continue on RR 166 toward Fort Davis, 25 miles east.*

Crossing occasional cattle guards, shoulderless RR 166 follows the route of the old Overland Trail, used by wagon trains between El Paso and Fort Davis. Outcroppings of red-and-white igneous rocks dot the landscape, and you glimpse an occasional ranch. Herds of fawn-and-white pronghorn antelope often graze on grasslands close to the road. One animal will always act as sentinel, ready to alert the others should danger threaten.

On the right at Mile 58 you see a "tin city" of metal buildings and travel trailers clustered in a grove of tall trees. A marker states that Bluys Camp Meeting has been held here each August since 1890. The elevation is 6000 feet, and it's pleasantly cool. But then the trees recede, and you're back pedaling across open prairie with no shelter from the wind.

Soon, however, a welcome oasis appears. At Mile 63 is Point of Rocks Picnic Area with tree-shaded tables on the left of the road. A marker on a boulder states that this was once a watering hole for wagon trains. As you approach Fort Davis, occasional ranch houses begin to appear, and a vineyard operation is visible on the left.

73.0 *Turn left at this junction with TX 17, and head north for Fort Davis.*

From here it's just 2 flat miles to Fort Davis where your ride began.

24
West Texas Loop: A 5-Day Tour (road bike)

Distance: 255 miles
Terrain: Suitable for fit, intermediate-level riders, this tour traverses hilly and mountainous terrain. Forty-eight of its miles involve steep, roller-coaster riding; the remainder roll along well-engineered roads, with long, steady climbs but few steep grades.
Nearest cities: Fort Davis, Alpine
County maps: Brewster, Jeff Davis, Presidio

The ultimate West Texas tour, this 5-day road-bike loop takes you from the high, cool Davis Mountains down to the sun-drenched Rio Grande and through a spectacular river-sculpted canyon on the Mexican border. Along the way you visit two well-preserved ghost towns and ride past a score of mountain peaks towering over a mile high. Among optional side trips is a wildly scenic 75-mile loop tour of the Davis Mountains (Tour 23); a colorful ride through the Mexican city of Ojinaga (Tour 24-B); and an all-day out-and-back ride to a pair of the most remote and isolated adobe villages in the US (Tour 25).

This tour crosses a wide, sparsely populated region with long distances between facilities and few trees to act as windbreaks. A sudden and sustained headwind strong enough to prevent you from reaching your destination is always a possibility. Assuming you have no support vehicle, it may be more prudent to turn around and ride back to your starting point. Again, even in midwinter, afternoons can become hot close to the border, and I recommend carrying three 24-ounce water bottles or the equivalent in a camelback.

I've broken this tour into five 1-day stages, each of which should be within the capabilities of a fit, intermediate-level bicyclist. To accomplish this requires staying at a couple of rather pricey motels, but when two or

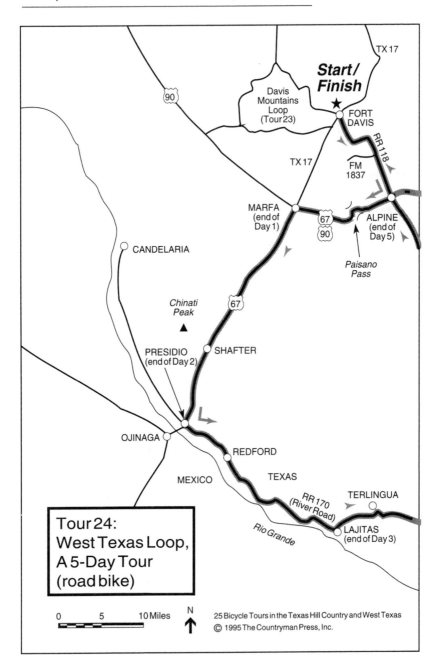

TX 17

**Start/
Finish**

Davis
Mountains
Loop
(Tour 23)

FORT
DAVIS

90

RR 118

FM
1837

TX 17

MARFA
(end of
Day 1)

67
90

ALPINE
(end of
Day 5)

CANDELARIA

*Paisano
Pass*

*Chinati
Peak*

67

PRESIDIO
(end of Day 2)

SHAFTER

OJINAGA

REDFORD

MEXICO

TEXAS

TERLINGUA

RR 170
(River Road)

Rio Grande

LAJITAS
(end of Day 3)

**Tour 24:
West Texas Loop,
A 5-Day Tour
(road bike)**

0   5   10 Miles

N

25 Bicycle Tours in the Texas Hill Country and West Texas
© 1995 The Countryman Press, Inc.

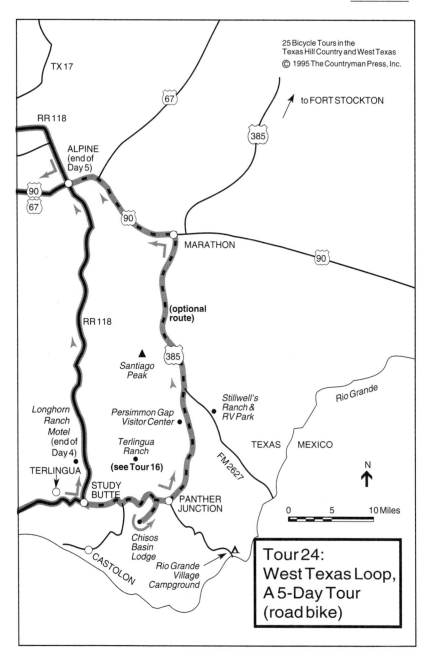

25 Bicycle Tours in the
Texas Hill Country and West Texas
© 1995 The Countryman Press, Inc.

to FORT STOCKTON

TX 17

RR 118

ALPINE
(end of
Day 5)

90
67

67

385

90

90

MARATHON

**(optional
route)**

385

RR 118

Santiago
Peak

Rio Grande

Longhorn
Ranch
Motel
(end of
Day 4)

*Persimmon Gap
Visitor Center*

*Stillwell's
Ranch &
RV Park*

TEXAS   MEXICO

TERLINGUA

*Terlingua
Ranch*

(see Tour 16)

STUDY
BUTTE

PANTHER
JUNCTION

FM 2627

N

0   5   10 Miles

*Chisos
Basin
Lodge*

CASTOLON

*Rio Grande
Village
Campground*

Tour 24:
West Texas Loop,
A 5-Day Tour
(road bike)

three riders share a room, the per-person cost is hardly excessive. I was unable to find a safe place to camp in or near Presidio, so if you're tent camping, you might want to schedule a night in a motel at Presidio.

You may prefer to schedule this tour in different stages. I've seen it done in 3 days with daily rides of 85, 65, and 79 miles respectively and with an elevation gain of 2800 feet on the final day. Go this way if you prefer, but it may take some hammering to do it. Some tours of this area also include Big Bend National Park. Certainly the Castolon and Chisos Basin roads are scenic, and the main east-to-west park highway takes you close to the Chisos Mountains. But the almost-shoulderless park highways carry a disproportionate share of large RV traffic, it is not possible to reserve a campsite in advance, and reservations at Chisos Basin Lodge (915-477-2291), the only motel-type accommodation in the park, usually must be made weeks or months in advance. Only Rio Grande Village Campground has an overflow area able to accommodate all comers. And the ride out of the park from Chisos Basin, or any other campground, to Marathon is at least 79 miles. (With a tent you can camp midway between the park and Marathon at Stillwell's Ranch (915-376-2244), located 6 miles east of US 385 on FM 2627; see Tour 21.)

In any case, I recommend confirmed advance reservations for all motels everywhere on this tour. And, if possible, I suggest a Monday-to-Friday tour rather than riding over the weekend.

This tour links with Tour 11, a 6-day tour from Kerrville in the Hill Country to Alpine or to Fort Davis in West Texas. Put Tour 11 and Tour 24 end to end and you have a magnificent 11-day tour of 576 miles to which you can still add several optional 1-day side trips. It is also possible to return to Kerrville a different way (see Tour 11), making a huge grand circle tour through both the Hill Country and West Texas.

DAY 1: Fort Davis to Alpine and Marfa
Distance: *51 miles*
Terrain: *A moderately strenuous ride with one long upgrade but no really steep hills*

0.0 *From the center of Fort Davis, head south on Main Street and fork left onto RR 118. Two-lane RR 118 has a 3.5-foot shoulder, and you stay on it all the way to Alpine.*

Car traffic on RR 118 averages about 45 vehicles per hour in each direction. On the left at Mile 4 you pass the Chihuahua Desert Visitor Center with its extensive collection of desert plants and cactus (open daily April 1 to August 31, 1–5 PM weekdays and 9–6 weekends). RR 118 then begins to wind through scenic hills. Beside the road at Mile 6.2 you pass the adobe ruins of the house of Manual Musquiz who ranched here in 1854 but was driven out by Native Americans. From here on, picturesque rock pillars, cliffs, and outcroppings line the road as it serpentines through a long, narrow valley bordered by juniper-clad hills.

13.8 *Junction with FM 1837, which branches right to Camp Mitre Peak. Stay left on RR 118.*

With Mitre Peak rising high on the right, the highway emerges from the valley and for the next 8 miles crosses a wide, treeless plain. Herds of pronghorn antelope often graze close to the road. At Mile 17 the wide patch of green visible ahead is the city of Alpine. You pass an airfield on the right and at Mile 23.5 enter Alpine's city limits. The final 0.5 mile takes you past a subdivision of new brick homes and into downtown Alpine.

24.0 *Alpine.*

Look up Alpine in the City and Resource Directory. You'll find several eating places in the downtown area as well as a supermarket and a convenience store.

24.0 *When you're ready to continue, head west as far as you can go on Avenue D, then jog 1 block south to Avenue E, which is westbound US 90. Avenue E passes under a railroad bridge, then enters US 90, a major two-lane highway with 7-foot shoulders. Although you may meet an occasional 18-wheeler, traffic on this road is usually quite light.*

From the western outskirts of Alpine, US 90 commences a gradual but scenic 11-mile ascent that winds between juniper-dotted mountains and peaks. At Mile 29 you pass a large picnic area on the right (a good lunch spot if you bought snacks in Alpine). At Mile 37 you reach Paisano Pass, and the long, uphill grade is over. A marker explains that Don Domingo de Mendoza camped at the pass in 1684, and during the 1850s, Paisano Pass was a key point on the Chihuahua Trail to California.

From the pass, US 90 emerges onto the yellow-green Marfa Plain. A marker at Mile 41 describes the Marfa Lights, mysterious and unexplained lights often visible from this location after dark. At Mile 46 the dome of Marfa's handsome courthouse is visible ahead, and by Mile 49 most of the city's buildings can be seen. US 90 crosses a bridge and enters Marfa.

51.0 *Marfa, end of today's ride.*

Look up Marfa in the City and Resource Directory.

DAY 2: Marfa to Presidio
Distance: *59 miles*
Terrain: *A fairly strenuous ride with many hills*

0.0 *From the center of Marfa head south on US 67, a major two-lane highway with a shoulder 4–5 feet wide and an average traffic flow of 30 vehicles per hour in each direction.*

On the right as you leave Marfa are the buildings of a former air base, now home of the Chinati Art Foundation (see Marfa in the City and Resource Directory). For 12 miles US 67 crosses a tawny, undulating plain, a favorite grazing ground for pronghorn antelope. Almost exactly at Mile 15, a highway cut reveals a curious mixture of ancient black lava flow and white volcanic ash. At Mile 17 the road begins a gradual 6-mile ascent through juniper-sheathed hills. It then crosses an open area with stunning views of nearby peaks and craggy distant mountain ranges.

At Mile 30 a sign points right to the 7000-foot summit of Chinati Peak. Then 3 miles beyond, at the impressive rock gateway to Cibolo Creek Ranch, a marker describes how pioneer rancher Milton Faver settled here in the 1850s and prospered against great odds. At Mile 34 the highway passes close to Elephant Rock, a mass of rounded igneous rock with an unusual resemblance to the hindquarters of a pachyderm. A few miles farther on, at the foot of a steep, winding descent, you sight the white church and rooftops of Shafter village.

40.0 *An unpaved side road leads left into the mountain-encircled ghost town of Shafter.*

Almost any road bike can negotiate the mile or so of unpaved roads that lead around this former mining town where once a thousand

The old post office at Shafter ghost town is
still open for business each morning.

people lived. Between 1883 and 1942, millions of dollars worth of
gold, silver, and lead were extracted here. Shafter was a company
town with its own church, hospital, store, school, and clubhouse,
and the post office and a small general store are still open for at least
part of each day. Some houses are still occupied, and services are
still held at the massive Sacred Heart Catholic Church out near the
highway. But much of Shafter remains a fascinating place of mem-
ories and crumbling walls. Follow signs through the village to the
old jail and past a ruined smelter to Shafter Memorial Historic Site
and the town's extensive cemetery. At the historic site, early-day
photos and captions tell the history of Shafter and how it closed in
1942 when the silver veins played out. Then ride around the cemetery. Though some tombs are fenced and well kept, the majority of
the more than 2000 graves here are just a heap of rocks marked by
a plain wood or metal cross that sticks up through the tangle of creosote bush.

Back on US 67, the road weaves uphill for another 7 scenic

miles. Vast panoramas of distant mountains reach away on every side, and a sign points right to a profile of Lincoln etched by nature on a mountain ridge.

Finally at Mile 47 the road tops out, and far below and miles away you can make out the city of Presidio in Texas and its much larger sister-city of Ojinaga, Mexico. From here it's a fast, easy downhill run of 9 miles to a signposted road that leads right to Presidio cemetery, known for its interesting headstones and unmarked graves. Back on US 67, it's just another mile to the wide bridge that spans Cibolo Creek on the outskirts of Presidio.

58.0 *As soon as you cross the Cibolo Creek Bridge, turn left onto the truck route, and continue to ride its wide shoulder for the next 0.5 mile. At Border Patrol headquarters turn left onto a two-lane road, and ride north for 100 yards to the Three Palms Motel.*

59.0 *Presidio, end of today's ride.*

Look up Presidio in the City and Resource Directory. Under Presidio, you will find additional information for staying at a motel in Ojinaga. Consider scheduling an extra day in Presidio to take Tours 24-B or 25.

DAY 3: Presidio to Lajitas
Distance: *48 miles*
Terrain: *A quite-strenuous, roller-coaster ride with one very steep hill*

Today's ride takes you over *El Camino del Rio* (River Road or RR 170), which follows an old Spanish trail more than 300 years old. Slicing through steep-walled limestone canyons carved by the Rio Grande, River Road is justly acclaimed as one of America's most spectacular river highways. About 34 miles into the ride, River Road climbs a mile-long hill with a 15 percent grade, then descends on the other side over an equally steep grade. The Big Hill, as it's called, effectively discourages most large trucks and RVs. But campers and tourist cars still buzz along this narrow, twisting road at the rate of about 25 per hour in each direction. Once outside Presidio, RR 170 currently still has no shoulder, and the edges are often rough and broken. Though scenically superb, and not to be missed under any circumstances, River Road should be ridden with care, and you should be alert for overtaking traffic.

0.0 *From the Three Palms Motel in Presidio, turn left and go 100 yards to the truck route. Turn left onto the wide truck route shoulder and ride 0.5 mile south to the junction with RR 170. Turn left onto RR 170, and ride on the wide shoulder until it ends 2.2 miles east. Stay on RR 170 all the way to Lajitas.*

For the first 2.2 miles RR 170 takes you through an area of small homes and businesses. En route you pass a café and a convenience store. Then the wide shoulder ends, and you're on the narrow, shoulderless two-lane road described above. On the right at Mile 3.4 you pass Fort Leaton State Historical Monument (described under Presidio in the City and Resource Directory). Often within sight of the Rio Grande, River Road winds on past miles of irrigated fields to Mile 18 and the small community of Redford. A dusty collection of scattered homes surrounded by farm equipment, Redford has two small stores with phone, soft drinks, and candy bars. One or both may be closed on Sunday mornings.

Leaving Redford, River Road plunges into a geological wonderland. Limestone layers thrust skyward, creating a jagged wall of mountains on both sides of the Rio Grande, and at Mile 24 you enter Big Bend Ranch State Natural Area. From the highway edge, deep canyons reach back into the wall of mountains on the left, and there isn't a flat spot anywhere. Expect lots of short, steep hills and some longer ones as well. At Mile 28, River Road threads through a sheer-walled canyon, then veers away from the river and heads through the Bofecillos Mountains for several miles.

At Mile 35 the big climb begins. Snaking through a huge boulder field, RR 170 climbs the side of a deep gorge. For 0.5 mile near the top the grade is 15 percent, and most riders walk it. Stop at the lookout on top, and view the deep gorge where the Rio Grande threads between two lava flows. Then ride down the equally steep descent on the other side. At the bottom, on the right, are three picnic tables, each shaded by a metal tepee.

Vivid panoramas of river and mountains continue as you ride down across arroyos and up over rugged, rocky hills. At Mile 42.5, at Fresno Creek, you can see across the river the historic Mexican village of Flores with its hilltop cemetery. Occasional riverside homes then appear on the US bank, and soon Lajitas comes into view, poised on a bluff above the river.

48.0 Lajitas, end of today's ride.

> Look up Lajitas in the City and Resource Directory. With a mountain bike available, you might consider stopping an extra day and taking Tour 17, or going on a 1-day raft trip through Santa Elena Canyon.

DAY 4: Lajitas to Longhorn Ranch Motel
Distance: *32 miles*
Terrain: *A moderately strenuous but leisurely day of hilly riding with a final 11-mile uphill climb*

From Lajitas you continue east on RR 170 for 19.5 miles through Terlingua to Study Butte. Since this narrow and shoulderless two-lane road is used by local residents driving to work, by starting at 9 AM or just after, you can avoid most of the commuter traffic. But at any time, RR 170 should be ridden with care throughout its length.

0.0 Lajitas. Turn right onto RR 170 and ride east.

> On the right at Mile 1.0 is Barton Warnock Environmental Education Center (915-424-3327) with 2.5 acres of cactus gardens and several exhibits of wildlife, rocks, and early ranching equipment. Also here is a splendid collection of regional guidebooks and maps for sale. Open daily 8–5, the center charges admission. RR 170 then follows a roller-coaster course across 14 miles of featureless foothills until the stone buildings of Terlingua appear on a hillside on the left.

15.0 A sign points left to Terlingua, and an unpaved road branches left for 0.5 mile to this once-thriving center of quicksilver mining. You can easily ride into Terlingua on a road bike.

> An historic marker on the highway explains that Terlingua was founded in 1890 following a cinnabar strike, and the city soon became the world's leading mercury producer. Over 2000 miners were once employed here. By 1922 Terlingua was supplying 40 percent of America's mercury needs. But a drop in mercury prices, and a flood in the mine, ended Terlingua's prosperity. Soon after World War II almost everyone had left.
>
> Visit the Chisos Mining Company store with its superb collection of regional guidebooks, cookbooks, and maps. The store's porch is a popular place to share a drink with the locals. All around, the hills are dotted with ruined stone houses and buildings, including a jail, a church, and an ice-cream parlor. The Starlight Theater, next to the

store, is still in business as is a café nearby. You also pass a small cemetery on the way in.

On past a small trailer park, RR 170 passes Easter Egg Valley Motel and reaches the intersection of RR 118.

19.5   Study Butte. Turn left onto RR 118 and head north.

Look up Study Butte in the City and Resource Directory. A café at the intersection is convenient for lunch.

For the first 6 miles from Study Butte, RR 118 is old, narrow, and shoulderless. But the rest of the way—including all of tomorrow's ride to Alpine—is on a new two-lane road with shoulders 5 to 7 feet in width. Unfortunately, the first 6 miles include a steep uphill climb. (But perhaps by now all of RR 118 has been widened.)

In any case, RR 118 cuts through the rugged Christmas Mountains, providing superb views of such major peaks as Bee, Hen Egg, and Packsaddle Mountains on the left and Willow Peak on the right. At Mile 25 you can get a cold drink at Wildhorse Station (915-371-2526), a curio shop with furnished cabins. Then at Mile 25.5 the wide shoulders begin. At Mile 28.5 you reach the crest of a hill, and visible there, a few miles away across a grassy plain, are the red roofs and white water tank of Longhorn Ranch Motel.

32.0   Longhorn Ranch Motel, end of today's ride.

Though rather isolated, Longhorn Ranch Motel (915-371-2541) has comfortable accommodations, and its Matterhorn Restaurant serves breakfast and dinner.

DAY 5: Longhorn Ranch Motel to Alpine
Distance: *65 miles*
Terrain: *A moderately strenuous ride that crosses 35 miles of flat grassland followed by 30 miles of hilly riding*

The shoulder on RR 118 varies from 5 to 7 feet in width and runs the entire length of today's ride. While you may meet RVs and an occasional large truck, traffic is fairly light, especially on weekdays. But do be prepared for a steady climb. Though the elevation of Alpine is 4483 feet, this road reaches an altitude of 5360 feet, which is 877 feet higher than Alpine. Starting from Longhorn Ranch Motel, that translates into an elevation gain of roughly 1800 feet.

0.0 *From Longhorn Ranch Motel, turn left and head north on RR 118. You stay on this highway all the way to Alpine.*

For the next 35 miles RR 118 crosses a treeless plain of yellow-green grass, and pronghorn antelope often graze near the road. At Mile 3.8 a large sign invites you to visit "Terlingua Ranch—it's worth the trip" (for more information, see Tour 16). You pass Agua Fria Mountain off to the left. And at Mile 10 you reach The Frontier Store, open 7–7 daily and your last chance for food or drink for the next 55 miles.

Several high mountains break the monotony of the immense flatland you are crossing. Off to the right lies the truncated cone of Santiago Peak, 6521 feet high. Then at Mile 35 a series of lava-topped mesas appear close to the road on the left, and RR 118 begins a gradual climb. At Mile 37 a sign points right to lava-capped Elephant Peak, 6230 feet in elevation and part of Elephant Mountain Wildlife Management Center that you pass on the right.

At Mile 39 a tree-shaded picnic site invites a stop, and there's another at Mile 48. Splendid views of massive, 6900-foot-high Cathedral Mountain open up on the left, and at Mile 49 a sign identifies the gate to Woodward Ranch, a popular place for hunting rare agates and other minerals (rock shop, camping).

At Mile 54 the highway crosses a lofty divide with an elevation of 5360 feet. It's high and cool up here with lots of juniper trees and magnificent views of the huge bulk of Mount Ord, 6815 feet high and about 3 miles away on the right. As you round a bend in the mountain road near Que Decie Ranch, a vast panorama suddenly appears, and you see the city of Alpine 4 miles away and almost 1000 feet below. You fly down the hills, and within minutes you're in downtown Alpine.

65.0 *Alpine, end of today's ride.*

For more information, look up Alpine in the City and Resource Directory. If your car is in Fort Davis, you can ride back there tomorrow morning over the same road you traveled on Day 1.

24-A

Ojinaga City Loop (road bike)
Distance: 11 miles
Terrain: A flat, easy ride through a colorful Mexican border town

Founded by the Spaniards in the 17th century, and later the headquarters of Pancho Villa, Ojinaga (oh-hee-nah-gah) is a thriving Mexican city on the south bank of the Rio Grande across from Presidio, Texas. Despite the considerable traffic, Mexican motorists are used to bicyclists and, in towns at least, they often seem more considerate than do many American drivers. Perhaps this is because, in case of any accident in which blood is drawn, the car driver may be jailed.

I suggest that female bicyclists be accompanied by a male rider. You should also carry some proof of US citizenship or legal residence for returning through US immigration. During late spring or early fall, the temperature in Ojinaga may reach 110 degrees in midafternoon. It's a dry heat that isn't too apparent. But I'd carry a full bottle of water. Soft drinks are also available at several places en route. If you stop to go into a store or café, one rider should remain outside to watch the bikes. Although the distance isn't far, most people take 2 to 3 hours to complete the trip. Though Ojinaga has a population of 55,000, many streets do not carry name signs. If you lose your bearings, almost any well-dressed person will speak English and can direct you to the *zócalo* (city center) or back to the international bridge. It's best to avoid crossing back into the US during busy weekend periods or during morning and evening hours when people are driving across the Rio Grande bridge to and from work.

0.0 From Presidio's Three Palms Motel, turn left onto a paved road, and go 100 yards to a junction with a truck route.

0.1 Turn right onto the truck route, and stay on the wide shoulder for 0.5 mile to the junction with US 67.

0.6 Turn left onto US 67, and ride on the wide shoulder for 1 mile to the Rio Grande Bridge.

1.6 Dismount at the bridge, and either walk or ride across on the sidewalk to the Mexican side.

Tell the uniformed Mexican immigration officer that you are going

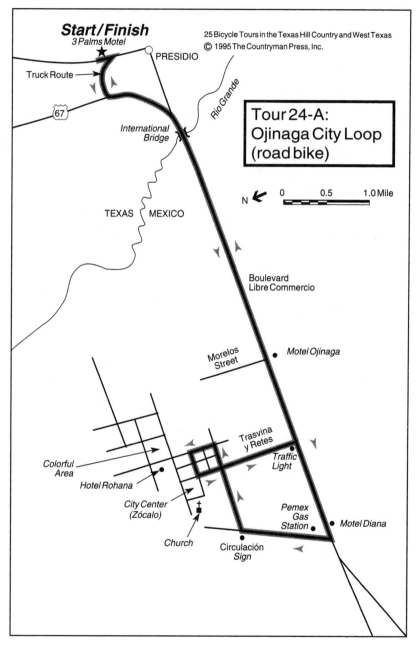

Start/Finish
3 Palms Motel

25 Bicycle Tours in the Texas Hill Country and West Texas
© 1995 The Countryman Press, Inc.

PRESIDIO

Truck Route

Rio Grande

(67)

International Bridge

**Tour 24-A:
Ojinaga City Loop
(road bike)**

N

0   0.5   1.0 Mile

TEXAS   MEXICO

Boulevard
Libre Commercio

Morelos
Street

Motel Ojinaga

Trasvina
y Retes

Traffic
Light

Colorful
Area

Hotel Rohana

City Center
(Zócalo)

Church

Circulación
Sign

Pemex
Gas
Station

Motel Diana

only to Ojinaga, and you'll be waved on. Immediately ahead is six-lane Boulevard Libro Commercio (Free Trade Boulevard), lined with warehouses and other commercial buildings. At Mile 2.6, on your left and at the corner of Morelos Street, is the comfortable Motel Ojinaga (phone 145-30311), a good place to stay. At Mile 3.6 is a traffic light and a green sign reading Ojinaga Centro and pointing right. (This is a shortcut to the center, and you'll be returning this way.) Keep straight on Libro Commercio for another mile until you reach a road junction with a Pemex gas station on the right. Across from the gas station is the Motel Diana (phone 145-31723), a more modest place to stay.

4.6 *At this junction turn right and ride 1 mile on a divided road to a large sign that says* Circulación, *meaning one-way.*

5.6 *At the* Circulación *sign, turn right and ride down this street to a traffic light and a sign that identifies the cross street as* Trasvina y Retes. *Go straight across this intersection, and ride 2 more blocks. At this intersection, turn left and ride 1 block up a short, steep hill and continue on for 1 block more. You are now close to the city center and can see the* zócalo, *or central square, 2 blocks to your left. Ride or walk over to it.*

Here in the heart of old Ojinaga all streets are narrow and one-way. An arrow on the wall at each intersection indicates which way traffic may travel. Do not ride a one-way street against the traffic flow. Get off and walk your bike on the sidewalk.

6.2 *The* zócalo.

Flanked by the municipal palace on one side and a handsome church with a bell tower on another, the *zócalo* of Ojinaga has seats and fountains, and local citizens can direct you to any place you wish to reach. Just 1 block from the *zócalo,* for instance, is the Hotel Rohana (phone 145-30078 or 145-30071), which was once shot up by Pancho Villa. Behind it is a new motel block with comfortable rooms. North and east of the Rohana are several historic blocks, and just beyond are colorful dirt streets lined with typical flat-roofed adobe homes. They're worth exploring on your bike.

For a tasty snack, visit Panadería Francesa at Calle Zaragoza #504, a block from the *zócalo.* The building it occupies was once the

You can ride your bike across the border and tour the Mexican city of Ojinaga, with its historic *zócalo* (square) adorned by fountains and its bell-towered church.

headquarters of Pancho Villa, and the bread and pastries are still baked in a traditional wood-fired oven and slid in and out with a long wooden paddle. Use a pair of tongs to select some crisp rolls (*bolillos*) or gingerbread cookies (*marranitos*) from the cooling trays. You can munch them while enjoying the sights of the *zócalo*.

6.2 *To return to Presidio, head east down Trasvina y Retes, one of few streets to be identified by signs. At the second traffic light it intersects with Boulevard Libro Commercio. Turn left onto this six-lane thoroughfare. From this point you retrace the same route you rode on the outward leg, but you will be on the opposite side of the road. Ride 2 miles back to the Rio Grande Bridge.*

At the bridge you must pay a small toll. It's best to walk or ride across on the sidewalk. Immediately ahead is the US Immigration building. You must wait in line with the cars to reenter the US. A green light will indicate when it's your turn to ride forward to the immigration inspector. You will have to surrender any fruit other than papayas.

9.3 *From the bridge return to the Three Palms Motel by the same route that you followed on the way out. Except for the last 100 yards, there's a wide shoulder all the way.*

10.9 *The Three Palms Motel.*

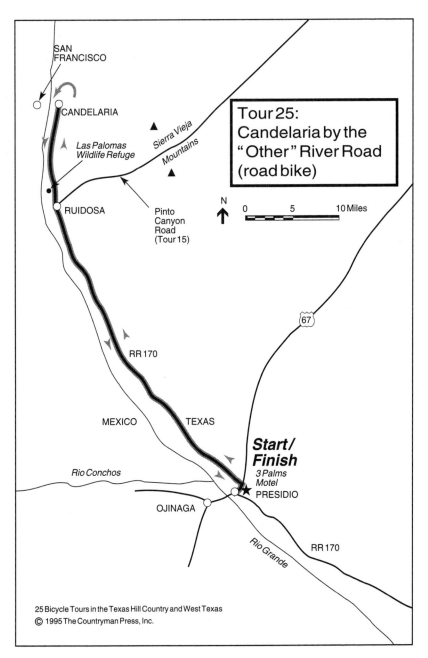

SAN FRANCISCO

CANDELARIA

Las Palomas Wildlife Refuge

Sierra Vieja Mountains

RUIDOSA

Pinto Canyon Road (Tour 15)

Tour 25: Candelaria by the "Other" River Road (road bike)

N

0   5   10 Miles

(67)

RR 170

MEXICO   TEXAS

Rio Conchos

Start / Finish
3 Palms Motel
PRESIDIO

OJINAGA

Rio Grande   RR 170

25 Bicycle Tours in the Texas Hill Country and West Texas
© 1995 The Countryman Press, Inc.

25

Candelaria by the "Other" River Road (road bike)

Distance: *96 miles*
Terrain: *A long but relatively level out-and-back ride to a pair of isolated adobe villages on the Mexican border*
Nearest city: *Presidio*
County map: *Presidio*

Every year thousands of tourists drive RR 170 southeast of Presidio, the River Road that hugs the Rio Grande for 50 miles through a wild extravaganza of mountain and canyon scenery. But RR 170 also follows the Rio Grande for another 48 miles *northwest* of Presidio. While it's not as dramatically scenic, this "other" River Road is a road biker's dream come true.

Narrow and winding but lacking any really long hills and virtually traffic-free, it's the sort of road where a bicyclist can reach out, spin those cranks, and really go for it. With high mountains a mile or two away on each side, you glide past a succession of ruined adobe houses, clusters of beehives, and weirdly sculptured monoliths. It's 37 miles to Ruidosa, the first hamlet, and 48 to Candelaria, the second. Once out here, you're in an unbelievable corner of the US that resembles south Mexico more than Texas. Coyotes and *javelinas* are common, people still gather on porches for a sing-along, and you may still meet cowboys on horseback and bearded old-timers with a repertoire of yarns.

Water and cold drinks are available at Ruidosa and at Candelaria (perhaps not on Sundays), but you should still carry at least two 24-ounce water bottles. No accommodation is available out here, so if a strong southeasterly wind springs up, consider turning around and heading back to Presidio. From Presidio to Candelaria and back is 96 miles. Once back at Presidio you

Beside the general store at Candelaria is an iron cage
that once served as the town jail.

can ride 2 miles north on US 67 and 2 miles back to complete a century.

If 96 miles sounds intimidating, try this: Drive to Ruidosa with your bike and park on the shoulder in the village. Ride the 11 miles to Candelaria and return. Have a snack at your car, then ride another 12 or 15 miles toward Presidio and return. This provides a total of 45 to 50 miles of great riding. You visit both villages. And you're never more than an hour from your car.

One thing you won't see on this ride is the Rio Grande River. That's because the river here has been badly depleted by irrigation. The wider, deeper Rio Grande River that you see below Presidio is boosted by water from a Mexican tributary, the Rio Conchos, that flows in at Presidio.

The itinerary below begins at Presidio's Three Palms Motel and takes you the full 48 miles to Candelaria. You return the same way.

0.0 *From Presidio's Three Palms Motel, turn left onto a paved road, and go 100 yards south to a junction with a truck route.*

0.1 *Turn right onto the truck route, and ride on the wide shoulder for 0.5 mile to the junction with US 67.*

0.6   *Turn right onto US 67, and ride on the shoulder across the long span of Cibolo Creek Bridge.*

0.9   *Turn left onto RR 170. No more turns are necessary. This same paved, two-lane, low-traffic road leads directly to Candelaria, where it ends.*

For the first 4 miles RR 170 is new and wide and runs past irrigated cantaloupe fields. Beyond the fields, the Mexican city of Ojinaga sprawls across the hills like some Oriental casbah. Then the road narrows and you soar on, pedaling briskly up and down a series of low roller-coaster hills and dips. On the left at Mile 14 is a hillside cemetery brightly decorated with paper flowers; none of the graves seem historic.

Spiny desert cacti line the road as you glide on across a series of vados, or dry arroyos, that are briefly impassable after a flash flood. Houses are so remote that it's an event to pass one. At Mile 30 the road winds up through a series of foothills. Then far ahead you see a cluster of white houses surrounded by trees.

37.0   *Ruidosa. On your right a dirt road leads to Pinto Canyon (see Tour 15).*

Ruidosa is a tiny cluster of white adobe houses with a general store called *La Estrella del Norte* (North Star). Soft drinks and junk-food snacks are available, and a sign announces it is open daily from 8–8. Beside the store are the remains of a ruined adobe Catholic mission built in the early 1900s.

As you ride on, watch for occasional bumpy cattle guards made of large-diameter iron pipe. On the left at Mile 38.6 is the Ocotillo Unit of Las Palomas Wildlife Refuge. It's primarily a riverside bird refuge. You're welcome to visit provided you sign in at headquarters just inside the gate. On past rugged juniper-sheathed mountains, the road switchbacks across a series of vados, and at Mile 46 you ride past a dried-up oxbow lake, once part of the Rio Grande. Ahead you see a low white church and the houses of Candelaria. Ride into the center and up to the store.

48.0   *Candelaria. Once a cotton-raising center, the village recently still had a one-room schoolhouse.*

Go inside the old-fashioned, high-ceilinged store, which carries soft drinks and staples. Every day a score of women walk several miles across the river from Mexico to shop here, and this is a good place to practice your Spanish. Behind the store is a compound with several flat-roofed Mexican-style houses, and next to the store is a roofless steel-cage "jail" with two iron bunks. Also here are some early-day tractors and farm equipment. From the compound, a trail leads south through tall brush for about a mile to the river. Here it crosses the shallow Rio Grande on a narrow, rickety wooden bridge to the Mexican village of San Francisco on the other bank. You could probably ride to the bridge, but crossing it with your bike is difficult. San Francisco offers little of interest.

48.0 Ride back on RR 170 to Presidio the way you came.

As always when you retrace a route and see everything from the opposite side, the trip back to Presidio is like taking an entirely different ride.

How to Plan a Grand 21-Day, 1184-Mile Bicycle Adventure Including the Best of Both the Hill Country and West Texas

Put together Tours 11, 22, 23, 24, 24-A, and 25 and you get a real adventure tour that looks like this:

Day 1: Tour 11, Day 1: Kerrville/Ingram to Junction, 48 miles

Day 2: Tour 11, Day 2: Junction to Sonora, 58 miles

Day 3: Tour 11, Day 3: Sonora to Ozona, 35 miles

Day 4: Tour 11, Day 4: Ozona to Iraan, 51 miles

Day 5: Tour 11, Day 5: Iraan to Fort Stockton, 63 miles

Day 6: Tour 11-B, Day 6: Fort Stockton to Balmorhea State Park, 59.5 miles

Day 7: Tour 22: Balmorhea State Park to Fort Davis, 32 miles

Day 8: Tour 23, Davis Mountains Loop: Fort Davis to Fort Davis, 75 miles

Day 9: Tour 24, Day 1: Fort Davis to Marfa, 51 miles

Day 10: Tour 24, Day 2: Marfa to Presidio, 59 miles

Day 11: Tour 24-A, Ojinaga City Loop: Presidio to Ojinaga to Presidio, 11 miles

Day 12: Tour 25, Candelaria by the "other" River Road: Presidio to Candelaria and return, 96 miles

Day 13: Tour 24, Day 3: Presidio to Lajitas, 48 miles

Day 14: Tour 24, Day 4: Lajitas to Longhorn Ranch Motel, 32 miles

Day 15: Tour 24, Day 5: Longhorn Ranch Motel to Alpine, 65 miles

Back in Alpine on the 15th day, you'll have ridden a total of 783.5 miles, much of it through some of the grandest scenery in Texas. Could you ride on and loop back to Kerrville without retracing the route you've already ridden?

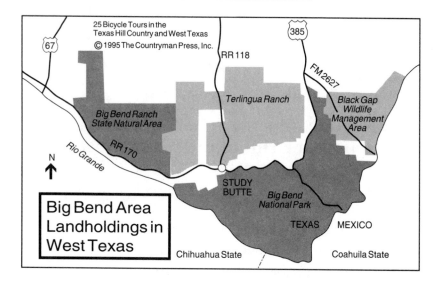

25 Bicycle Tours in the
Texas Hill Country and West Texas
© 1995 The Countryman Press, Inc.

Terlingua Ranch

Black Gap
Wildlife
Management
Area

Big Bend Ranch
State Natural Area

Rio Grande

RR 170

STUDY
BUTTE

Big Bend
National Park

TEXAS   MEXICO

Chihuahua State

Coahuila State

**Big Bend Area
Landholdings in
West Texas**

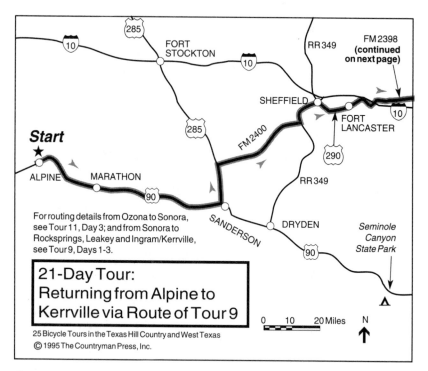

FM 2398
**(continued
on next page)**

FORT
STOCKTON

SHEFFIELD

FORT
LANCASTER

Start

ALPINE   MARATHON

FM 2400

For routing details from Ozona to Sonora,
see Tour 11, Day 3; and from Sonora to
Rocksprings, Leakey and Ingram/Kerrville,
see Tour 9, Days 1-3.

SANDERSON   DRYDEN

Seminole
Canyon
State Park

**21-Day Tour:
Returning from Alpine to
Kerrville via Route of Tour 9**

0   10   20 Miles   N

25 Bicycle Tours in the Texas Hill Country and West Texas
© 1995 The Countryman Press, Inc.

Returning to Kerrville by US 90

For years, the standard route to Kerrville has been to go east on US 90 to Marathon, Sanderson, Comstock, and Del Rio, then to head northeast on US 277 and US 377 to Rocksprings, and finally to go east on TX 41 and TX 27 back to Kerrville. While this route is scenic in parts, and US 90 has a wide shoulder, three long stretches exist between motels. One, from Sanderson to Comstock, is 88 miles; the second, from Del Rio to Rocksprings, is 77 miles; and the third, from Rocksprings to Ingram/ Kerrville, is 69–73 miles. By comparison, the maximum distance between motels on Tour 11 is 65.5 miles and on 4 of the 6 days of Tour 11, food and drink are available at some point along the way.

Again, the first tent campground east of Sanderson is Seminole Canyon State Park, located 80 miles east of Sanderson. If you have vehicular support, or are confident you can make these distances, ride back to Kerrville this way. From Alpine, the total distance is 324 miles, which could add 5 or 6 more days of riding. This would make a grand tour of 1108 miles in 20 to 21 days.

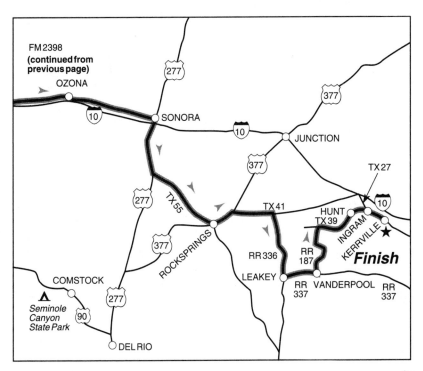

Returning to Kerrville via Tour 9

To exclude the long distances between motels, another possibility is this: From Alpine ride east on US 90 to Marathon and Sanderson. After overnighting in Sanderson, head north on US 285 for 14 miles, then turn right on FM 2400 for 39 miles, and turn left on RR 349 for 9 miles into Sheffield. Neither food nor water is available during this 64-mile ride. At the village of Sheffield, stay overnight at the small Oases Motel and Cafe (915-836-4438) or camp at Eagle Nest Trailer Park. A confirmed advance reservation at this motel is essential before starting out to ride here. Once the stompin' grounds of raiding Apaches, and later the headquarters for Black Jack Ketchum's gang of train and bank robbers, Sheffield today is almost a ghost town.

Next day, continue east on US 290 past Fort Lancaster, and ride east for 4 miles on the shoulder of I-10. Continue east on the north side I-10 frontage road and FM 2398 into Ozona, a total distance of 45 miles. The same day you can probably continue another 35 miles east to Sonora, following the same route as in Tour 11.

After overnighting in Sonora, I suggest following the first 3 days of Tour 9 in reverse back to Kerrville. This gives overnight stops at Rocksprings and Leakey. From Alpine to Kerrville this way is a ride of 400 miles with overnights at Marathon, Sanderson, Sheffield, Sonora, Rocksprings, and Leakey.

Add this return route to our 15-day itinerary, and you have a 21-day, 1184-mile grand tour of Texas that includes not only the best of West Texas but also some of the biggest hills and most exciting river canyon scenery in the Hill Country.

Here's a final tip for anyone planning to ride the full 21-day grand tour and return via Tour 9: For minimal exposure to traffic, I suggest *starting out* by riding the first 3 days of Tour 9 from Kerrville/Ingram to Leakey, Rocksprings, and Sonora. On the return trip, you would then follow in reverse the routing for the first 2 days of Tour 11, from Sonora to Junction and Kerrville/Ingram. Though this may sound slightly confusing, following this route takes you on wide-shouldered roads for the last 14 miles into Ingram, which is not the case if you return from Leakey to Ingram via the routing in Tour 9.

City and Resource Directory

This directory supplies essential touring information and guidance for all towns and cities on or near our bike rides that have overnight accommodations. This information is often hard to come by because small, isolated communities such as Iraan or Rocksprings are seldom listed in any guidebook or directory, and obtaining the names and phone numbers of motels or campgrounds in these places is often difficult. Yet communities like these are key touring bases or stopovers for anyone exploring the area by bicycling or driving through.

This directory also focuses on less-expensive and more-affordable accommodations and omits mention of some pricey, deluxe resort-type motels. Hotels or motels are named as a convenience for cyclists and are not recommended for quality, comfort, or price. The symbol (E) after a motel name indicates that lower rates may be found at neighboring establishments. I also mention a few atmospheric and historic hotels at which rates may be higher. Bed & breakfasts are generally not listed because many close after a year or two. For more current information, including bed & breakfasts, call the chamber of commerce or visitors bureau listed, or send them a postcard requesting a complete set of their literature including a street map of their city, a map of their historic area with a walking or driving tour, a list of accommodations, tent campgrounds and restaurants, and any other specific information you require.

Alpine (Brewster County; Pop. 5655; Alt. 4483 feet)

Information: Chamber of Commerce, 106 N.Third St., Alpine, TX 79831 (915-837-2326).
Home of Sul Ross State University and gateway to the Big Bend and Davis Mountains country, mountain-rimmed Alpine is also a stop on transcontinental AMTRAK and bus services. Alpine's Big Bend Medical Center at 801 E. Brown (915-837-3477) provides hospital facilities and 24-hour emergen-

cy service. Alpine has two supermarkets and a number of motels, restaurants, convenience stores, a Western Auto store, and other stores providing basic necessities. US 90 traffic travels on one-way streets through Alpine: westbound on Avenue E, and eastbound on Holland Avenue. You can avoid most traffic by riding on Avenue D, which is one block north of Avenue E. Topographical maps are available at **Apache Trading Post** (915-837-5194) at the west end of Alpine. For a half- or all-day out-and-back ride on a scenic paved road try RR 118 north toward Fort Davis (see Tour 24); RR 118 south toward Study Butte (see Tour 24); or US 90 west to Marfa (see Tour 24).

Campgrounds
Tent camping has been available at **Danny Boy R-V Park** (915-837-7135) on East US 90 and **Pecan Grove R-V Park** (915-837-7175) on West US 90.

Motels
Antelope Lodge, west side on US 90 (915-837-2451).
Bien Venido, central at 809 E. Holland (915-837-3454).
Days Inn, east side on US 90 (915-837-3417).
Highland Inn (E), east side on US 90 (915-837-5811).
Siesta Country Inn, 1200 E. Holland (915-837-2503).

Balmorhea State Park (Jeff Davis County; Pop. 250; Alt. 4750 feet)

Information: *Superintendent, Balmorhea State Park, PO Box 15, Toyahvale, TX 79786 (915-375-2370).*
Balmorhea State Park, 4 miles west of the small community of Balmorhea (located on US 290 near I-10) is widely known for its huge spring-fed swimming pool: 1.75 acres in extent and 30 feet deep with a constant temperature of 72 to 76 degrees. Also in the park are picnic tables, tent campsites, and the **San Solomon Springs Court,** a motel with some kitchenettes. For an overnight stay, an advance reservation is essential. Four miles east at Balmorhea are two other small motels: the **Country Inn** (915-375-2477) and the **Valley Motel** (915-375-2263).

Bandera (Bandera County; Pop. 925; Alt. 1258 feet)

Information: *Convention and Visitors Bureau, 1205 Cypress, Bandera TX 78003 (210-796-3045 or 1-800-364-3833).*
An authentic western town ringed by dude and working ranches, Bandera

began as a cypress-shingle camp in 1852, then became the site of a Mormon colony and a Polish community. Pick up a "Historical Tours of Bandera" brochure from the visitors bureau (corner of Main Street and TX 16). Then ride around on adjacent side streets and see St. Stanislaus Church and the various historical sites, identified by markers, scattered in and around the courthouse square. Bandera also has two supermarkets, several cafés, a convenience store, and other basic stores. Roads best avoided include shoulderless RR 173 to Kerrville and TX 16, which carries traffic to and from Bandera Downs Racetrack. However, unpaved county roads, plus the trails in nearby Hill Country State Natural Area, offer traffic-free, off-road riding through some of the most rewarding sections of the Hill Country. Reservations are advised on weekends and holidays throughout the year. The visitors bureau has listings of bed & breakfasts and dude ranches.

Campgrounds
Bandera Beverage Barn RV Park, at city edge on TX 16 north (210-796-8153).
Hill Country Natural Area, 11 miles south via FM 1077, open Thursday through Sunday (210-796-4413).
Yogi Bear's Jellystone Park, Maple Street and RR 173, riverside RV park with tent sites (210-796-3751).

Motels
Frontier Hotel, downtown at 701 Main Street (210-796-4100).
River Front Motel, downtown on Main Street (210-460-3690).

Fort Davis (Jeff Davis County; Pop. 900; Alt. 5050 feet)

Information: Chamber of Commerce, PO Box 378, Fort Davis, TX 79734.
Set in the Davis Mountains, and the highest town in Texas, Fort Davis's cool summers annually attract thousands of visitors. The town originated in 1854 to serve the needs of the US Army's Fort Davis, located 1 mile north. The fort, restored by the National Park Service, draws thousands of tourists each year. Davis Mountains State Park, 5 miles west, is another major attraction. Fort Davis is also the hub city for visiting McDonald Observatory and the Chihuahua Desert Visitors Center, and for driving the Davis Mountains Scenic Loop. Reservations are advised, especially June through August.

211

Indian Lodge, nestled in the hills of Davis Mountains State Park, is a popular stopover for bicyclists touring the Davis Mountains.

To experience the town's lingering frontier flavor, cycle the 1-mile Historic Loop, which is marked and runs a block or so west of Main Street over the original Overland Trail, then jogs east to the old town square, still surrounded by historic buildings. Fort Davis has several restaurants and cafés, an old drugstore with fountain, and two small markets. Not to be missed are:

Fort Davis National Historic Site, 1 mile north on TX 17. Built in 1854 to protect the trail between San Antonio and El Paso, Fort Davis was closed during the Civil War but was reactivated in 1867 and remained in service until 1891. So-called "buffalo soldiers" of African descent served in infantry and cavalry units here after the Civil War and fought the Apaches and Comanches. Twenty-five of the original buildings are now preserved including the original officers' row cottages, the parade ground, barracks, and other buildings, and the entire post appears much as it did in 1891. The visitors center has an interpretive program and bookstore. A scenic hiking trail winds through a canyon for 4 miles to Fort Davis State Park. Open daily except Christmas and New Year's, 8–5 in winter and 8–6 in summer (915-426-3224).

Davis Mountains State Park, 5 miles west of Fort Davis on TX 118 and Park Road 3. This popular 1869-acre park has scores of shady tent campsites served by toilets and hot showers. Also in the park is **Indian Lodge** (PO Box 1458, Fort Davis, TX 79734; phone 915-426-3254), a rambling New Mexico–style lodge with restaurant and pool nestled in a mountain basin. It is closed the middle 2 weeks of January. Reservations are advised at all times and should be made by calling the number just given rather than the state parks central reservation number in Austin. However, campsites should be reserved through the central reservation number.

Motels
Fort Davis Motor Inn (E), on TX 17 north of RR 118 intersection (915-426-2112 or 1-800-80-DAVIS).
Hotel Limpia, town square. A historic high-ceilinged hotel built in 1912 and now restored (915-426-3237 or 1-800-662-5517).
Prude Ranch, guest ranch 10 miles north (1-800-458-6232).
Stone Village Motel, on Main Street (915-426-3941).

Fort Stockton (Pecos County; Pop. 8525; Alt. 2955 feet)

Information: *Chamber of Commerce, PO Box C, Fort Stockton, TX 79735 (915-336-2264).*

A supply and trading center for a vast ranching, oil, and natural gas area, the city of Fort Stockton grew up around a military post established here in 1859 to protect wagon train and stagecoach routes from raiding Native Americans and bandits. The big attraction was Comanche Springs, an enormous natural spring that gushed 65 million gallons of water daily. But irrigated farming has depleted the spring, and it now feeds an Olympic-sized swimming pool in James Rooney County Park.

From east or west, bicyclists usually approach Fort Stockton by riding on the I-10 frontage road. From the east, take Exit 261 into Fort Stockton. This brings you onto wide East Dickinson Boulevard, and you pass several affordable motels as you ride west toward downtown. From the west, take the first Fort Stockton exit, which leads you onto wide West Dickinson Boulevard. You will see the Motel Six and several other motels clustered here. Dickinson Boulevard (US 285, US 290, and US 365) is the city's principal east-west thoroughfare. Fort Stockton has 800 motel rooms plus two supermarkets, a K-Mart, and most other basic stores. For bicyclists, the motels at the east end of Dickinson Boulevard seem more central and closer to supermarkets and the city tour.

Although this flat city looks nondescript, it has an interesting historic-area tour that you can make by bicycle. A tour map is available from the chamber of commerce at 222 West Dickinson Boulevard (near the junction with US 385) or you can send for a map beforehand.

Campgrounds

KOA Kampground, 3.5 miles east on I-10 at Exit 264, Warnock Road (915-395-2494 or 1-800-447-6067).

Motels

Budget Inn–Silver Saddle Lodge, east side at 801 E. Dickinson (915-336-3311).

Comanche Motel, older, east side at 1301 E. Dickinson (915-336-5824).

Econo-Lodge (E), east side at 800 E. Dickinson (915-336-9711 or 1-800-643-2666).

El Rancho Motel–Economy Inn, east side at 901 E. Dickinson (915-336-2251).

Motel Six, west side at 3001 W. Dickinson (915-336-9737).

Fredericksburg (Gillespie County; Pop. 7500; Alt. 1745 feet)

Information: *Convention & Visitors Bureau, 106 N. Adams, Fredericksburg, TX 78624 (210-997-6523).*

Named for Prince Frederick of Prussia, leader of a mid-19th-century German immigration movement, Fredricksburg was founded in 1846 by a group of German families led by John O. Meusebach, a former nobleman. After the settlers had signed a peace treaty with the Comanches, Fredericksburg began to thrive and grow. Soon ranchers began building small "Sunday houses" so that they could stay in town for Sunday church services. Today Fredericksburg remains a showplace of pioneer houses, churches, and stores, many built of native limestone, and the city is filled with reminders of its German heritage. You'll find its most famous landmark, the "coffee mill" church—a replica of the original octagonal *Vereins Kirche* built in 1847—on the north side of Main Street. Surrounding the *Vereins Kirche* is a historic district that embraces at least 25 blocks. You can pick up a Historic District Tour Map at the visitors bureau located close to the center and just north of Main Street at 106 North Adams. Ask also for a combination street map and road map of Gillespie County, a priceless guide that shows by name many of the back roads you'll be riding in this area.

Because of traffic on Main Street, I recommend exploring its 7 historic blocks on foot. Housed in 19th-century buildings are German restaurants with robust cuisines, beer gardens, bakeries, antiques shops, and even a dulcimer store. At 340 East Main is the unique Nimitz Steamboat Hotel, a famous frontier-day hostelry, now a museum depicting the World War II naval victories of Admiral Nimitz, a native of Fredericksburg. Behind the hotel is a Japanese Peace Garden and, nearby, a History Walk lined by rare World War II tanks, guns, and aircraft.

You can explore the rest of the Historic District by bike. Let your map be your guide as you ride past the old jail, the European-style *Marienkirche,* and a score of Sunday houses and other historic homes with wide verandas and gingerbread decor.

Fredericksburg also has two supermarkets, including a large HEB superstore on South Adams (TX 16) and a smaller Super-S store on North Milam (RR 965). **Hill Country Memorial Hospital** at 1020 Kerrville Road (210-997-4353) has a 24-hour emergency room. Bicycling around town is much more enjoyable if you travel on side streets instead of Main Street (TX 16 and US 87). For this reason I strongly recommend obtaining a street map from the visitors bureau well before your visit. Roads to avoid include TX 16 to the north, US 290 both east and west, and US 87 south of the city; and on weekends and holidays RR 965 leading north to Enchanted Rock State Natural Area. (This caveat aside, Gillespie County is webbed by a labyrinth of quiet, traffic-free back roads, and most are readily accessible from Fredericksburg.)

Fredericksburg draws hundreds of tourists on weekends, and advance motel reservations are advised. A list of atmospheric bed & breakfasts can be obtained from the visitors bureau.

Campgrounds
Enchanted Rock State Natural Area, 18 miles north on RR 965 (915-247-3903). Over 100 tent-only sites in beautiful setting.
KOA Kampground, 5 miles east on shoulderless US 290 (210-997-4796).
Lady Bird Johnson Municipal Park, 3 miles south on TX 16 (210-997-4202). 50 tent sites.

Motels
Budget Host Deluxe Inn, 901 E. Main (210-997-3344).

215

The Wahrmund-Weirich-Weigand House is one of many early-day homes on Fredericksburg's historic district tour.

Dietzel Motel, junction of US 290 west and US 87 north (210-997-3330).
Frederick Motel, 1308 E. Main (210-997-6050).
Frontier Inn, west side on US 290, kitchenettes (210-997-4389).

Iraan (Pecos County; Pop. 1365; Alt. 2200 feet)

A small, dry, dusty West Texas oil town, Iraan is surrounded by brown hills dotted with oil pumps and rigs, for here, in 1928, one of the largest oil fields in the US was discovered. It was named the Yates Oilfield for Ira and Ann Yates who owned the townsite. The couples' first names were then joined to name the town itself. From a hastily constructed camp of tents and frame buildings, Iraan has grown into a small but prosperous-looking community with a motel, an IGA food market (closed Sundays), a deli, and a 40-acre city park. At the park, on the city's west side, are several giant statues immortalizing comic-strip character Alley Oop, his girlfriend, Oola, and his dinosaur, Dinny, 65 feet long and 16 feet tall. All were created by artist V.T. Hamlin while he lived in Iraan. Iraan has only a single small motel, and an advance reservation is strongly advised.

Campground

The city park offers unimproved tent camping with running water and toilets nearby.

Motels

Trail West Lodge, on east side at 416 E. Sixth St. (915-639-2548).

Junction (Kimble County; Pop. 2780; Alt. 1710 feet)

Information: *Kimble County Chamber of Commerce, 402 Main St., Junction, TX 76840 (915-446-3190).*

Named for its location at the junction of the North and South Llano Rivers, Junction is a major motel stop for travelers on I-10 and an important center for pecan, wool, and mohair production. Although several buildings on or near the Courthouse Square bear medallions with dates in the 1870s, Junction lacks a true historic district. Rather than sightseeing, we suggest swimming at the riverside city park.

Another interesting spot is South Llano State Park, 5 miles south on US 377 (wide shoulders), a wooded 500-acre riverside park with swimming and tubing. Adjoining the park is the 2123-acre Walter Buck Wildlife Management Area with a large population of deer, fox, *javelina,* turkey, and armadillo. At various times, sections of the park may be closed to protect wildlife. Otherwise, a variety of single- and double-track trails are open to hiking and mountain bicycling. Inquire at the visitors center as you enter to check which trails are open. Two supermarkets and at least a dozen very affordable motels line Junction's Main Street, which runs east and west. The city's **Kimble Hospital** at 2101 Main Street has a 24-hour emergency room (915-446-3321).

Campgrounds

City Park, east end of city on riverbank.

KOA Kampground, west end of town at 2145 N. Main St.; tree-shaded riverbank tent sites (915-446-3138).

South Llano State Park, 5 miles south on US 377; excellent shaded tent sites, hot showers (915-446-3994).

Motels

Carousel Inn, 1908 Main St. (1-800-876-9171 or 915-446-3301).

Hills Motel, 1520 Main St. (915-446-2567).

217

Kimble Motel, 1110 Main St. (915-446-2535).
Lazy T Motel, 2043 Main St. (915-446-2565).
Sun Valley Motel, 1611 Main St. (915-446-2505).

Kerrville (Kerr County; Pop. 21,000; Alt. 1640 feet)

Information: *Convention & Visitors Bureau, 1700 Sidney Baker, Suite 2, Kerrville, TX 78028 (1-800-221-7958 or 210-896-1155).*

Sprawling along the Guadalupe River and surrounded by wooded hills, Kerrville is the Hill Country's largest city. Together with smaller Ingram 6 miles west, it has become a popular river resort and retirement town and a center for the scores of summer camps, religious retreats, and ranches that dot Kerr County. Although the city dates back to the mid-1800s, it lacks any significant historical district.

Art buffs enjoy visiting the Cowboy Artists of America Museum at 1550 Bandera Highway (RR 173), located just west of Kerrville State Park (210-896-2553). Also worth seeing at Ingram—you pass them on Tours 9 and 11—are the murals on the outside walls of T.J. Moore's lumberyard in the center of Ingram. Painted by local muralist Jack Feagan, the 16 panels form a panoramic scene which chronicles 150 years of Kerr County history.

Larger than any other city in this directory, Kerrville has three supermarkets, a K-Mart, Walmart, two health-food stores, and the only fully equipped bicycle shop in the Hill Country. Also here is **Sid Petersen Memorial Hospital,** in the city center at 710 Water Street (210-896-4200), which has a 24-hour emergency room.

Since 1993, all single- and double-track trails in Kerrville State Park have been open for mountain bicycling. Call 210-257-5392 to ensure that the trails are still open, and pick up a trail map at the park visitors center at 2385 Bandera Highway. The park is located in southeast Kerrville on RR 173 just east of the intersection with Loop 534. The trails are in the southern half of the park. For some technical single-track challenges, ride the outermost loop up to the white water tank, and stay on the outer perimeter as you ride completely around the park. Then try some of the other trails. Most offer ledges, rocks, tree roots, and other obstacles favored by riders of fat- or knobby-tired bikes.

For another outstanding opportunity to ride some really challenging single- and double-track mountain-bike trails, call **Mountain Sports** (210-238-4400) and ask about riding at Kelly Creek Ranch. This privately owned ranch 7 miles west of Ingram has 40 miles of single- and double-track trails and has become a popular site for the Texas State Cross-Country and Downhill NORBA races. It has been open to individual bikers for a small daily fee.

Although the annual Hill Country Bicycle Rally is held in Kerrville each Easter, Kerrville is not a particularly good town to bicycle in, nor is it the starting point for many good rides. The truth is that the Kerrville area has too much traffic for enjoyable riding. True, Tours 9 and 11 start from Ingram, but if you're looking for a pleasant, low-traffic ride, I recommend putting your bike in the car and driving out to Bandera, Tarpley, Harper, Fredricksburg, or Comfort rather than trying to ride close to Kerrville. Other than early on Sunday morning, RR 173 to Bandera or RR 783 to Harper are best avoided; TX 16 north to Fredericksburg has wide shoulders, but many motorists use the shoulder as a second lane. All in all, Kerrville is an excellent place to stay if you have a car and can drive out each day to the starting point of our various rides. But as a place to bicycle in or out of, you can do better elsewhere. If you *must* cycle in town, send for or pick up a street map, and plan a route that keeps you on side streets. Traffic is particularly busy on Sidney Baker Street (TX 16), which runs north-to-south through Kerrville; on Main Street; and on Junction Highway (TX 27), which runs east-to-west through the city. For these reasons I recommend that anyone starting on Tours 9 or 11 stay at a motel or campground on the west side of Kerrville or at Ingram. Starting about 1.5 miles west of downtown Kerrville, Junction Highway (TX 27) has wide shoulders all the way to Ingram, another 4.5 miles to the west. Because of numerous driveways and entrances to commercial businesses, be alert for traffic turning across the shoulder the length of Junction Highway.

Bicycle Shop
Mountain Sports (210-238-4400) is on TX 39, a mile west of Hunt and 13 miles west of Kerrville. Proprietor Ron Duke stocks Ritchey, Marin, and Cannondale, sells components and accessories, and has a fully equipped repair shop. Open Monday through Saurday; closed Wednesday. Nearby, **Outpost Wilderness Adventures** (PO Box 511, Hunt, TX 78024; phone 210-238-4383) holds professionally led mountain-bike training camps.

Campgrounds
Kerrville State Park, east side on RR 173. Shady tent sites in a 500-acre park; swimming, mountain-bike trails (210-257-5392).

KOA Kampground, west side at 2950 Goat Creek Road, 1.75 miles south of I-10, Exit 501 (1-800-874-1665).

Motels

Econo-Lodge, north side, 0.25 mile south of I-10, Exit 508, at 2145 Sidney Baker (210-896-1711).

Flagstaff Inn, west side on TX 27 West at 906 Junction Highway, economical rates (210-792-4449).

Hunter House Motor Inn (E), at west end of Ingram on SR 39 (1-800-655-2377 or 210-367-2377).

Sands Motel, west side on TX 27 West at 1145 Junction Highway (210-896-5000).

Save Inn Motel, north side, 0.5 mile south of I-10, Exit 508, at 1804 Sidney Baker (210-896-8200).

Lajitas (Brewster County; Pop. 75; Alt. 2440 feet)

Information: Lajitas on the Rio Grande, Star Route 70, Box 400, Terlingua, TX 79852 (915-424-3471).

People had lived in the village of Lajitas for decades when General Black Jack Pershing established a cavalry post here to keep out Mexican bandits in 1917. But it wasn't until 1977, when a development company restored this frontier town, that Lajitas became a stopover for bicyclists riding the River Road (RR 170). Today the village is a privately owned resort grouped around a row of old-time western buildings fronting a boardwalk. Lajitas on the Rio Grande, as the development is called, is a complex of pricey hotel, motels, and condos with tennis, golf, and swimming. There's also an RV park with tent camping, a bakery, washateria, old-fashioned drugstore with soda fountain, and a trading post with occasional fresh produce. Lajitas (pronounced lah-hee-tas) occupies a bluff above the Rio Grande and looks across the river to the village of Paso Lajitas on the Mexican side. All around on the US side are the mountains and canyons of Big Bend Ranch State Natural Area, a vast primitive preserve.

Worth visiting is Warnock Environmental Education Center (915-424-3327), a mile east on RR 170, with an interesting display of desert plants and a bookshop filled with regional guidebooks and maps. The center also supplies information on Big Bend Ranch State Natural Area. (Although the preserve will be open to mountain bicycling, these trails are not accessible from Lajitas.) If you're seeking a short bicycle ride in the area, I suggest riding *west*, not east, on RR 170.

For a number of years, Lajitas has hosted the Chihuahua Desert Challenge Mountain Bike Race and Festival, usually the third weekend in February. Besides group bicycle tours in the area, it includes the first Texas State Offroad Championship series of the year and a series of NORBA-approved cross-country races and time trials. (The trails used for the races are on private property and cannot be accessed the rest of the year.) During the festival, virtually all accommodations and tent sites are filled, including those at nearby Study Butte. Lajitas is also a starting point for 1-day raft trips through sheer-walled Santa Elena Canyon, and reservations can be made the previous day. Tip: If you have a car and are staying at motels, you may prefer to stay at the less-expensive Easter Egg Valley Motel, 17 miles east in Study Butte (see Study Butte in this directory).

Campgrounds

Lajitas RV Park and Tent Campground, on grassy area near river, showers (915-424-3452, ask for RV Park).

Motels

Lajitas on the Rio Grande, includes the Badlands Hotel and three motels plus condos (915-424-3452).

Leakey (Real County; Pop. 500; Alt. 1610 feet)

Information: *Frio Canyon Chamber of Commerce, PO Box 743, Leakey, TX 78873 (210-232-5222).*

Pronounced lay-key, this picturesque small town on the Frio River is surrounded by high, wooded hills dotted with camps, ranches, and resort lodges. A marker at the historic native-stone courthouse describes the city's founding by settlers John and Mary Leakey. Other examples of early Hill Country architecture are the First State Bank Building and Leakey School, both located on wide-shouldered US 83. Riverside lodges and camps line the Concan area, which reaches south along US 83 to Garner State Recreation Park, 11 miles south. With two groceries, a café, and one or more motels, Leakey offers superb road cycling on quiet roads among some of the highest hills and most exceptional river-canyon scenery in the Hill Country. For emergency medical service dial 210-232-5300.

Campgrounds
Garner State Recreation Park, 11 miles south on wide-shouldered US 83; shady riverside tent sites (210-232-6132).

Motels
Welcome Inn, south side on US 83, motel units, cabins (210-232-5246).

Llano (Llano County; Pop. 3150; Alt. 1030 feet)

Information: Chamber of Commerce, 700 Bessemer St., Llano, TX 78643 (915-247-5354). Open weekdays only.

Originally settled by German pioneers, Llano enjoyed a brief boom during the late 1800s as a mining and quarrying center. Today this ranching and deer hunting center on the wide Llano River is famed for its historic town square. If you haven't already sent for one, you should pick up a "Historic Walking Tour" brochure from the chamber of commerce located just north of the river bridge. It's probably easier to walk than to bicycle through the compact historic blocks. Let your map guide you to the courthouse, the old county jail, and the Southern Hotel, all on or near the square, and to Badu House and the Llano Museum north across the river bridge. All date from the late 1800s. Robinson City Park offers river swimming; it's located a mile or so west of Courthouse Square via Main Street (RR 152). For information on camping at the park, call the **Llano County Community Center** at 915-247-5354.

Bicyclists on our Tour 4 (See Cross-Country Capsule Routings) from Ingram follow lightly trafficked Wright Street to within a block of the Courthouse Square. Llano's motels are located north across the river. To get there from Courthouse Square, walk your bike 1 block north on the west side of TX 16 to the river bridge and cross the bridge on the footway—you can usually ride across but watch for broken glass. Once across the bridge, turn left onto the first street (Tarrant Street), go 1 block, and turn right onto Pittsburgh Street. Go 2 blocks north on Pittsburgh and turn left onto Dallas Street. Go 5 blocks west on Dallas and turn right onto Ames Street. Ride 1 block north and you will emerge onto TX 29 where the motels and a supermarket are located. It's helpful to have sent in advance for a street map from the chamber of commerce; not all these streets may be paved but it's much quieter than riding TX 16 and TX 29. Reservations are almost essential at weekends and in summer, and are advised at any time.

Motels

Classic Inn (E), on TX 29 west at 901 W. Young (1-800-347-1578).
Chaparrel Lodge, on TX 29 west at 700 W. Young (915-247-4111).
Llano Motel, on TX 29 west at 507 W. Young, older, kitchenettes (915-247-5786).

Marathon (Brewster County; Pop. 800; Alt. 4043 feet)

This small crossroads community at the junction of US 90 and US 385 began with the establishment of Fort Peña in 1879. With Native American uprisings quelled, Southern Pacific trains began to roll through Marathon (they still do), and the town became a thriving cattle-shipping center. Nowadays this high desert town owes much of its fame to former cattle baron Alfred Gage. In 1927 he built the elegant Gage Hotel on US 90 in the middle of town. Restored to its original appearance, the Gage is filled with 1920s memorabilia. Together with its new, pueblo-style Los Portales Motel annex, the Gage Hotel remains in business and has a popular dining room. The original hotel rooms, with bath in the hall, are quite adequate and much more affordable than the pricey motel. Marathon has a small market with a produce section, and a café on US 90.

Motels

Gage Hotel, central on US 90, described above (915-386-4205).
Marathon Motel, west side on US 90 (915-386-4241).

Marfa (Presidio County; Pop. 2984; Alt. 4690 feet)

Information: *Chamber of Commerce, PO Box 635, Marfa, TX 79843 (915-729-2942).*

Popular for sailplane soaring and headquarters of the US Border Patrol, this West Texas ranching center is also known for its freedom from crime, pollution, and summer heat. The handsome Presidio County Courthouse, built of local brick in 1886 and topped with a life-sized statue of Justice, dominates the city. Ride around Courthouse Square and see the iron-cage jail. A block south on broad Highland Avenue is the southwestern-style Paisano Hotel, built in 1927 and once the city's social center. It is still open, and you can stay here. Ride next through some of the streets on Marfa's south side. Adobe homes—some in ruins, others over a century old—line these streets.

When these homes were built, some of the last Native American battles in Texas were being fought nearby against the Mescalero Apaches.

Finally, ride south on Hill Street to the Chinati Foundation complex. Until the end of World War II the 15 buildings here were part of Fort D.A. Russell, an army post. Today they house the Chinati Foundation's collection of monumental sculpture (open 1–5 Thursdays, Fridays, and Saturdays; a donation is expected; phone 915-729-4362).

Motels
Capri and **Thunderbird Motels,** west side on US 90; both motels under same management (915-729-4326 or 915-729-3145).
El Paisano Hotel, historic hotel at 207 N. Highland (915-729-3145).

Mason (Mason County; Pop. 2125; Alt. 1550 feet)

Information: Mason County Chamber of Commerce, Box 156, Mason, TX 76856 (915-347-5758).

The establishment of Fort Mason here in 1851 ended Native American attacks, but in the 1870s a bitter range war swept the county as ranchers defended their cattle against strong bands of rustlers. After Fort Mason was deactivated in 1869, local residents used sandstone blocks from the fort to construct homes and buildings. As you walk or cycle through Mason's extensive historic district, you'll recognize the brown sandstone walls contrasting with white gingerbread trim on scores of older houses.

Mason's National Register Historic District reaches from the Courthouse Square area for a mile south to the remains of Fort Mason. Many bikers begin their tour with a doughnut and coffee at Busy B's Bakery, located on the square. Close by is the chamber of commerce, where you'll want to pick up a map of the historic district if you didn't write for one earlier. The entire town square has been restored to its original appearance. A short distance north at 400 Broad Street is the exquisite 17-room Seaquist Home, ringed by two classic verandas and a charming example of birthday-cake architecture. More than 50 other historic buildings lie on or close to Post Hill Street, which leads south to Fort Mason.

Fort Mason City Park, 1 mile south on US 87, has 125 wooded acres and tent camping may be permitted (call 915-347-6449). The chamber of commerce has a list of local bed & breakfasts in historic homes. Motel reservations are advised, especially on weekends.

Motels

Carter's Motel, 0.75 mile west on US 87, older (915-347-5259).

Hill Country Inn, 2 blocks west of center on US 87 west, good value (915-347-6317).

Menard (Menard County; Pop. 1775; Alt. 1960 feet)

Information: *Menard County Chamber of Commerce, PO Box 64, Menard, TX 76859 (915-396-2365).*

Menard's first settlers were Spanish missionaries who established the Mission Santa Cruz de San Saba here in the mid-1700s. To protect the mission from hostile Native Americans the Spaniards built a fort, the Presidio de San Saba, 2 miles west of present-day Menard. By 1770 both fort and mission were abandoned due to Native American attacks. Then in 1858 cattle drovers began using the old mission's compound as a huge corral. Modern Menard grew here astride the San Saba River. The ruins of the mission and the fort remain. Mohair and wool production have replaced beef-cattle raising as the leading industries. And nowadays this small, quiet town on US 83 makes a pleasant overnight stop while bicycling.

With a street map, sent for beforehand, you'll have no difficulty finding your way around this small community. There's a tree-shaded city park on the river near the center and the ruins of the presidio are 2 miles west off US 190. The chamber of commerce can also send you a map of Ditch Walk, which takes you through the city's historic blocks, as well as a map to the Menardville Museum. US 83, the main street, crosses the San Saba River on a long bridge (sidewalk available). Alternatively, you may prefer to cross by the quieter Decker Street bridge, 2 blocks east. Menard also has a food market and cafés. **The Shamrock Clinic** at 110 East San Saba Street offers 24-hour emergency service (915-396-4612).

Campgrounds

Pie in the Sky RV Park, west of center, shaded riverside tent sites (915-396-2059).

Rabbit Haven RV Park, 1.5 miles east on FM 2092 (915-396-4745).

Motels

Navajo Inn, south end on US 83, near food store (915-396-2362).

83-Motel, north side on US 83, older (915-396-4549).

Ozona (Crockett County; Pop. 3110; Alt. 2350 feet)

Information: *Chamber of Commerce, 1110 Avenue E, Ozona, TX 76943 (915-392-3737).*

Center of an oil and mohair industry and seat of Crockett County, unincorporated Ozona was founded in 1891, and its courthouse was completed in 1902. A walking-tour map, available at the chamber of commerce, takes you to a total of 13 historic sites that include the distinctive native-limestone courthouse, the county jail, the old Ozona Hotel, Crockett County Museum, and several historic homes. You can also bicycle up "Silk Stocking Row," a lineup of stately homes that reaches north for 0.5 mile on tree-canopied SR 163.

Motels
Daystop (E), 820 Loop 466 (915-392-2631).
Flying W Lodge, east side on US 290, good value (915-392-2656).
Hillcrest Motor Lodge, west side on I-10 frontage road at Exit #365, older section offers lower rates (915-392-5515).

Presidio (Presidio County; Pop. 3300; Alt. 2595 feet)

Information: *Chamber of Commerce, PO Box 1405, Presidio, TX 79845 (915-229-3199).*

A hot, dusty, windblown, and unlovely border town at the confluence of the Rio Conchos and Rio Grande, Presidio was named for the Mexican fort, or presidio, that once stood here. A modern highway bridge spans the Rio Grande and leads to the adjoining and much larger Mexican city of Ojinaga (oh-hee-nah-gah). Despite its unimpressive appearance, Presidio's main street is lined with stores selling luxury items that are eagerly purchased by visiting Mexicans. Also here are three small food stores, each with a produce section, plus several restaurants and other stores supplying basic necessities.

Presidio is an important base for anyone exploring this isolated area by bicycle. Besides offering scenic road rides in both directions along the river and north to Shafter ghost town, plus an excursion into Ojinaga, Presidio is the gateway to mountain biking in Pinto Canyon and in the not-yet-fully-opened Big Bend Ranch State Natural Area (see below).

Many people, including bicyclists, prefer to stay at a motel in Ojinaga. To get there, ride southwest to the international bridge, and ride or walk across the bridge on the sidewalk into Mexico. Tell the Mexican immigra-

Fort Leaton State Historic Site, a massive adobe fortress built in 1848, lies close to River Road and the Rio Grande.

tion inspector that you are going only to Ojinaga. Ride straight on, and you will emerge into broad, six-lane Boulevard Libro Commercio. Pedal about a mile down the boulevard, and at the corner of Morelos you will see the Motel Ojinaga across the street. This is a large, comfortable motel with restaurant, but you are still 2 miles from the center of town. So if you prefer, continue riding south on the boulevard for another mile to a traffic light. A sign here points right and reads *Ojinaga Centro*. Turn right here. You will now be on Avenida Trasvina y Retes. Ride along this divided avenue for about a mile to the *zócalo* (square) at the center of town. From here you can see the Hotel Rohana, a traditional hotel that was once raided by Pancho Villa. Walk or ride your bike over to it, and go through the side entrance into the modern Rohana Motel.

Bicycles are quite common in Ojinaga, and riding here should present no problems. Many people speak English. You must pay a small toll to return across the bridge into Presidio. Back on the US side, you must wait in line with cars to pass through US immigration. Proof of citizenship may be required to reenter the US. It's best to avoid crossing during busy weekend periods or during morning and evening rush hours. For more about cycling in Ojinaga, see Tour 24-A.

Four miles east of Presidio on RR 170 is:

Fort Leaton State Historic Site, a massive adobe fortress built by pioneer rancher Ben Leaton in 1848 on the site of an earlier Spanish mission. Leaton built his fort close to the Rio Grande and astride the Chihuahua–San Antonio Road. It was used as a fort and trading post until the Civil War. Of the original 40 rooms that once faced the inner patio, 24 have been restored and roofed over with beams and cane roofing and will eventually be furnished in frontier style. The visitors center is open daily 8–4:30 (915-229-3613) and has a fine collection of regional guidebooks and maps for sale. The visitors center also supplies information on Big Bend Ranch State Natural Area, a vast primitive region occupying most of the land bordering the Rio Grande as far east as Lajitas and reaching north for many miles.

Big Bend Ranch State Natural Area is a former 300,000-acre ranch of spectacular desert wilderness, purchased by the state in 1988 and in process of becoming the centerpiece of the Texas state parks system. While the date of opening the natural area to the public remains indefinite, it will very likely occur during the life of this edition. The ranch contains a huge geological caldera (a collapsed volcano dome) called *El Solitario* that is 8 to 9 miles in diameter, as well as a prehistoric Indian camp, Indian pictographs, and the original ranch buildings at Sauceda slated to become park headquarters.

When the park is open, approximately 50 miles of existing unpaved roads will be open to vehicular traffic, including mountain bicycles. An additional four trails will be open to both four-wheel-drive vehicles and mountain bicycles. Another trail designated for mountain bikes only will run south from the Sauceda Visitors Center and still another will loop around the caldera. From the caldera you should then be able to bicycle over a four-wheel-drive route through Fresno Canyon. Although permits are likely to be needed for biking on trails, Big Bend Ranch should provide fat-tire bicyclists with miles of scenic riding through steep-walled canyons and past mesas and bat caves. Tent camping will also be permitted at designated sites.

As this was written, you could ride a mountain bicycle from Presidio or Fort Leaton to the natural area entrance by taking RR 170 east as far as the sign pointing to Casa Piedra Road. Turn left and ride up this unpaved two-lane graded road for 6 miles until you come to a Y-fork. Take the right fork, which will be signed for Big Bend Ranch when the park is open. The road then dips down across a deep valley and climbs for several miles to the park entrance. Some trails were announced open just as this book was going to press.

Parts of the southern sector of Big Bend Ranch State Natural Area bordering the Rio Grande are already open, and primitive campsites are available along RR 170 between Redford and Lajitas. To obtain one, you must first request a permit either at Fort Leaton or at Warnock Environmental Education Center near Lajitas. For literature on **Big Bend Ranch**, write the Superintendent, Big Bend Ranch State Natural Area, PO Box 1180, Presidio, TX 79843 (915-229-3613).

Motels in Presidio
La Siesta Motel, Highway 67 north, older (915-229-3611).
Three Palms Inn, Highway 67 north (915-229-3436).

Motels in Ojinaga
Ojinaga Motel, 1 mile south of bridge on Blvd. Libro Commercio at corner of Morales (phone 145-30311 or 145-30191).
Hotel-Motel Rohana, 1 block from central square called the *zócalo* (phone 145-30071 or 145-30078).

Rocksprings (Edwards County; Pop. 1375; Alt. 2450 feet)

Established in 1891 and the seat of Edwards County, Rocksprings was an early-day water source for Native Americans and settlers. Nowadays it is a major Angora wool and mohair center. The old town square may have seen better days, but the courthouse and jail, both built of native stone, are worth a look. Some bicyclists report enjoying the fried catfish dinner served Friday evenings at the Rocksprings Inn. The hotel, with its traditional veranda, bears a medallion explaining that it was originally built as the Gilmer Hotel in 1916. Rocksprings has a well-stocked IGA supermarket and convenience store, and most necessities can be found, though the town lacks modern accommodations.

Motels
Mesa Motel, a rustic motel near town center (210-683-3241).
Rocksprings Inn, a traditional hotel on the square, café (210-683-3186).

Sanderson (Terrell County; Pop. 1125; Alt. 2980 feet)

A ranching and railroad center, this frontier western town was almost destroyed by a disastrous flash flood in 1965. Following a heavy downpour, a dam in Sanderson Canyon gave way, and a wall of water roared through the city, killing 26 people. Within minutes the waters receded. But

229

much of Sanderson never recovered, and today this partial ghost town is mainly a stopover for travelers on US 90. A small market supplies limited produce and there are several cafés, an RV park with possible tent camping, and several comfortable motels with reasonable rates.

Motels
Desert Air Motel, west side on US 90 (915-345-2572).
West Texan Motel, an older motel with its own food store (915-345-2332).
Western Hills Motel, east side on US 90 (915-345-2541).

Sonora (Sutton County; Pop. 2800; Alt. 2120 feet)

Information: *Chamber of Commerce, PO Box 1172, Sonora, TX 76950 (915-387-2880).*
Settled around 1880, this relaxed town is a trading center for hundreds of sheep and goat ranches in the area. A small historical area around the courthouse includes the city's first jail, the 1889 Miers Home Museum, and the former Santa Fe depot. A walking-tour map is available. Fifteen miles southwest are the Caverns of Sonora, deep caves famed for their delicate crystal formations; a 1.5 mile guided walking tour leaves every half hour. While the caves are accessible by bicycle, it may be simpler to visit them by car if you have one along (the road to the caves is narrow, and someone must watch the bikes while you are underground). Sonora has a large supermarket and a hospital with emergency service.

Motels
Holiday Host Motel, 2 miles east on US 290 (915-387-2532).
Twin Oaks Motel, west side on US 290 at 907 SW Crockett (915-387-2550).
Zola's Motel, west side on US 290 at 1108 SW Crockett, older (915-387-3000).

Study Butte (Brewster County; Pop. 135; Alt. 2510 feet)

Between 1909 and 1970, when mercury ore was mined here, as many as 600 miners lived in Study Butte. But when the mines closed in 1970, the miners left and Study Butte became a ghost town. Named for Will Study, the first mine manager, and pronounced "stew-dy," the community is ringed by mountains and is famous for its color-splashed sunrises and sunsets. Study Butte's unique "last frontier" flavor has also lured a number of refugees from the big-city rat race to this isolated region. You can often meet the locals after work on the porch of the Study Butte Store, a mile east on RR 118. For decades this store was located at the mine entrance; it was moved here when the mines closed. On this same porch where miners once watched movies, local people bring their musical instruments for an impromptu sing-along over a beer. This tells you something of the frontier character and spirit that linger here and in Terlingua ghost town, another former mercury mining community 4 miles west on RR 170. Many locals live in renovated adobe or stone houses originally built by miners.

Tent camping is available at Big Bend RV Park, 2 miles west of Study Butte on RR 170; also here is La Kiva, an underground bar and restaurant and a popular spot for locals. Terlingua also has a café and a dinner theater with entertainment. The store at Terlingua ghost town stocks an excellent collection of regional guidebooks and topo maps. The Study Butte Store stocks food supplies, and there's a café near the motels. Highways 118 and 170 leading east, west, and north out of Study Butte are narrow with blind bends and should be ridden with care. In contrast, limitless miles of traffic-free dirt roads take you through magnificent mountain scenery.

Campgrounds
Big Bend RV Park, 2 miles west on RR 170 (915-371-2250).
Terlingua Oasis RV Park has cabins and tent sites (915-371-2218).

Motels
Easter Egg Valley Motel, west side on RR 170; ask about their prefab economy units in rear (915-371-2430).
Mission Lodge, town center at junction of RR 118 and RR 170; next door is more expensive **Big Bend Motor Lodge** (E), under same management, café (1-800-848-2363 or 915-371-2218).
Wildhorse Station, 8 miles north on RR 118, cabins, reasonable (915-371-2526).
Longhorn Ranch Motel, 12 miles north on RR 118 (915-371-2450).
Terlingua Ranch Resort, 16 miles north on RR 118 then 16 miles east on graded dirt road; quiet, remote, beautiful; motel, tent sites, pool, café, reasonable rates, good off-road biking on bulldozed roads (915-371-2416).

Also from Backcountry Publications and The Countryman Press

Regional Bicycling Guides

25 Bicycle Tours in Coastal Georgia and the Carolina Low Country, $13.00
30 Bicycle Tours in Wisconsin, $14.00
25 Bicycle Tours in Southern Indiana, $10.95
25 Bicycle Tours in Ohio's Western Reserve, $12.00
25 Bicycle Tours in Maryland, $12.00
25 Bicycle Tours on Delmarva, $12.00
25 Bicycle Tours in and around Washington, D.C., $10.00
25 Bicycle Tours in New Jersey, $10.00
25 Bicycle Tours in Eastern Pennsylvania, $12.00
20 Bicycle Tours in and around New York City, $11.00
25 Bicycle Tours in the Hudson Valley, $10.00
The Bicyclist's Guide to the Southern Berkshires, $14.95
25 Bicycle Tours in the Adirondacks, $13.00
30 Bicycle Tours in New Hampshire, $11.00
25 Bicycle Tours in Vermont, $10.00
25 Bicycle Tours in Maine, $10.00
25 Mountain Bike Tours in Massachusetts, $11.00
25 Mountain Bike Tours in Vermont, $11.00

A Sample of Our Other Outdoor Books

Food Festival: America's Best Regional Food Celebrations, $16.00
Camp and Trail Cooking Techniques, $20.00
Fishwatching: Your Complete Guide to the Underwater World, $18.00
Fishing Small Streams with a Fly Rod, $15.00
Fly-Fishing with Children: A Guide for Parents, $19.00
Backwoods Ethics, $13.00
Wilderness Ethics, $13.00

We offer many more books on hiking, walking, fishing and canoeing—and many more books on travel, nature and other subjects.

Our books are available through bookstores, or they may be ordered directly from the publisher. For shipping and handling costs, to order, or for a complete catalog, please contact: The Countryman Press, Inc., P.O. Box 175AP, Woodstock, VT 05091-0175; or call our toll-free number: (800) 245-4151.